Andrew

Andrew had his first Jake Dillon crime thriller published in 2006. He lives in Dorset, where he positions many of Dillon's assignments. Powder Diamonds is the fifth in the Dillon series. Andrew's writing reflects his interest in travel and perpetual observation of national security and covert operations. Andrew lives with his family and is currently working on yet another novel in the series of Dillon crime thrillers.

Powder Diamonds

Andrew Towning

First published in the United Kingdom in 2014
Published by Andrew Towning
www.andrewtowning.co.uk

For you...

...as we haven't yet met, or have only a glancing acquaintance - perhaps we haven't seen each other in a while, or we are in some way related, or perhaps are not destined to meet at all but will - I trust - despite all of that, always think fondly of each other... therefore Powder Diamonds is for you.

Thank you to Zoe Wilson once again for her help with the Dillon process and the Powder Diamonds' jacket concept and to Jennie Franklin for the photography.

Forward

POWDER DIAMONDS

Present Day

The chair legs scraped against the concrete floor as Jasper Nash stood up and stretched the tension out of his body. Enough of this chit-chat he thought. He was terminating the interview. They would have to arrest and caution him before he uttered another word. But he questioned who 'they' were and who this man was, asking so many questions?

Dillon recognised the stance. It was something he had seen many times during interrogations; and this was no ordinary interrogation and Nash was no ordinary suspect, but his silence only implied guilt; Dillon was damned if he would release Jasper Nash so easily. He fired a warning shot at him.

"Tell me something, Jasper. Are you still on talking terms with Maximilian Kane?" Dillon paused. There was no answer. "I reckon it was Kane who had something to do with your recent troubles. It wouldn't surprise me if it was Kane who had got you out of Hong Kong. Now you feel that you are indebted to him. I don't believe you're so bad. A bit misguided, maybe. You might even possibly be a fool. But Kane's a really hard-core career criminal as you well know. He and I go back a long way - but that's another story for another day. I want you to know that he is under twenty-four hour surveillance. Whatever he does and wherever he goes he will be watched. If you're smart you'll keep him at arm's length, you might even consider staying well clear of him." Jasper continued to ignore Dillon. "So you're the silent type, eh Jasper? Well OK have it your way. There will always be more time to talk at our next meeting..." Dillon paused just long enough for his words to sink in, and then continued. "When we next meet, and we most certainly will. I want you to know that I'll give you one opportunity to do what's right. Remember that. I'll give you one chance only."

Prologue

Cornwall UK - 1985

Dillon walked back along narrow country lanes towards the small Cornish coastal village. He lit a cigarette and looked up at the gathering clouds overhead. He was glad to be home on leave for a while. It would be blowing a gale before the night was out. Only a few small sailing craft and dinghies remained moored out in the bay, with all of the larger craft having made for the safety of the harbour. Their owner's racing against the ebbing tide towards the clubhouse of the local Yacht Club.

He flicked his cigarette over the edge of the quay as he made his way to see Anna. As he turned the corner at the far end of the quay he caught sight of a ocean-going yacht approaching the channel. The tide was already on the turn with the sandbanks just starting to show. The yacht would be lucky to find enough water. He watched as her skipper nosed his way towards him, throttling back the inboard motor as it passed the high sided breakwater of the harbour entrance. The craft entered the harbour and came to within three foot of the quayside.

Dillon walked to where the yacht was manoeuvring alongside. He immediately noticed she was sitting low on her flotation marks, most likely stocked to the gunnels with equipment and provisions for a long trip. Her teak decks pristine, she was an expensive toy and wouldn't like her shiny blue hull being pressed up against the harsh stone of the quayside. Dillon watched as the crew threw the fenders over the side rail and readied her to berth, one of them looked up and called out to Dillon, who caught the bow line thrown up to him and pulled hard before tying it off on a cleat, he walked back to the stern and repeated the exercise. Dillon looked at the three crew, they were in their mid-to-late thirties. The one who had thrown the rope gave a brief smile, raised his hand in acknowledgement and carried on squaring away the boat. Dillon walked on towards his girlfriend's house.

That night Dillon saw the yacht's crew in the bar of the local pub.

Where he stood waiting to be served, a tall man who looked a little older than the other crew members approached him. "My name is Max Kane," he said. "I'm the skipper of that yacht you helped berth earlier. Please, let me buy you a drink as way of a thank you."

"Jake. Jake Dillon. I'll have a pint, thanks."

"We're on our way to Ireland," explained Kane. We had to put into harbour as our main-sail has a bloody great rip in it."

Dillon said nothing. He nodded.

"This is a quiet place," commented Kane. "Does much ever happen around here?"

"Depends on what you're looking for," replied Dillon reticently.

Kane nodded. Locals, he thought, they had no idea about the cut and thrust of engaging conversation. "Is there any chance of getting some decent food somewhere local?"

"It's a bit late for most places, but the landlord's wife might knock you up something." Dillon picked up his pint.

"Thanks for the drink," he said, and went and joined an attractive blonde girl who had just entered the bar.

* * *

Dillon sensing that someone was looking over his shoulder, turned and found Kane standing there. "Sorry to butt in, Jake. But I'd like to invite you on-board before we leave, for a spot of supper one evening. My way of saying thanks to you properly."

It takes more than that to buy friendship, thought Dillon.

"In fact why don't you come for a sail when we've got the mainsail fixed?" Kane asked.

"I'm only here visiting for a couple of days and then I've got to get back to work."

"Is that your yacht that's dwarfing all the other boats in the harbour?" Anna asked enthusiastically.

"Yes," said Kane. "Do you sail? Please forgive me. We haven't been introduced properly. I am Max Kane and that is my boat, Freebase."

"Oh hello, I'm Anna Westcott."

"Well Miss Westcott, perhaps you would like to come out on her too. We could do with someone who has local knowledge of the waters around here. We almost landed on a sandbank or two on the way in!" Kane smiled disarmingly at the attractive blonde haired girl.

"Are you staying long, Max?" Dillon asked pointedly.

"Just until we get the sail fixed. But then I might decide to stay longer. After all, it's such a beautiful part of the English coastline; it would be such a shame to miss the opportunity of exploring all that it's got to offer, fully." Kane looked at Anna as he spoke. Dillon frowned.

"I'd love to sail on a proper ocean racer," said Anna, naively.

"Splendid. It would be my pleasure to have you aboard, Anna."

Dillon looked away; he'd decided that he didn't like Kane. "Come on Anna, let's go." Dillon led the attractive girl out of the bar. She looked back over her shoulder as she was going through the door. Max Kane smiled.

When they had left, Kane pulled out his mobile phone and made a call. He'd got the measure of this place and there was nothing to raise alarm bells.

* * *

For the second and last time in his life Jasper Nash drove down the narrow country lanes into the Cornish coastal village. He stopped the Mercedes Sprinter van by the quayside, got out, and stretched. He put on his jacket. He was in no hurry. He remembered with clarity every inch of the waterfront from the images he took the first time. Behind him the local pub, to the right the Yacht Club, and to his left an Italian restaurant. In front of him the boats strained at their moorings as the early morning wind blew in from the sea. He went in search of a hot strong coffee. He'd let Kane track him down. After all, he wasn't supposed to know what Freebase looked like. He walked off of the quayside and found a café a couple of streets back. It looked clean and there were already a few local fishermen sitting at tables. He went inside and ordered strong black coffee and a full English breakfast with a round of toast. When he'd finished eating he ordered another coffee and sat smoking a cigarette, thinking that by nightfall he would have earned in one day what some people could only dream of earning in their entire lifetime. Momentarily the thought unsettled him. He got up and walked back to the quayside and spotted Kane standing by the side of the van.

* * *

At midday Dillon was disappointed to find Max Kane holding court in the lounge bar of the pub, with a small audience surrounding him for whom he'd bought drinks. He couldn't help overhearing Kane's running commentary on the Sail Maker's progress. If Kane was so smart he should have checked the condition of the sail before he'd left wherever it was he had come from; but then men like him had more money than sense. Dillon glanced at his watch; it was five minutes to one. The Landlord turned up the radio for the shipping forecast.

* * *

That evening Kane and Jasper Nash were in the bar, talking loudly about the repair to the main-sail, playing out their little charade for the benefit of any eavesdroppers sitting nearby. Kane was complaining about the amount of time it was going to take to repair the sail, Jasper was telling him that he was waiting for a special thread to be delivered down from London and that was the reason for the delay. The locals listened to this exchange, every now and then one or more of them would nod, sympathising with the Sail-Maker. Wealthy yachtsmen were all the same: they expected everything to be done at once.

Now it was time to leave. Jasper stood up and shook Kane's hand. As he returned his glass to the bar he overheard a conversation between two twenty-something girls. He glanced at them briefly. One was attractive with blonde hair. She was being a sulky mare because her boyfriend didn't want her to go sailing. Jasper wanted to tell her to do it. Go for the adventure; it didn't matter what was right. There was always time to reflect afterwards. "Go for it," he said to her as he passed by their table. "You might never get another opportunity like it." The girl looked up, surprised, and smiled hesitantly.

As he drove back to Dorset, Jasper thought about the girl in the bar. He envied her innocence and her caution. He wove a few dreams around her, and imagined a life with her in a luxury house on the water's edge. As he drove into Bournemouth he forgot about her. He had a job to do.

* * *

Anna went sailing with Kane and his friends. The days turned into weeks. A high pressure system established itself over the Southern half of England and a mini Indian heat wave arrived to the joy of the tourist trade along the coast. The local Cornish fishermen were busy and their daily catches plentiful.

In early September, Kane left the harbour of the small Cornish fishing village for the last time. Five days later the Coastguard found a young woman's naked body washed up on a beach seven miles along the coast, deposited by the ebbing tide. She had been beautiful. Her naked body and limbs askew on the sand screamed 'murder'.

Anna's body was quickly identified. Her capsized dinghy was later found half a mile away. There was no murder enquiry. The caressing action of the water and waves always stripped corpses of their clothes before returning them to land.

* * *

After the inquest Dillon sensed a conspiracy. Anna's family had completely blanked him at the funeral and he had stood bewildered by the grave side; he felt some irrational responsibility for her death. Occasionally he intercepted an awkward glance. Afterwards he looked to see who had sent flowers. There were none from Kane, and that made him feel angry. Kane knew about Anna's death all right, because he had been summoned to the inquest.

* * *

It was two Metropolitan Police Officers from the serious drug squad who inadvertently sent him in search for the answers. They interviewed him at length about the yacht. They asked if he was aware it had sailed up from Morocco. They warned him he could have committed an offence by helping, and not reporting its arrival. They said they were investigating Maximilian Kane and his yacht Freebase because of intelligence received about the boat being used for smuggling drugs into the UK and he had known about it.

Dillon felt like he had be drawn into a very bad dream. He didn't care that someone had tried to implicate him. He wanted to know why Kane had left with the tide on the morning that Anna had disappeared. She would never have capsized her dinghy, and the weather that day had been calm and sunny. He wanted to know why the police didn't think her death was suspicious.

Once he had finished reading the Coroner's report he realised why a conspiracy of silence had descended upon the small village community. Anna had drowned, but a high level of cocaine had been found in her bloodstream. The Coroner's verdict was 'death by misadventure'. The autopsy revealed nothing else, other than Anna had been healthy and physically fit at the time of her death.

* * *

Dillon didn't want to sleep - couldn't sleep. He wasn't prepared to abandon Anna. He didn't want to forget her. He was constantly being haunted by her ghostly-figure on the foreshore. Her eyes, once so invitingly curious, now stared back at him from the sea. He remembered too many things - their first kiss, and the first time they had made love. Even the sound of the breeze off the water and the smell of salt air conspired to keep her memory alive, conjuring the times they had sailed together and walked hand in hand along the beach on hot summer nights.

Dillon escaped from the claustrophobic confines of the village which had betrayed Anna and had enrolled in the Army Officer Training Programme at Sandhurst. He spent long days and nights studying and training to gain his commission. After forty-four weeks he passed out of training and had gained the rank of Second Lieutenant. His past had ended with Anna's death. His emotional development stopped because Anna's death was never resolved. He changed. He didn't like people who overly cared about trivial things. He didn't like people generally.

When Dillon became a commissioned officer he chose to join the Army Intelligence Corp where he learnt the art of collecting information from within and outside of Battle Space, to evaluate analyses, integrate and interpret this information to provide intelligence for those in most need. And along the way he'd picked up and developed other skills that had kept him alive on many occasions.

It was twenty-six years later that he ran into Maximilian Kane again.

For Dillon it was like it had only been yesterday, but the hatred of this man was still there, it had remained hidden - until now...

Chapter 1

For Martha, it all began with the entry intercom. She stopped painting and walked away from her easel to where the handset was located. As she stood there about to answer the annoyingly persistent sound, she had a premonition that her life was about to change. The small screen lit up as she lifted the handset. The tall man standing outside had a particular look about him. He was ruggedly handsome and had obviously been round the block a time or two, and clearly knew how to look after himself. It was the look in those blue eyes, she had seen it before - dangerous, calculated, intelligent. Most of all he had an air of authority and inevitability about him. She knew that this visit had been coming for a long time.

Martha released the lock on the main door and then, with her own front door still securely locked, she asked the man for ID, which he held up to the spy viewer. Once satisfied she unlocked the heavy oak door and found the man somewhere in his mid to late forties standing in the hall, he had two younger men with him. Before he entered Martha's apartment, he thrust the ID card towards her once again for closer inspection. She didn't look at it. She heard him say, "My name is Jake Dillon. I am attached to Her Majesty's Home Office. I have something to tell you." His voice was not loud or harsh but seemed to silence the whole of the Sandbanks peninsula. Martha stepped back into the room and smiled weakly. Dillon followed her in. The two younger men, who were both wearing black suits, remained outside in the hallway and Martha closed the door. She knew the visit concerned Jasper, but she didn't know why. Immediately she was convinced that he was dead. She really didn't want to hear what Dillon had to say. "Can I get you something to drink Mr Dillon?" She asked stupidly.

"No thanks," said Dillon. "Perhaps you should sit

down," he added, alarmed by Martha's pallid complexion. Martha sat down convinced that Jasper had met with an accident in Hong Kong.

"You are Martha Hamilton?" Dillon asked. Martha nodded and bit her lip. "And Jasper Nash is your partner?"

"Yes," Martha replied quietly.

"I don't suppose you've heard, but he's been arrested by the Hong Kong police department." He let this revelation sink in. "He was in possession of ten kilos of un-cut cocaine which he intended to smuggle into the UK. But there's also something else I'm afraid, and it's the reason why I'm here."

"Something else, that sounds serious?"

"It is serious! You see Martha, Jasper wasn't only smuggling cocaine. He has been trading in something with a much higher value in return for the drugs. As yet we don't know what that other something is."

Martha sighed, and her shoulders shook with the relief. She closed her eyes tightly and two small tears formed in the corners of her eyes and rolled down over her cheeks.

"Jasper, oh Jasper," said Martha quietly.

Dillon looked away embarrassed. He was angry that someone like Jasper Nash should have risked and squandered so much love.

"I'm sorry," he said, not understanding the precise reason for her emotion, only knowing that he was somehow responsible.

"No, don't be sorry," said Martha hurriedly. "I expected..." she began, but then said nothing.

"Listen, Martha. The people I work for know that you're not involved. They know because they've had you under surveillance as part of the investigation into Nash's dealings. I'm afraid I have to search this apartment." Dillon saw the look on Martha's face, and added. "I can do it with or without your permission. The choice is yours."

"Go ahead, but please don't damage anything. What's going to happen to Jasper?"

"He'll go to a high security prison."

"How long will he get?"

"I don't know. I'm not an expert on the subject. The Chinese have strict sentencing. But I'd guess somewhere in the region of ten years minimum."

"Can't you extradite him to a prison in this country?"

"That isn't possible at the moment. Although, the British Government might intervene with this case as they'll want to question him."

"Oh," said Martha. The reality of what she was embroiled in, beginning to take hold. She had been taken aback by the revelation that Jasper was smuggling drugs, but not entirely surprised. But what the hell was this other stuff? All sorts of thoughts raced through her mind and now she had to fight to keep her composure intact.

"Could you show me where Jasper keeps his personal papers, address books, bank statements, and stuff like that? I'd like to have a look through them."

Martha was helpful. There was no reason not to be. She knew that Jasper kept no incriminating evidence in the apartment. He kept names and telephone numbers in his head, and his bank accounts were meticulously in order. Jasper had always been proud of that. His earnings and expenditure all tallied down to the last penny. But Jasper owned nothing. He'd never been tempted to buy a house. He always rented. If he needed money in the bank he bought something for cash at an auction and then sold it elsewhere for a small loss if necessary. Martha's friends admired Jasper's entrepreneurial skills. Martha had thought the charade ridiculous, until now.

The two younger men came in and helped Dillon search the apartment. They found little, and removed the bank statements which they promised to return along with a laptop.

"There doesn't appear too many of his belongings here," commented Dillon. "He wouldn't have a second address, by any chance?"

"No not that I'm aware of." Martha said.

Having had a good look round, the three men left Martha alone to contemplate ten years or more without Jasper Nash.

At the door, Dillon turned and said, "If you think of

anything that might be of interest, or you just want to talk then please call me." He handed Martha a card with his mobile number on and grinned a disarmingly lopsided smile which she had noticed when she had first opened the door to him.

* * *

Two weeks later Martha heard from Maximilian Kane that Jasper had been sentenced to ten years. She was shocked. For the last three years she had lived with the possibility that something might happen to him, but it hadn't prepared her for the reality. Three of his business associates phoned nervously, fishing for information, trying to find out if there was an investigation which might jeopardise their own freedom. Once reassured, they all promptly forgot her. She never heard another word from Kane who had called, that one time, from a pay-as-you-go mobile phone that had withheld the number. It was sometime before her friends noticed Jasper's prolonged absence. He'd always led a surreptitious life, appearing and disappearing without explanation. When they asked where he was, she lied and said he was setting up a business in the Far East. The lies distanced her from everyone and merely accentuated the loneliness. Only one or two of her closest friends knew the truth.

It had always been lonely. She was never able to tell the truth. People were always curious about how Jasper made his money. She told them that he was involved with buying and selling commodities. Her parents thought that he flew by the seat of his pants and was definitely not the marrying type. She pointed out to her father that it was no different to selling used cars as he had done all his life. She was drawn into the lie, expanding on it; and eventually was corrupted by it. She explained how Jasper researched his target markets, looking for medium to large return trading opportunities. She agreed he flew by the seat of his pants, because that was the nature of what he did. Her parents didn't understand. They asked too many questions about the sort of things he sold. As a result she was forced to create a romanticised career for Jasper, in which he was surrounded by advisors and assistants who traded globally in anything from an ocean going tanker of crude oil to containers of granite and quartz for the building industry. Then, whenever they met friends or family, she reminded him to talk about his latest deal, and give credence to the lie. Lying was second nature to Jasper. He said the lies never hurt people. But Martha knew they did. They were insidious. The illusion of his exciting life made others dissatisfied with their own.

Five months later Martha found she missed Jasper more than ever. She forgot how insecure life had been with him. She forgot how frightened she felt every time he went out of the front door, scared that he would end up in a body bag with a bullet through his skull. She craved those experiences she resented so much before his disappearance; the sudden weekend trips to Berlin, Venice or Amsterdam; expensive dinners; first class travel and five-star hotels.

Her yearning for Jasper became unbearable. She wondered if she was going mad. She began to believe the lies she told others. She made herself believe that Jasper was really setting up a business in Hong Kong and would be returning soon.

One time she was sure she had seen him on a busy Saturday afternoon walking along Westover Road in Bournemouth. She recognised him from the slight hunch of his shoulders; his profile, the turn of his head, the flare of his nostrils and the curl of lips beneath high cheekbones. She rushed, pushing her way through the crowds of shoppers and holiday makers, her heart beating faster, but he was gone. Suddenly she vividly recalled making love to him. She was self aware as her body reacted feverishly to the memory.

She longed to touch herself, in the midst of hoards of shoppers, of all places. She did not know whether to feel aroused or disgusted at how it moved her. There were days when he haunted her. Everyone seemed to have blue eyes. She looked up into a beautiful blue sky and sighed. She walked off towards the seafront, her top caressing her hardening nipples as she reminded herself that she was a single woman again. Ten Years! Would he haunt her for all that time?

It was because she couldn't find out any information

about Jasper which drove her to make the telephone call. She wondered if there was any chance that he would be released before he completed his sentence. She was frightened about the future and had never doubted that she was attractive, but would anyone want her now she was that little bit older? Her body's curves were still good for now, but it wouldn't be long before she had to work harder at the gym and cut down on the carbs. "What the hell" she thought. She wanted to talk to someone who understood her situation, knew about Jasper's circumstances, and who would tell her what to do. She was desperate, and so she called Jake Dillon.

* * *

The armed response Police Officer had been walking through the departure lounge at Heathrow Airport when he spotted the suspect. He watched the man as he queued to present his boarding card and passport. The official on the Custom's desk swiped the passport through the barcode scanner. This information immediately raised a Suspicious Movement Alert on the Central Custom's Database. Armed with the suspect's name, Maximilian Kane, the data was bounced around and transferred to the National Drugs Intelligence Unit at New Scotland Yard, which allowed access to the Police National Computer. He read the information which instantly appeared on screen. Kane had a criminal record. Kane's image on the passport didn't match the one on file...

The dedicated departure gate for the British Airways flight to Paris had closed and the Custom's officer went to the computer terminal, and typed in the command that would show where and when a ticket was purchased and whether there was a connecting flight. As he looked at the information being displayed on the screen he was sure of one thing. Maximilian Kane was definitely up to no good. He had bought the ticket for cash, but in the name of Mark Cane. Which meant that he was using a false passport and an alias? There was also a connecting flight booked to Amsterdam three days later. Why stop over in Paris? But, cash and Amsterdam suggested one thing. Dirty money - someone, somewhere, would welcome this snippet of information about Maximilian Kane.

Meanwhile, Kane settled into the business-class seat of the British Airways flight to Charles De Gaulle, Paris. A Financial Times draped over his right knee, held lightly between long manicured fingers. He was wearing an expensive hand-tailored dark blue pin-stripe suit and highly polished black leather shoes. His white shirt was one of a dozen he had packed into his suitcase. After all, he had the money and when travelling only ever wore a shirt once, discarding it in favour of the crispness of a new one. The round tortoiseshell framed reading glasses placed lightly upon his nose made for the finishing touch. Over the years he had worked hard to create the image of old money and blue blood. Only an old-school boy would smell a rat. But his immaculate dress sense was a result of frequenting Savile Row tailors who were more than willing to offer their advice about; what to wear and when to wear it. Right down to what colour cufflinks should be worn and when. His Sartorial elegance had been an expensive exercise, but it was the attention to detail which made all the difference.

Kane's family was new money from developing property on the Sandbanks peninsular and in the Borough of Chelsea, London. The family blood was distinctly red, but who gave a shit about all that in this day and age. He certainly didn't. He peered across to the window, watched the black tarmac speeding past, and imagined his brand new Bentley Continental racing along just under the jets turned up wing tip. He heard the engine pitch change and the aircraft lurch as it became airborne, and he relaxed. Despite his apparent comfort, airports always made him uneasy. There was always that underlying fear that he would be stopped as he boarded the plane. There was always the fear that he had forgotten or overlooked something. Perhaps the authorities knew that he carried another identity. Perhaps he hadn't spotted their surveillance.

He was tall and slim, physically fit, didn't smoke and had never tried. His once Dark hair was now a light silver colour, cut short. The lines of age and worry were being slowly etched across his tanned face. He looked in his mid-forties, ten years younger than he really was.

Kane's thoughts were broken by something unpleasant. An ordinary looking woman had changed seats and was now sitting across the aisle from him. She was somewhere in her mid-thirties, wearing a dark grey business suit which could have done with a good dry-cleaning. She was somewhat sweaty, and Kane could smell her body odour from where he was sitting. Why did so many people lack style and good taste when they tried to look smart? Why did they bother to dress for flights? Then Kane noticed her footwear. Cheap tights in shoes that were virtually worn out, the light grey suede uppers scuffed with ground in grime, the heels worn down. He always looked at a person's shoes. "You can tell a lady by her shoes," his mother once told him. Ladies and women who were really police officers, Kane had learned.

Kane felt a flutter in his stomach. He knew why. He was paranoid. He knew all about surveillance. There were small incongruous signs; the satellite engineers van parked over the road from his Kensington flat all day, and not an engineer in sight; the florist's van which no business could afford to leave idle; odd incidents at bars when he caught people looking at him. The same two or three cars following him on the motorways at weekends down to his Dorset home.

The plane hit an air pocket. Kane looked up and realised the woman was addressing him. "What?" He said.

"I said; it's amazing how these planes stay in the air."

"I'm led to believe that it has something to do with the wings!" Kane replied sarcastically.

Some people have no idea about personal space, thought Kane. Especially the police, and again there was the little flutter in the pit of his stomach.

The woman seemed to ignore Kane's sarcasm. "Do you often use the shuttle?"

"First time," Kane lied easily. He hadn't once looked the woman in the eye. She was definitely a member of the other firm. No one would have the gall to pursue a conversation in the face of such a taciturn response.

"It's my first time as well. I've a meeting in Paris. Where are you going?"

"Paris," replied Kane laconically. "Unless we've both got on the wrong flight and we're heading for Morocco."

"Oh no, I'm sure we're going to Paris. Well I'm going there on business." This one had definitely undergone a personality and humour by-pass.

"I might never have guessed. After all, you are travelling business class." Kane said.

"Yes, I work in publishing. The firm I work for has an office in the city."

Kane didn't reply. He hoped that the woman would shut up.

"What's your line of business, if you don't mind me asking?" The young woman chirped again.

Kane minded very much. "Architect," he snapped, and wondered how to terminate the conversation. One thing was sure. He wasn't under surveillance. After all, if you could see them then they weren't watching you. They'd have stopped him at the airport and asked him a question or two if they were interested. They weren't shy, but they were tenacious; and this irritating woman didn't look like giving up.

The flight was turning into a nightmare. He had some talkative female sitting next to him, who might or might not be an undercover police officer. Next time he would travel on an aircraft with a First Class option. In the meantime he had to stop this chit-chat. He stood up and went to the toilet. When he returned, he opened his briefcase and retrieved his Financial Times and studied the share prices. It was hard to concentrate. He couldn't remember what was exactly in each of his off-shore accounts in Geneva and the Cayman Islands.

"Sorry, I talk too much."

Kane ignored her.

"I've not been to Paris before Mr Kane."

Kane blinked. He hadn't told her his name. Perhaps he had introduced himself. No. He never gave the woman his name. The little bitch must have looked in his briefcase. Yes. She'd peered at his passport which was poking out of a side pocket inside. Or had she known his name before she embarked? Nasty, he thought. "Try the..." he was about to say, "Beck's," instead he decided, "Moet". That would put a large dent in the little bitch's expense account. She'd have a hell of a job claiming that on expenses. It would probably send the entire publishing industry into a spiralling slump.

"Could you spell that for me?" She proffered a small note pad and pen.

Kane looked at her hand which was ordinary, like the rest of this unremarkable young woman. If she thought she was getting a set of his fingerprints on that paper she had another thing coming. Maximilian looked squarely at his fellow traveller. He stared unblinkingly into her eyes and said very quietly and with cold firmness, "Look, why don't you go fuck yourself, can't you see I'm busy?" He turned back to his newspaper.

"That's nice. That's bloody charming," commented the woman. "I was only trying to be friendly. Trust me to pick a seat next to an arsehole..." She blushed. "You bloody jerk," she finished lamely.

* * *

"What did I do?" Thought Kane. "She was, after all, most likely to be a publishing assistant going about her business and I treated her like an undercover copper."

Kane had hopped in and out of taxis all over Paris in case he was being followed. He had too much to lose through carelessness. "I'm getting too long in the tooth for this game," he mumbled to himself. It used to be fun but now it was business and he was tired of looking over his shoulder. However, a chance encounter wouldn't force him into retirement. He was at the pinnacle of his career. Even the smallest deal made him five hundred thousand; and he wouldn't lift a finger for anything less. As governments cracked down on organised crime, the street price of drugs soared to reflect the much higher risks involved. Things had never been better. So long as he didn't take chances there was no reason why it should ever end.

It had been remarkably stupid of him to tell a perfect stranger to go fuck herself. However, it wasn't surprising if he overreacted sometimes. He was under pressure; and it wasn't helped by continual anti-drug campaigns across all media and a Parliament always trying to push through tougher new laws and harsher penalties for those involved in peddling drugs onto the streets of Europe. But this meant having to be vigilant in the extreme, especially when setting up deals with the Russians or the Chinese and when dealing with the Columbian cartels. It was all very stressful.

At last, convinced that he had not been followed, he made his way to the rendezvous. The Hotel Des Grandes Ecoles on the Sainte Genevieve Hill, a fairy-tale place in the historical heart of the Latin Quarter in the 5th Arrondissement, where each paving stone is charged with history. In the picturesque streets surrounding the famous Sainte Genevieve church, restaurants of all nationalities flourish. The Pantheon, the ancient Polytechnic School, the Sorbonne are the hotel's neighbours. This substantial pink mansion with tall, slate mansard roofs, fancy wrought iron balconies, louvered shutters and an azalea-filled courtyard is one the most charming in Paris. A hundred metres from the entrance to the hotel, Kane turned down a narrow pathway that would take him around the impressive building, and allow him to approach from the opposite side. There was still cause to remain cautious.

* * *

Two hours later Kane was sitting in the best suite of the Hotel Des Grandes Ecoles, trying not to think about his hidden agenda. He found it hard to act naturally with his Russian business associate, Aleksey, now he knew the truth. The two men were sitting in near darkness, for which Kane was grateful. Now and then Aleksey poured another flute of Krug Grande Cuvée from the Champagne magnum. Outside, the street lights shone crisply in the icy autumnal dusk. Winter was coming.

It was a time of year when criminals schemed and planned for the next twelve months, and double crossed their partners. At last Aleksey stood up and turned on the light. He was a man with an arrogant air about him, tall and upright, eyes the colour of coal and a look of too much good living and wealth about him. His clothes were expensive and handmade by the best tailors money could buy. Even at fifty-five, he was still a handsome man, relatively slim and when it suited him - fit. The features which had made him attractive to women when he was young, still had them falling at his feet. It was amazing what the skilled hand of the surgeon could achieve. Kane imagined him smelling of death under all the bling. The size of his wallet was his most endearing feature. The gold medallion around his neck and heavy gold chain bracelet on his wrist were Aleksey's bling. Kane didn't like to be seen in public with him anymore; and he never said when he was arriving at the airport in case Aleksey came to meet him in his Lamborghini. Nevertheless, Aleksey was one of the few men he'd been forced to trust and who knew him by his real name. They had done business together from the very beginning. He supplied the drugs when Kane had been studying Russian at Moscow University and then afterwards in Paris, where Aleksey had moved. Kane had made a lot of money from selling drugs while living in Paris and had purchased the ocean going racing yacht, Freebase ll, with some of the profits. Now, however, Aleksey was careless. There was nothing more dangerous than a Russian drugs baron exercising the last throes of power. Aleksey knew far too much about Kane and it made Kane nervous.

Aleksey flopped in a chair. "So what is it you want, my friend?" He asked. He had obviously decided the pleasantries were over.

"I have a client ready to take a half-ton shipment of candy within the week."

"This is not a problem."

"What's the country of origin?" Kane eyed the Russian closely.

"Colombia," said Aleksey evasively. "Don Rafael's cartel has taken over down there!"

"What about the price?" Kane asked.

"We are partners," said Aleksey. "We will share the profit."

"Fifty percent of nothing is nothing," Kane said.

"What's the shipment costing you?" Kane knew exactly what it cost; and now he knew how Aleksey had ripped him off for years, he wanted to see how good an actor he was. He wanted to hear the figure from Aleksey's lips.

"We've done business before, Kane. We don't need to talk prices."

"I need to know the prices now, Aleksey. Not later. I can then make a firm commitment to the half-ton shipment."

"Half a ton of candy is not such a big deal." Aleksey almost sneered. He had made his point. He was one of the biggest drug barons in Northern France. In the early days he and Kane had only dreamed of moving half a ton of drugs.

Kane had to keep the Russian sweet. "This is a one-off deal. After that, I'll be looking for one ton a month. That's twelve tons a year, Aleksey."

"So, you are now in the shipping business," said Aleksey quickly, with a smile. He knew that when people wanted precise figures they were restricted to a schedule.

"That's my business."

"I am assuming that you will be shipping the product over sea, concealed inside petrol tanks, so it must be a good route. But my supplier cannot give you credit, as the risk is too high."

Aleksey was talking bollocks; but then he didn't know that Kane had made direct contact with his supplier. Don Rafael, and already arranged a credit line with the Colombian cartel. "I never said it was being transported inside the tanks. How I do it is my business, and I want to keep it that way for security reasons. However, if there's no credit, then there is no deal and definitely no partnership. You're having serious problems finding safe outlets in the UK. That's why I work with you Aleksey. You have big options on the Cocoa crop in Colombia but you're in the middle of a drugs territorial war here in France. You need me, but you need the UK more because it's the biggest single market in Europe."

"Sure Max, but the pound is always weak. If your country's deficit gets any bigger and it devalues, I lose big time."

"Right now the pound is stable and looks like staying that way for the time being. Your problem is the transport into the UK and I've solved that."

"Things are not that bad, Max. I can get the candy out

of Colombia; especially now I have new methods."

"But you can't land that much product in the UK, can you?" Sometimes Kane wondered if he was talking Penguin instead of English. It was like talking to a five year old. "Right now I want a credit price for the material. Good quality and ready to go."

"Five thousand Euros per kilo," said Aleksey. Kane nearly gagged on his Champagne. Aleksey liked to haggle over the figures, but that price was daylight robbery. The Russian had obviously never heard of Dick Turpin, who would have at least had the decency to wear a mask when he robbed people at gunpoint.

Aleksey would never know that Kane was only feigning an interest in the deal to keep him quiet. That interest would die as soon as he took possession of the initial sample consignment, which belonged to Don Rafael. Aleksey's days in the business were numbered. He had made too many enemies along the way and now he had become too greedy. He'd bought options on material he didn't have a hope in hell of selling; and now he was irritating genuine buyers who were forced to negotiate with him as the middle man. Don Rafael was cutting up rough because Aleksey had inflated the prices, and failed to pay on time. Aleksey was cutting his own throat, and Kane was enjoying the show.

Kane had powerful friends. And now he had Don Rafael on his side. He only had to pretend to agree to Aleksey's price. The price was immaterial because Kane was going to pay Don Rafael a fraction of what Aleksey wanted. Kane had gone through the back door and Aleksey was being pushed out the front. Aleksey's last deal would be to pass Don Rafael's product, which he was holding on credit, to Kane. All Kane had to do was make sure that Aleksey didn't suspect anything.

The door from the adjoining suite opened and an attractive woman, somewhere in her late forties, walked into the room. She was scantily dressed in expensive underwear but nevertheless Kane stood up politely. Aleksey laughed and waved him down. "This is Natalya," he said. "She's a very dear friend of mine from Moscow."

"And you are?"

"Adam," said Kane. "My name is Adam," he lied instinctively.

Natalya cast a glance in Kane's direction and ignored him. She walked to the mini-bar, opened it, leant forward and stared inside, closed it. She pouted, but she was past the point where she was impressed and it had little or no effect. "I'm hungry Lexi," she complained.

"We are still talking," said Aleksey, casually. Natalya left the room. "She is very good in the sack. But I'm sending her back to Moscow. Hookers don't cost so much money as women who have aspirations of marriage. You can have her if you like." He roared with laughter, but wasn't joking.

Kane looked at the Russian blankly without comment. He didn't find Natalya to be his type. Real floozies were two a penny. He was calculating percentages. They were far more rewarding. He reckoned the dollar would fall against the pound and the Euro over the next three months, which in turn meant that by transferring the money to a numbered account in Switzerland; that would be worth another six percent.

"Tell me something," asked Aleksey curiously, "why is it that you are scared of making a really decent size deal? Why not ten tons? Why do you bother with half a ton consignments all the time? After all, you only increase your overheads."

"After all these years Aleksey, I'll let you into a little secret. It's why I'm still in business and a free man and my bigger competitors have been put behind bars. The UK market is the biggest in Europe but the quantity you are talking about would be enough to saturate that market for a long time. After that, marketing slows down, which means the product needs to be warehoused for longer periods. Most Police raids occur because of storage. You need people to mind the warehouses. You keep visiting and collecting the stuff for distribution. After a while everyone, including the Police, knows that the drugs are in storage. Then you get nicked. If you import half a ton at a time the whole lot is on the streets within two to three days. No storage. No evidence."

"I have people in the UK who say they can take ten

tons."

"That's fine Aleksey. Work with them," said Kane. Aleksey was always a pain - always chipping away. If he knew the UK market so bloody well he should have been over there doing business himself. But, the Russians were scared shitless of England; the trouble was Her Majesty's Revenue and Customs, the Drug Squad and the prison sentences. The Russians had good reason to be scared, thought Kane wryly.

Kane suddenly remembered he had to make the negotiations look good. "I want one more condition on this deal. I want an exclusive contract with you. You don't work with any other firm in the UK."

"My business is my affair, Max."

"Not when you work with me. I have to market the product. If two firms have the same product we stand the danger of a price war. The dealers shopping around for the best prices and then it starts to all get messy. I hope Aleksey, you're not under the delusion the product sells itself. It requires marketing, just like any other. It's a business, with quality control and price points. Sometimes you forget that. I don't want you complaining that the product isn't selling quick enough because you've flooded the market to my competitors and the white stuff is all over the country but not selling. In the end, the only winners are the Police."

"You always drive a hard bargain, Maximilian." Aleksey held out a fleshy palm for Kane to grasp. It was evidently a deal.

No way could Aleksey suspect Kane of a double-cross now. "I'm paying you over the odds, and you know it," said Kane. "Otherwise, you wouldn't have done the deal so eagerly."

Aleksey almost smirked.

"My client will collect on Thursday, at 3.00 pm, from the usual location in Amsterdam."

"Very well, that is not a problem. But I want you to think about something else I have."

"What is it" asked Kane, his attention already starting to wander.

"I want you to consider planes, Max."

"I am not going to consider planes," said Kane firmly,

his mind quickly returning to reality. There was no point wasting time on this subject, with a man at the end of his career.

"Planes are a nightmare to organise. You send them up on a thousand mile journey to pick up the candy. When they get back to the UK they look exactly like they've been involved with drug smuggling. Flight plans that cost a fortune to falsify and cargo that will get the pilot and crew at least twenty years in a maximum security prison. That's if they don't get frightened and jettison the entire cargo over the Channel or decide to go into business for themselves and rip us off. Just forget about it, I've been there done that, Aleksey. I've also lost a lot of money playing with aircraft. And I'm not going down that route ever again."

"OK, Max. Listen to me. This time is different. This time I am the co-owner of a VIP air charter company that has a fleet of Cessna Citation Sovereign long range jets flying all over Europe and to the USA. I can get the cocaine on board with minimum risk. You tell me when you're ready. I ensure that one of the aircraft is within easy reach and I send in the team to clean up the aircraft once it lands and take the product off with the rubbish. Each aircraft can safely hold up to a hundred kilos each trip. You can have as many consignments as you can take, each and every week."

Kane knew he had to humour Aleksey. Once upon a time he would have been interested in his schemes. But times had changed. He had lost Jasper, the only person who could deal with the logistics of an operation like that. Now he was running back-to-back deals, instead of marketing, because Jasper had got himself locked up in a Hong Kong high security prison for ten years.

"That's not of any interest to me Aleksey," said Kane. "And anyway Jasper is not around at the moment."

"So find someone else."

"Not so easy. Jasper has the contacts for an operation like that."

"Oh come now, Max. Everyone is available for a price."

"Not Jasper. He's serving ten years in Hong Kong. They grabbed him when your Chinese friend Wong's import-export business was rumbled by the Hong Kong Drug Agency." Kane watched Aleksey's reaction closely.

"I'm sorry to hear that. I wasn't aware that you'd lost someone as important as that." Aleksey stared at Kane for a moment. "Everyone is available for a price. Even your friend Jasper - and I have excellent contacts in Hong Kong. Maybe they can get him free."

"What's it going to cost?"

Aleksey thought for a moment. "One hundred thousand American Dollars should do it."

"How long will it take to get him out?"

"The last time was extremely fast. Ten to fourteen day stops. Just as long as there are no complications, after all, how long does it take to get one piece of paper from the Justice Department to the prison?"

Kane's mind was racing ahead of itself. Jasper would be out of prison. Jasper would be very useful at the moment. It would make this new venture simplicity itself. He wouldn't have to recruit anyone else. He hoped Aleksey stayed alive long enough for Jasper to be released.

"You have a deal," said Kane. He smiled. He was fifty-six in two weeks time and a cash millionaire many times over, so a hundred grand was like petty cash to him.

Kane smiled. White teeth flashed as he smiled. "So now we fix a price for my new deal?"

"Four thousand Euros," offered Kane.

"OK." Aleksey said after a moment's thought. "Only this one time", though Maximilian.

Kane smiled. Aleksey thought he'd made a bargain. It was almost pitiful.

* * *

The fearsome looking baton clattered noisily over the bars of the prison cell, the guard taking pleasure waking the inmates in such a manner. "Wake up, English." Shouted the short Chinese guard with the big smile on his fat sadistic face. It had been the same routine every morning since Jasper had been incarcerated here. It simply made his resolution to escape more determined! Unfortunately the signs weren't favourable, and the day was starting as any other. A guard would usually come and summon him to the Governor's office. But not this morning, this morning he walked with the others looking casually around the prison yard. The walls were ten metres high, topped with broken bottles and razor wire. A million shuffling feet had long trodden the earth into concrete, so there was no chance of digging a tunnel even if he could organise murderers, lunatics, thieves, corrupt politicians, smugglers and all the filth and trash. On the face of it, the only quick escape was in a coffin.

The fat Chinese punched the young scrawny prisoner who was forced to give sexual favours in return for extra scraps of food. The other inmates standing around smirked. It was a perverse sort of entertainment. One of the other inmates muttered words of disgust in Spanish, spat forcibly onto the ground and walked off. The Chinese guard registered the insult. The Spaniard had money and status which bought him protection. But one day the money would run out, and then the Chinese would have his day.

The Chinese guard ruled Jasper's wing with brutality and violence. Soon he would be bored of tormenting the youngster and search for another victim. "Hey English!" He shouted. He was too late.

Jasper had slipped away to hide among the lesser criminals for the time being. Only seven months of his ten year sentence had elapsed. He thought obsessively about escape. Each day his escape plan moved forward. He only hoped he wasn't making a terrible miscalculation.

The guards relied on supplementing their wages from money the prisoners gave them in return for American cigarettes, extra food and drugs. Foreign prisoners were the most valuable because they had money, and consequently they were nurtured and cherished for the duration of their sentences. Penniless foreigners were always a problem. They tended to appeal against their sentences but didn't have the funds available to pay a top-flight lawyer. Worst of all, without family or friends they received visits by an assigned Liaison

Officer from their Embassies who were invariably dismayed at the degenerating condition of their nationals. The Spaniard would serve his full time. He was arrogant and unrepentant for the heinous crimes he had committed; including, multiple murder, rape, drug smuggling and distribution. Jasper had once tried explaining to him the workings of a Chinese high security prison but he wouldn't listen. He wasn't interested in suffering briefly in return for his freedom. The Spaniard optimistically expected a reprieve from the three life sentences that had been meted out to him.

In the meantime Jasper was sustaining himself with the real belief that he would soon be free. Free or very dead from trying to escape, he scratched the soft flesh just under his right armpit at something that felt like it was making its home under his skin. He could feel the raised areas of skin that went down his side to just below his rib cage. He'd already dropped two stone in weight. He was sure he had lice and his back felt like he'd been kicked by a mule. He didn't know how much longer he could survive without asking the British Embassy to cable for money from... whom? Martha? He'd rather not worry her.

Max Kane knew where he was and what had happened. He was surprised he hadn't heard from him already. Max would be on the case. Jasper was confident of that.

Of course he could write to Martha. He would have to borrow the money from the Spaniard to bribe a guard to post the letter. The guard would take the money and then most likely not post the letter anyway. Jasper wondered what he would say in the letter. "Hello from Hong Kong, I'm having a blast of a time. Goodbye, see you in ten years or never again." Of course he could always get himself put in hospital. It would be much easier to escape from there that is if he had the strength.

Jasper glanced towards the far end of the prison compound, sectioned off for the two executions that were taking place the following morning. The gallows had been erected and the seating for the VIPs and local dignitaries set out in an orderly fashion. It was rumoured that there would be a reprieve for one man. But the other would surely drop. No one knew which prisoner would be reprieved, yet.

"Who gives a shit? They're both murderers," said the Spaniard apathetically, offering a cigarette, which Jasper accepted in a moment of weakness. "Every day we are all dying a little more."

Early the next morning; the two prisoners were manhandled up onto the scaffolding. Jasper observed that neither of them appeared to have been given any sedation and both were praying as they were being positioned. There was an unnatural hush over the prison as all inmates contemplated their own mortality. The Prison Governor stood up and made a speech. Two trap doors sprang open. No reprieve came for either man. The two dangling bodies twisted and turned, delivering a spasm or two at the end of the ropes. Jasper now knew that death by hanging was not instantaneous.

"Hey English," shouted the Chinese guard. "You like our little show?" The fat faced Chinese laughed and punched Jasper on the arm. It was a playful friendly gesture under the circumstances. Jasper thought he was going to be sick. Suddenly he snapped, and all his pent up frustration and rage exploded.

"You're an arsehole; you haven't got a fucking clue." The Spaniard had disappeared. The Chinese guard's smile froze. This was a moment he'd been waiting for. The English had made a big mistake. He'd snap his bones like kindling.

"English!" Shouted a guard from a doorway of the main building.

Jasper turned towards the guard. "The Governor wants to see you immediately. Two guards were standing behind him, one of them jabbed him hard in the back with his baton stick.

"Move it English."

Chapter 2

Max Kane relaxed in his seat. He was more careful now than he had ever been. He was taking safety into another dimension. They won't catch me again, he thought. He had prebooked a flight-ticket to Amsterdam which he had never intended to use. Instead he was on his way to Switzerland. His flight into Geneva International Airport was on time and had just landed; he hired a BMW five-series saloon and drove to his bank in the city. The UK Serious Organised Crime Agency or SOCA would have to work with Interpol, who might know that he was up to something, but they would have to find out where he was going and what was going on first. To do that they had to follow him, and he was keeping an eye on his rear-view mirror. That time he had done on remand had been time well spent, he thought. He had laundered a large sum of dirty money and if anyone asked him what he was living off he had over a million pounds tax-paid. When HM Revenue and Customs had carried out a routine inspection they had found the usual anomalies and had set about investigating his entire business affairs. After he had paid over what was due, he had invested what money was left in the UK, and made it work for him. The dirty money - they would have to find it first and that would be hard, especially when he had completed this latest trip.

The numbered accounts of the Swiss banking system were not as secure as they once were; but still provided the account holder with a greater degree of protection from scrutiny while minimizing the exposure of the account holder's name in public settings. Of course things had changed since the signing in 2009 of bilateral treaties with a number of European countries, which had weakened the protection previously offered and now allowed an exchange of information between the UK agencies and the Swiss. This was something that had bothered Kane for a while and the reason why he was making this inconvenient journey.

One of Kane's acquaintances had recently been investigated by a Revenue and Customs team. They knew the man was involved with the smuggling of cannabis but had only been able to convict him on a relatively minor charge of 'possession with intent to supply'. They carried out a thorough investigation of his living standard and discovered that he was living beyond his means. They found he made frequent trips to Switzerland and deduced that he had secret numbered accounts, but they didn't know where or which bank. When the trail went cold they had to resort to a process of elimination and eventually struck gold. The investigators then requested that the account details be divulged because they were the proceeds of crime. The transactions from one account had led to numerous other accounts of individuals now having to defend themselves at the Old Bailey.

There was no way that Kane was going to end up like that, he thought, as he walked through the double revolving glass doors leading to the cavernous main reception hall of the prestigious bank. A suited young woman came and admitted him to the inner sanctum of the building. He was led to a familiar room which was minimally furnished with a long elegant contemporary oak table and two chairs at both ends, and a sumptuous royal blue carpet from wall to wall. He stared at the carpet that had been recently vacuumed while he waited for Herr Leitner.

The door opened. "Good morning Mr Kane. Good morning."

"Good morning Herr Leitner." They exchanged a few pleasantries and then settled down to business. It had been like this for the last twelve years. They never asked each other personal questions or used their Christian names. Leitner grew a little older and became a little thicker around the waist.

"Now, what can I do for you?" Leitner produced an expansive smile, revealing perfectly capped white teeth.

"I wish to rearrange my portfolio with the introduction of a trust fund."

"We have talked of this many times in the past. Very

wise, and which options do you wish to consider?"

"I was thinking of Belize."

"Ah yes, Belize is a very sound option." That was enough for Leitner to know exactly what his client required. Of course, that was why he had clients. They didn't have to spell out their wishes to him and he was under no illusions. The kind of money which passed through his department's hands seldom originated from legitimate enterprises. He even had a number of eminent politicians from around Europe who entrusted their ill-gotten gains to him. "I have an associate in Belize who is a lawyer. He will set everything up for us and I would highly recommend that we take this route. His firm will act as the 'Settlor' who is the person or legal entity that will create the Trust by placing the assets that you own into the Trust. You will obviously be the 'Beneficiary', and I will act on your behalf as the 'Trust Protector'. I will open the company for you," Leitner paused for a brief moment and took out a gold fountain pen.

"Is there perhaps a specific name you would prefer?"

Kane thought for a moment and then smiled. "I think it should be Oceanic Leader Industries?"

"Very well, we will incorporate a Belize International Business Company in the name of Oceanic Leader Industries. Firstly, I must run a thorough check to ascertain that there is no other company existing with this name, but I think that this will not be the case." Leitner was highly intellectual, but had no sense of humour at all. That was the trouble with the Swiss. If they needed to laugh they had to leave the room and go to the bathroom. "The Settlor will hold the theoretical stockholding of this company. You see, there will be nothing remaining to connect you with your company. And now we will make the secret trust agreement between us, which you will keep. I will arrange for your company to open a numbered account here, at this bank. Of course, your old account will be closed today and a new one opened at the same time and a new number will be assigned."

"What would happen if, for example, the accounts of Oceanic Leader Industries are examined?"

"That is very simple. On inspection, it will show that

Oceanic Leader Industries is a company operating from Belize. It will show that I am the officer, and I am above suspicion, I can assure you. The only proof of ownership of Oceanic Leader Industries is the trust agreement, which will be prepared for your scrutiny and signing by tomorrow midday."

"I am not available tomorrow. Perhaps I could meet with you in say, three day's time?"

"As you wish, I will have my secretary draw up all of the necessary documents."

"Is that all Herr Leitner?"

"Yes that is all Mr Kane. The rest will not be a problem. We must provide a minimum capital of twenty-five thousand Euros, but once the company is formed this will be returned to you. Apart from that we must pay a figure to be determined, but not more than two thousand Euros per annum, every year to the lawyer who is also the director of Oceanic Leader Industries. I hope that everything is clear?"

"Yes, thank you. I am perfectly clear on all points Herr Leitner. I will see you on Friday morning?"

"Certainly, I will be available at eleven-thirty." Leitner stood up. Kane looked at the Swiss banker's face and had a brief moment of panic. He wondered if he could really trust this man with his entire fortune. Leitner interpreted the look.

"Don't worry, Mr Kane. There is nothing to be concerned about. This is all entirely normal."

"You must not forget that here in Switzerland we rely on making arrangements like this. If anything should go wrong we would lose our credibility and no longer be the banking capital of Europe."

"Of course, I do not doubt the arrangement for one moment."

Leitner led him to the door, opened it, and bowed indiscernibly. The heavy door closed behind Kane. He was pleased. He had safeguarded his money and provided a comfortable home for the proceeds of his next major deal.

Kane's European meetings were not over. After a quick lunch he was back in the hired BMW five-series saloon heading for Italy. He'd stop the night at the five-star Hotel Splendide

Royal in Lugano overlooking Lake Ceresio to indulge himself in absolute luxury. In the morning he'd drive to Venice, where he had meetings with Abdul-Malik Al-Jazari and another man. This man, whose existence was unknown to all Kane's business associates, was the only person Kane truly feared; and discovery of their relationship would be dangerous for both of them.

This man had provided Kane with details of Jasper's arrest in Hong Kong. He told Kane what had happened, and that Abdul-Malik Al-Jazari was reputed to be Aleksey's source. Most important of all, this man told Kane how Aleksey had tipped off the Hong Kong Drug Enforcement Agency about the consignment. At last, the pieces slotted into place. Aleksey kept Kane's advance payment because Jasper had taken possession of the candy before the bust. Then, Aleksey bought the candy back at a discounted price, and it never reached the narcotics disposal incinerator on the outskirts of Hong Kong. Aleksey's only insurance was one hundred kilos stashed in a warehouse somewhere just outside Amsterdam; and when that was delivered, he was dead. Good riddance to bad rubbish.

* * *

Some mornings were better than others, but since his last assignment; taking on Ramus and his female Assassins, every day started the same - in a bad way. Jake Dillon constantly promised himself that he would try and get a proper night's sleep every now and again. He'd stop smoking and cut down on the drinking too. Somehow the habits of many years kept interfering with his good intentions. It was eight-thirty and the Ferran & Cardini International building was just coming to life. Standing on the roof of the building he had a view across the skyline of London in all directions; he pulled out a packet of cigarettes and lit the first of the day with the gold lighter that Tatiana had given him many years previously. The headache which would surely develop over the course of the day made a few tentative stabs. It had nothing to do with his habitual nightcaps, or his eyesight. Dillon knew the air-conditioning caused it, the whirring of the computer hard drives and the constant ringing of telephones all merged into a blinding cacophony. The lighting in the department had never agreed with Dillon and was far too bright. He crushed the cigarette butt with the sole of his shoe; breathed in the smog of the city and thought about drug smugglers and serious organised criminals who were sitting on Caribbean beaches, breathing pure Atlantic air, and living off of their vast immoral earnings. It was galling.

Dillon checked his emails and flipped through the various sheets of paper that Edward Levenson-Jones had left on his desk in preparation for their meeting later that morning. He was in his late forties and the oldest and longest serving Field Operative in the department with a long list of successful assignments to his name. He opened a drawer and popped some painkillers into his system, washing them down with the last of his lukewarm black coffee. It was best to deal with the headache before it took hold and dealt with him.

He was back on the firm's payroll after a long period of convalescence in an exclusive Italian clinic, recovering from the numerous injuries he'd sustained during his last assignment; all courtesy of HM Government. He was going to be working with Vince Sharp again, and that made him smile. The big Australian was one of only handful of computer hackers considered the best in the world. Together, Dillon and Sharp were considered the best intelligence gathering team in the business.

Edward Levenson-Jones' report of the assignment and intelligence briefs landed on his desk first, informing Dillon of the budget and procedural protocols. Dillon always felt calm before embarking on an assignment, success gauged by how many criminals, megalomaniacs and narcissistic fanatics were brought to book. His alter ego measured the success of the assignment by the number of body bags lined up in the morgue.

Dillon attracted the jobs that the younger Field Operatives couldn't or wouldn't undertake. His peers mistakenly believed he expected to be given these arduous and highly dangerous assignments that were issued at the monthly op's meetings. He didn't give a damn. After all, he had retired once and it had nearly killed him!

Dillon's attention was caught by an email that stood

out from all the others in his in-box. He opened the file and read carefully through the text. It had come from the Ferran & Cardini station in Nassau. He wasn't working on anything connected with the Bahamas so he doubted it would provide any links with his current assignments. However, it might lead to a jolly overseas trip, which would be no bad thing.

Gathering intelligence soon put paid to any belief in the probability of coincidence. Anyone who'd been flagged by the world's intelligence and crime agencies in the past and who suddenly reappeared usually indicated some new conspiracy in the making. The email surprisingly concerned Jasper Nash. It had been intercepted and forwarded to the Home Office. It concerned the Chinese who had apparently released him after he'd served only nine months of a ten year sentence for cocaine smuggling on an enormous scale. The email came from his old friend Dunstan Havelock at the Home Office and gave a flight number and time of arrival at Heathrow. Dillon looked at his monitor screen for a moment deep in thought. If Havelock was involved then it meant that he was now involved because of the 'secrets for drugs' element involving the North Koreans. This was obviously far more sinister than drug smuggling and concerned the safety of the UK.

Dillon thought back to the meeting he'd had with Martha after she called him.

"Thank you for agreeing to meet me," said Martha, awkwardly.

"It's no problem," said Dillon. "What's on your mind?"

"Oh no," she said quickly. "Nothing really," she paused.

"Look Martha to be honest, I agreed to come here tonight because you sounded a little distressed when you phoned me." There was an uncomfortable silence.

"I'm sorry. It's just that I can't come to terms with what's happened. There's no one I can turn to. I can't seem to grasp the enormity of it all. Is there really no hope? No chance that Jasper could be freed early?"

"There's always a chance," said Dillon, cautiously. "But the charge is a serious one and the Chinese authorities are harsh with meting out maximum sentences. Early release is virtually unheard of. If I were you, Martha, I'd put Jasper Nash behind you." He knew it was a mistake to become too friendly with the enemy or their women. It had a nasty tendency of affecting judgement. "Start again. Put bluntly, he was willing to sacrifice you, and now you have to make a decision."

"It's not as easy as that," Martha said angrily.

"Why?"

Martha looked at Dillon for a brief moment, "Have you ever been in love Jake? I mean so truly deeply in love with someone that they are all you can think about. That it becomes unbearable when you're not with them. Have you Jake?"

"I'm afraid, Martha, that I haven't. I've loved, but unfortunately I can't say that I've ever met anyone who does that to me." Dillon felt awkward and looked around the bar they were sitting in. "I'm sorry for what I've just said; it must be awful for you."

"Oh don't be sorry, you're just doing your job. Whatever that is? I really only wanted to talk. You see there isn't anyone else who knows the whole truth."

"What was it like with Jasper?" Dillon asked curiously. "What is it exactly that you find hard to leave behind?"

"Jasper's such good fun," said Martha. "We always enjoyed ourselves."

Dillon knew all about that. Of course they enjoyed themselves. They had money, lots of money. He'd seen it many times before. There was a rosy glow which ready cash brought to the cheeks of criminals. "You know," he said, "this is not unusual, in the world you've experienced, to find that relationships never get past the honeymoon stage. All those dinners, all those five star hotels, all those exotic far flung holidays: neither of you had to face up to the trials and tribulations of everyday life."

Martha was silent, digesting what he had said.

"I know I'm being blunt and it appears that I don't give a damn about your feelings. But I believe that it keeps things real, being honest."

Martha smiled weakly. "Of course, what you say makes sense."

"Forget him," said Dillon. "You're young, you're beautiful. You still have a life ahead of you. Jasper is not going to be released; he might not even survive the experience of a high security Chinese prison."

Martha's eyes widened and tears started to roll down over her cheeks.

"Sorry. I shouldn't have said that. But you're worth more than being left in the lurch by Jasper. You can pick up the pieces and start again." Inside, he wanted to say how happy he would be to look out for her. But that wouldn't be right and he wouldn't jeopardise the entire assignment because of some middle aged soft spot he had for this dark eyed beauty. He was doing it again, what the therapist had warned him of: getting too involved. What did the therapist know anyway, she thought she was treating him for post-traumatic stress syndrome? But once again he had concealed his secret - the alter ego that only surfaced when his life depended on it.

"Look, I have to go now. But if you need someone to talk to, then give me a call," he offered as he stood up.

"That won't be necessary, thank you anyway." Martha shook Dillon's hand and walked out of the bar.

Dillon watched Martha walk away, and glanced around the bar area for anyone who might follow her out and left.

* * *

Martha never called him back. Now he knew how she felt about Jasper, he should let her know about Jasper's imminent release. It was far better if she heard it from him and not someone else, and then jump to the wrong conclusion. He picked up his mobile phone and dialled Martha's number. It was still early in the morning. He heard her voice, "Hello?"

"Martha, it's Jake Dillon."

"Oh. Hello?"

"I thought I should let you know I was completely wrong the other evening. I've just heard that Jasper was released from prison last night."

"I know," said Martha. "It's marvellous news. I can't believe it."

Dillon hesitated a moment. "How did you find out?" He asked suspiciously.

The line went very quiet for a long second in response, before Martha's voice, a few degrees colder, replied, "Someone told me."

"Oh," said Dillon. "Well, I'm very pleased for you."

"Thank you," said Martha. "It was kind of you to think of me."

Dillon wanted her to tell him who had told her, but decided not to be too pushy. "Well, I'll leave you in peace Martha. Goodbye."

"Thank you Jake. See you around."

"Yeah, maybe," Dillon said doubtfully. He pressed, end call, and Martha Hamilton was gone.

Dillon knew who had told Martha the news of Jasper Nash. It was Maximilian Kane.

Jasper Nash was freed because someone knew exactly where to place an accurate bribe. By no stretch of the imagination was six months a respectable proportion of his sentence, however tough the prison conditions. What irritated Dillon more than anything else was a memory. Jasper Nash was Max Kane's right hand man, and Dillon had been assigned the duty of nailing both of them to the floorboards. No doubt Kane was responsible for springing Nash. If Kane wanted Nash out of prison then he was planning something big. It fitted together. Kane, after months of inactivity, had suddenly started to appear on the reports of various agencies around Europe. The most recent being a report from Customs at Heathrow when he boarded a flight for Charles De Gaulle Airport, Paris, using the name Mark Cane.

Dillon picked up the Glock pistol and felt its reassuring weight in his grip. He felt the coldness of it and remembered how many times it had snuffed out a life to protect his own. For a moment his thoughts drifted back in time, to Anna Westcott. For a moment he felt melancholy. He pictured her all those years ago, beautiful and vibrant. He had experienced loneliness like never before after her death. And now he was chasing the man who was responsible for her death. His thoughts came back to the present, as he slotted a fully loaded magazine into the base of the grip.

* * *

Dillon walked along the dimly lit corridor to his meeting, it was seven-thirty and he'd already been working for two hours.

As he entered the large office he always felt a shiver run up and down his spine at the austerity of the room. The man sitting behind the highly polished desk carried on writing, only after a few awkward moments did he look up from over his wire framed spectacles.

"Good morning Jake. Please take a seat." Edward Levenson-Jones gestured for Dillon to sit down.

"Good morning LJ."

The Head of Covert Operations opened the file on his desk and placed his hands palm down on the highly polished surface. "The Home Secretary wishes me to convey his thanks to you for undertaking this assignment. That said I believe you are most definitely not the person for this assignment." Dillon was about to comment, but LJ stared him down and continued. "Dunstan Havelock has arranged for you to have unlimited resources at your disposal, and a special licence to carry that Glock 20 of yours. However, the Partners and I would prefer it if you could possibly refrain from killing everyone with whom you come into contact with. The problem is old son; it creates such a lot of paperwork." LJ raised his right eyebrow as he leaned back in his chair.

It had been a long time since Dillon had spoken to Max Kane and he relished the idea of reacquainting himself with him once again.

LJ continued with the briefing. "Kane has been under surveillance for just over a year. The Serious Organised Crime Agency suspects that he has been involved with importing substantial shipments of cocaine and Marijuana for many years but the evidence to-date has all been circumstantial. He never touches the drugs himself; instead he hires intermediaries to carry out the dirty work. However, he did make a mistake about two years ago by picking up a suitcase full of money from a courier at Heathrow Airport and was arrested by an undercover drug team. The suitcase contained fifty pound notes to the value of half a million pounds sterling. He was charged with receiving illegal currency and money laundering. In court, he pleaded not guilty and produced a Russian businessman who provided documentation supporting that the money was in fact the operating capital for a property development deal. Apparently the judge didn't think it unusual tender for that type of investment, and decided to acquit Kane on that charge. But he didn't get away completely unscathed, he was ordered to pay all legal costs and the Value Added Tax on the total amount. It was a hollow victory for the authorities and Kane knew it. Afterwards, Revenue and Custom's officers spent many months investigating Kane, which merely served to effectively legitimise all of his assets and money in the UK." LJ handed Dillon a file, the name on the front cover, Maximilian Kane.

Dillon thumbed through the detailed report sheets inside the file and decided he would make his way to Heathrow and take a look at Max Kane's lieutenant. Jasper Nash, and welcome him back to the mother land. While he was sitting in an interview room, he'd take his picture through a two-way mirror to bring his file up to date. He might even hold him for a few hours just to make him more agitated. Kane might even be at the airport to meet Nash, which would be rather fun, but if not he would have a little chat with the lieutenant, perhaps Nash would provide a lead. One day Maximilian Kane would make a mistake.

Chapter 3

Martha had never really liked Kane. She'd met him when she first met Jasper while she was studying art at Bournemouth University, twelve years ago. He'd always been aloof and very vague about his life. She thought he was emotionally inept. She knew he resented her relationship with Jasper and had competed for his attention in the early days. When she had found out that he and Jasper were involved in smuggling she had made it clear that she didn't want Jasper bringing his work home. That meant that Jasper didn't bring Kane to their home. As a consequence Kane drifted out of her life. They occasionally bumped in to each other around town, but they seldom did more than exchange pleasantries. Over the years people had come to assume that they hated each other, though Martha thought that too strong a description for the indifference she felt toward him.

When Kane phoned to give her the news about Jasper's imminent release from the Chinese prison he asked her if she would like to have dinner with him. Her first impulse was to refuse him point blank; but she accepted. She wanted to know exactly what had happened to Jasper. After she replaced the receiver she wondered why he had made the offer. There were times during the last six months when she would gladly have welcomed dinner in the hope of knowing a little more about Jasper's whereabouts.

* * *

"I thought that this was a good opportunity to celebrate Jasper's release," said Kane, pulling the Bentley Continental up outside of the multi award-winning Chewton Glen hotel located on the edge of the New Forest National Park, in Hampshire.

"Have you dined here before Martha?"

"No. I thought only celebrities and the very wealthy

came here, to be honest," replied Martha sarcastically

"The food really is quite exquisite," said Kane unperturbed.

Martha said nothing as they entered the five-star opulence of the country house hotel and spa. "This is nice, very nice," she thought. "So this is how you live while Jasper takes the fall for you?" She bit her tongue.

From the moment they walked through the main entrance through to the dining room, Kane was greeted with an air of respect by the hotel staff. The maître d' showed them to a reserved table which was obviously Kane's usual by a window overlooking the hotel grounds.

"I do so like it here," said Kane. "You're treated like royalty and it's so peaceful." Kane said gazing out the window, and smiling added. "I'm very happy that you accepted my invitation Martha."

Martha supposed the remark was meant to be friendly and flattering. Perhaps Kane had serious delusions of grandeur.

"Why haven't you called me in all the time that Jasper has been locked up? You are after all, supposed to be Jasper's oldest and closest friend. I think I might have deserved a call."

Kane picked up his napkin and then laid it down again and looked at Martha. "Why do you suppose Jasper is being released? I've been working tirelessly on his case to find the right people to overturn his sentence. It took a lot of time, effort and money. I didn't want to raise your hopes by calling you before I had something positive to tell you."

"I'm sorry," said Martha, quickly. "That sounded very churlish of me."

"It's quite alright," said Kane graciously. "You were entitled to an explanation." He turned his attention to the menu. "What have you chosen?" Kane asked at last.

"Seared scallops, smoked duck and Asian broth, followed by the roast halibut."

"Excellent choice," said Kane enthusiastically. "I like a decisive woman." He closed his menu and the Maître d' immediately sent a waiter over to Kane's table. He ordered, while the sommelier poured the 2009 Olivier Leflaive Meursault.

Kane sipped and then hesitated. He sipped again, discovering the many layers that this wine offered. Kane always thought that if you still have doubts. Like sex, you'll regret it if you're not sure. He turned to the sommelier and nodded.

"You do know that Jasper is going to retire when he returns?" Martha said sipping her wine.

"Really?" Said Kane, raising his eyebrows. "I hadn't realised." He placed his hands together as if he were going to pray. "Does Jasper know about this imminent retirement?" Kane's tone was derisory.

Martha's contempt for Kane's arrogance and smugness almost got the better of her. "Of course we spoke about it just before he left for Hong Kong."

Kane nodded. "Well Martha, it's an interesting concept. But Jasper has never mentioned this to me, and as you already pointed out. He is my oldest and closest friend." Kane nodded. "I don't know if Jasper is ready for retirement. He might get bored."

Martha didn't react. They sat in silence until the first course arrived, and Kane didn't waste any time devouring everything on his plate with gusto. He wiped his lips with an over zealousness that made Martha wince. "Delicious!" He commented. Martha thought her starter was an inspiration to her senses.

Kane embarked on a monologue about his property development company. It didn't interest or impress Martha in the slightest as she savoured her main course. Kane ordered another bottle of wine. Occasionally he tried to draw her into conversation. "You ought to buy more property. High end stuff, that's where the money's to be made even during these times of austerity, they're always in demand to rent down here. You tell Jasper, it'll set you both up for life."

"Perhaps we will, one day," said Martha. "When we decide what we want to do and which direction our lives need to take."

"Oh you don't want to wait too long Martha. Time doesn't stand still for any of us. I'd be delighted to arrange everything for you both, should you wish."

"That's kind," said Martha, and guessed it somehow helped him launder money. She wondered why he was going to all this trouble to pretend that he was a legitimate businessman.

"What happened to Jasper in Hong Kong? What went so badly wrong for him that he ended up getting caught with his hand in the sweetie-jar?" Martha asked.

"I really wouldn't know," said Kane, casually. "I mostly look after Jasper's financial affairs these days. You see, I've retired. But he was up to his old tricks again. I heard about it through a third party and felt I should use my contacts in that part of the world to help him."

"I'm not stupid," said Martha.

"I know you're not Martha," replied Kane. "You're not stupid and you are extremely attractive."

"You've drunk the best part of two bottles of wine."

"That has nothing to do with it. I've always thought you were attractive. There's something about you I've always desired. You're always so radiant Martha."

"You haven't seen me first thing in the morning."

"It wouldn't matter." He smiled.

"Well lucky for you, you'll not be finding out, Max."

Unfazed, Kane asked. "Would you like anything else?"

"No thank you," said Martha. "I should be getting home. I'm really tired."

"I think I'll have a brandy and coffee. Are you sure you won't join me?"

"No. Really, I have to be going."

"Very well, then. I'll give you a lift home." He gestured to the Maître d' and indicated he wished for the bill.

"Actually," said Martha. "I don't think you should be driving and I don't think it wise for you to come to my home. I had a visit from the Home Office this morning, or that's where he said he was from. He told me that Jasper was on his way home."

Kane's face stiffened making his angular features look stony and chiselled. "Did this person say anything else?"

"No."

He looked at the bill and reached into his jacket for his

wallet. He counted out the crisp fifty pound notes, and placed them on the silver salver. "The feel of new bank notes never ceases to bring pleasure to me, and it always looks so flash to pay with cash," he said.

"I think it's rather common," said Martha. "But thank you for dinner."

They stood up and Kane followed Martha to the main entrance of the hotel. He hadn't suggested driving Martha home again and a taxi was waiting for her. As she opened the taxi's door, he leaned forward to try and kiss her. She moved her head at the last moment and avoided his lips.

"Goodbye Max," she said.

Kane stood and stared coldly at her as the Mercedes pulled away.

* * *

When the Cathay Pacific Boeing 747-400 took off, Jasper knew he was free and that the Hong Kong authorities were not playing some malicious Chinese trick. He swore he would never gamble with his liberty again. Nothing on earth was worth the risk of losing his freedom and being sent to prison. One thing was certain. He would give up the drug smuggling. He would have enough money when he collected it from Kane. He could buy a small country hotel or something by the coast. He might start a property development company and use it to launder some money. That would please Martha, developing not laundering. He knew that his activities had increasingly perturbed her of late. She had long wanted him to retire. He only hoped that she had not taken him at his word to move on if he ever disappeared or was sentenced to a long term in prison.

He smiled up at the stewardess as she handed him the first class menu. She didn't smile back; she had seen him handcuffed to a police officer at the first-class departure gate. Jasper didn't care, though he'd liked to have had an excuse to flirt with her a little. He turned his attention to the menu and gourmet dishes on offer. After the shit he'd eaten over the past six months, he was looking forward to lunch and dinner during the thirteen hour, twenty-three minute flight. The straight-faced stewardess returned and took his lunch order of various Chinese dishes and a half bottle of Veuve Clicquot Brut NV Champagne.

Jasper stood up and stretched his legs by going to the bathroom. As he walked back to his seat he looked at his fellow affluent travellers and realised how much the last six months in a Chinese high security prison had taken out of him. In the past he prided himself on his physical fitness, not to the extent of being a muscle bound bodybuilder, but well-toned. He was a tad less than six foot one inch with a slim build. He had fair hair and blue eyes. He could melt into a crowd within seconds. Now he stood out like a sore thumb. People looked at his shaven head as if he were some sort of escapee from a religious cult, but the hair would grow back, and they stared at the tailored Savile Row light grey suit which hung on his scrawny frame. They averted his gaze from bloodshot blue eyes, just in case he was a recovering alcoholic.

After a month or so of good living he would soon put on weight. And with his hair back to normal, he would start to be himself again. The past would be a nightmare. He began to picture his life moving forward, a brand new start with Martha; somewhere they could live a normal life in peace and quiet. He'd tried retirement from the business once before, but hadn't really given it a chance and had returned after only eight weeks. He found the boredom too much and domesticated life had soon led him to one drink too many. Then there was the spending, fast cars and frequent visits to the casino which soon started to eat into the money in his quest to find something that even came close to the excitement of smuggling cocaine. He finally recognised that he was on his way to a stay at The Priory and the bankruptcy courts. So he made the decision to return to the business and the rush of adrenaline and the thrill of survival. He came out of retirement and submersed himself back into what he now knew was his fate.

Now, things had changed. He had heard the rumours and been told things that he now knew to be true. No amount of money made prison acceptable. He recalled the ambitions he had aspired to while studying at Cambridge, before he had met up with Max Kane and got into the smuggling game. Smuggling had been exciting. It had provided the means to travel and had supported him through university with a first-class degree in English Literature as the end result. It had given him the escape from conventionality and the routine driven lives of ordinary hard-working people. Now he envied the rest of humanity. He wanted to do what normal people did everyday of their lives. He wanted to buy a car, anything, on credit. He wanted to go shopping in a supermarket and know what food actually cost. By the time the aircraft was on its final approach to Heathrow he had started to warm to the idea. He was about to come down to earth with a bump and join the real world at last.

When the aircraft landed Jasper felt physically drained and emotionally weakened. As he approached passport control, his pallor was noted by the immigration officer.

"Is something the matter, sir?

"Six months eating Chinese prison food."

"Oh." The passport was handed back quickly and Jasper shuffled off along the walkway.

* * *

Dillon was concealed behind the one-way observation glass, snapping images of Jasper Nash on his smart phone that were automatically uploaded to Vince Sharp's server at Ferran & Cardini. The word from Immigration that Nash had landed was sent via a secure link from their mainframe that Vince Sharp had set up specifically for this assignment to monitor the comings and goings of Maximilian Kane and Jasper Nash. Vince was also the only other person who knew the real significance of Dillon agreeing to this assignment.

Dillon made his way to the baggage hall to speak to the duty officer in the 'Red' and 'Green' channels. No one paid any attention to Dillon. None of the passengers would have guessed that he was a specialist covert field officer working for what looked like a private company who answered exclusively to HM Government. His mousy brown hair was always unruly, and looked as if it needed a good cut. His physique gave the impression that he was fit, but the years and the job had taken their toll on his body and mind. With stainless steel pins and titanium plates holding the majority of his bones together and anti-depressants keeping his head in order, he managed to keep going. Luckily he had always retained his keen sense of humour and the ability to laugh at himself. All of this made his ability to get into the psyche of his adversary's one of his specialities.

Five minutes later Dillon caught sight of Jasper Nash standing by the baggage carousel. He wondered what designer luggage Nash would have, probably Rimowa or Victorinox. Wealthy criminals liked tough expensive looking luggage as it gave the impression of sophistication and a globe-trotting lifestyle. He watched Nash reach out and retrieve a heavy looking bag and then wheel it away towards the Green Channel. It wasn't a designer Rimowa case after all. Dillon nodded at the uniformed customs officer standing on duty and indicated Nash. "Even if I didn't know Nash," he thought, "I'd still have him stopped. He's just stepped off a flight from Hong Kong wearing an expensive handmade suit and looking decidedly fatigued. But not from the first class flight."

The customs officer looked at Jasper Nash and said with authority. "Excuse me, sir. Would you mind stepping this way?" The uniformed officer indicated for Nash to place his case on the metal surface of the bench in front of his position.

Nash closed his eyes, opened them, forced a smile, and said with geniality, "Of course officer."

"Where have you come from?"

"Well my flight ticket tells me that I've just flown in from Hong Kong."

"May I see your passport?"

He offered it without a word.

"What were you doing in Hong Kong? I see that you have been there for the last six months."

"I was in prison."

The officer looked up sharply. Although Dillon had briefed him, he hadn't expected such a truthful answer. "Oh dear," he commented. He looked down at the passport again, flipping through the pages to see if Nash had visited any other dubious places. There were plenty of them. "What were you in prison for?"

"I was in the wrong place at the wrong time."

The customs officer raised an eyebrow, especially as he knew that Nash was a drug smuggler. "How unfortunate for you," he remarked. He tapped the battered suitcase with his hand. "Can you open the suitcase, sir?" He asked with a straight face.

"Be my guest." Jasper Nash looked casually around.

"Perhaps you would open it up for me."

Nash sighed in exasperation. He leaned forward and unlocked the catches on the suitcase. The officer said quietly, "Did you know that a lot of 'class A' drugs are smuggled out of Hong Kong, sir?"

Nash jerked his head up and blinked at the customs officer. "No I didn't know that. But thank you for telling me."

The officer carefully rummaged around, under, and over Nash's belongings looking for any suspicious. He felt all around the lining of the case and ran his hands over the lining of the lid. "No souvenirs, sir?"

"No."

The customs officer looked carefully over the suitcase. He picked at the corners and pushed the areas that could conceal a hidden compartment. He was merely playing for time. He didn't know if Dillon wanted to interview Nash. "I'm wondering if you're concealing drugs sir. I'm also thinking if I should call for a sniffer dog."

"Do what you want. You won't find any drugs in the case or me!"

"Of course I am only thinking out loud sir." Rapid eye movement, the suspect was uncomfortable. Not surprising, really, under the circumstances.

"You're not looking too well sir."

"I must admit I'm not feeling a hundred percent. I need to see a doctor."

Through his earpiece the officer heard Dillon's voice.

"Take him to a free interview room and then leave him on his own."

"If you'd follow me to an interview room sir, I'll call for a doctor to check you over."

"No thanks. I'll see my own private doctor if it's all the same."

"Let me put it another way sir. I believe you might have been taking drugs. Please follow me."

"What the fuck is going down here?" Nash demanded as he followed the customs officer. "This is harassment for God's sake." He snapped between clenched teeth.

"We won't detain you for long sir." The officer asked Nash to take a seat, placed his suitcase by the wall and closed the door as he left.

Jasper Nash looked around the bare room. The walls were white with only a one way observation mirror facing him.

"Jesus Christ," muttered Nash. "This is definitely a set up."

Dillon stood behind the one way mirror, arms crossed, wondering whether to interview Nash, watching him becoming more agitated by the minute.

Nash looked older than forty-five. Perhaps prison didn't agree with him. Dillon smiled to himself. Nash had wasted his life. He could probably have been very successful in any field he had chosen, but he had chosen crime. He had a university degree, a lovely girlfriend and was more gifted than the average person, but something was missing in his make-up. He lived on the edge of life. He enjoyed taking risks. Dillon recognised the symptoms. He had empathy with characters like that. Risk-takers, from gamblers to prostitutes that lived outside of society. They took chances every day and it distorted their view of reality. Unfortunately, luck tended to run out with youth; and there was nothing more pathetic than an old criminal.

Six years ago Nash had shown up on the files of MI5. At that time they could find nothing on him and the file was suspended - until now. The instruction had come from Dunstan Havelock the Home Secretary's private office to pass the file to Ferran & Cardini International. Dillon had been assigned to handle the investigation and to discover who Jasper Nash had been acquiring highly classified military secrets from, and then passing on to the North Koreans for undisclosed sums of money. The priority had been to find this person or persons. Dillon's initial search threw up nothing more than dead ends. But this time Jasper Nash was going to lead him straight to whoever it was...

Dillon had gained a grudging respect for Nash during the days and weeks he had spent on the case, and had even come to understand him. He learned that Nash was generous; he didn't lend money he gave it. He was also very professional in the way he conducted both his business and personal life. He was street wise and a little paranoid, and almost impossible to follow if he thought for one moment that he was being watched. Dillon once put a dozen good men and women in six cars on to him and he still managed to give all of them the slip. Dillon couldn't resist the opportunity to talk face to face with Nash for what could be the first and last time.

As Dillon placed his hand on the door handle he reminded himself, "There are no whole truths; all truths are half-truths. It is trying to treat them as whole truths that plays the devil." And Dillon liked nothing better than to play the devil's advocate. If Nash was inquisitive enough to know who and what this temporary incarceration was all about, then Dillon had a fair chance of finding out much more about Nash and Kane's business.

Nash looked with disinterest at Dillon when he entered the interview room. Finally he leaned back in the chair and stretched his legs out under the table, waiting for Dillon to introduce himself. Even then he remained silent, waiting for Dillon to explain why he was being detained. Dillon pulled the only other chair out from under the table and sat opposite Nash.

Dillon grinned. "Not very talkative are you?"

"It's not surprising." Nash replied.

"I see that you've spent the last nine months in Hong Kong, and that six of those were in a high security prison. I was wondering if you'd mind telling me about that Jasper?" Dillon asked.

Nash thought for a moment. He contemplated saying

nothing, but there was little point in antagonising the opposition. Dillon appeared to be different from the usual gloating customs official. There was something about him that was familiar, and yet Nash couldn't pin-point what it was. But he might learn something to his advantage from a conversation. "Well it's not something I'd want to repeat. The sooner China gets a human rights programme, the better."

"Perhaps you could tell me about your arrest?"

"I told the customs chap the story."

"Being in the wrong place at the wrong time, story?"

"That's the one."

"That was just a yarn. I want the version where you got busted because you were caught with your hand in the candy jar."

"You seem to know so much that there's little point asking me." Nash smiled.

"There's a small matter to clear up. You most likely know that conspiracy to import drugs into the United Kingdom, even when committed on foreign soil, is an offence." Dillon could have shown his hand and mentioned treason as well. But it was too early in the game to demonstrate that he knew about that.

Jasper Nash said nothing. "They'd have a hell of a job proving it. The case in Hong Kong would never have reached the courts in England."

"Is your silence an acceptance or a denial of your conspiracy?"

Nash chose his next words very carefully. "It's the first time I've heard of this conspiracy. I was convicted on a trumped-up charge. You'll see for yourself when you investigate the facts. I don't know what you mean by conspiracy. Where are my fellow conspirators? Perhaps you'd like to elucidate. Then I'll decide if I should speak to my lawyer."

"Well Jasper, you haven't answered any questions so far."

"I would like to leave now. I've just stepped off of a thirteen hour flight and I'm not in the mood for playing your silly little games."

"I'm sorry to hear that Jasper. Think of it like this, the narcotics trade does not leave many people in the best of health."

The chair legs scraped against the hardwood floor as Jasper Nash stood up and stretched the tension out of his body. Enough of this chit-chat, he thought. He was terminating the interview. They would have to arrest and caution him before he uttered another word. But who were they, he thought?

Dillon recognised the stance. It was something he had seen many times during interrogations; but this was no ordinary interrogation and Nash's silence only implied guilt; and Dillon was damned if he would release Jasper Nash so easily. He fired a warning shot at him.

"Tell me something, Jasper. Are you still on talking terms with Maximilian Kane?" Dillon paused. There was no answer. "I suspect Kane had something to do with your recent troubles. It wouldn't surprise me if it was Kane who had got you out of Hong Kong. Now you feel that you are indebted to him. I don't believe you're so bad. A bit misguided, maybe. You might even possibly be a fool. But Kane's a really hard-core nasty piece of work. He and I go back a long way. And I want you to know that we're keeping him under surveillance. Whatever he does and wherever he goes. If you're smart you'll keep him at arm's length, you might even consider staying well clear of him." Jasper continued to ignore Dillon. "When you discover the truth about Maximilian Kane, I want you know that I'll give you one opportunity to do what's right. Remember that. I'll give you one lifeline only."

Nash resisted the temptation to tell Dillon to fuck off. That would be a foolish move. Anyway he had no plans of becoming an informer.

"Now you are free to go," said Dillon and then added. "I haven't finished questioning you Jasper, but I can see you're fatigued and there's no point taking this any further here. I will want to question you again and the relevant agency may bring charges against you sometime in the near future. In the meantime your girlfriend, Martha, must be looking forward to seeing you."

Jasper Nash opened his eyes. "Martha has absolutely nothing to do with any of this," he said. He then stared at Dillon.

Dillon smiled. He'd made his point, without giving away the whole game. He wasn't really interested in the drugs smuggling, customs would get that one, his assignment was to catch a traitor or traitors of the realm - and to find whoever it was in the Ministry of Defence or at the highest level of Government leaking the highly classified information to Nash.

"Would you like a lift back into town? After all, I only came here to talk to you."

Nash suddenly felt very uncomfortable. He certainly didn't warrant that much attention. He looked suspiciously at Dillon. "No thank you. I'll get a taxi."

"No problem. I thought you'd say that." Dillon said with a smile.

Chapter 4

Aleksey placed the phone down onto the highly polished surface of the coffee table. He was sitting on one of the sofas in his suite of the Hotel Des Grandes Ecoles, which he now regarded as his home. Don Rafael's courier was waiting downstairs. He put on his cashmere jacket and turned for the door. He looked at Natalya contemptuously. She had dressed up for the evening. He dropped two five-hundred Euro notes onto the floor. "That's for your dinner. I have to meet someone now." Natalya reached down and snatched up the notes, stuffed it into her purse and followed him out of the room.

They'd barely spoken a word all day. The writing was on the wall; but Natalya wanted a pay-off before she left for good. She had given six months of her life to Aleksey. The next time that son-of-a-bitch left a large wad of cash lying around she was taking it back to Moscow; and from the nature of Aleksey's phone calls, she thought this might be the night.

Natalya reached the lift first and pressed the button to summon it. Aleksey hesitated for the briefest of seconds, and then decided to take the stairs. As he walked he reflected that he found Natalya most attractive when she was in a stroppy mood. He'd tie her up and fuck her for that later. She liked that.

Downstairs in the hotel foyer Aleksey expected to see a South American tanned face. The only man waiting had a pale complexion, fair hair that was thinning on top, and a paunch that had obviously grown out over his trousers over the years. He was wearing a badly fitting dark brown suit and tan coloured leather shoes that were scuffed on the toe. Aleksey stretched out his hand. "You are Don Rafael's courier?" He asked.

"That's right," said the small man, returning a limp damp handshake.

"I am Aleksey. It's a pleasure to meet you."

"I know," the man nodded. There was tiny broken thread vanes scattered across his cheeks. His eyes were brown and darted nervously around the foyer, which was deserted except for the receptionist and the concierge. Under each of his eyes he had hound-dog fatty pouches which Aleksey couldn't stop himself from looking at. The lift announced its arrival with a chime, and Natalya emerged. She stared at Aleksey as she left the hotel.

"Who's she?" Asked the man.

"No one," said Aleksey. "Let's go to the square for a drink."

The two men left the hotel, turned left onto Rue Du Cardinal Lemoine and crossed to the other side of the road towards the Place de la Contrescarpe.

"What name did you say?" Asked Aleksey.

"I didn't," said the man.

He thinks he's a clever bastard, thought Aleksey. These couriers didn't trust anyone. Cold fish - and this one was no exception. He walked with his shoulders hunched and he didn't look people in the eye; he most likely couldn't with those huge bags under his eyes.

"My name is Mr Kipper," said the man, suddenly.

"That's a strange name, but OK. Mr Kipper it is," commented Aleksey. He looked at Mr Kipper, and realised that the badly fitting suit hid a muscular fit body.

"Is this bar very far?" Mr Kipper asked.

"No, it's not far. Just around the corner off the square. Have you been to the Latin Quarter before, Mr Kipper?"

"No, never before and I doubt I will ever again."

They reached the café, took a table inside, and ordered cognac and espresso coffee.

"I do not have the money with me. We will have to go and collect it." Mr Kipper talked with a cockney English accent. Aleksey found it hard to understand some of the man's words.

"That's OK. We can take our time."

Normally Aleksey wouldn't bother to meet a courier for money. He'd send one of his minions. But this time Don Rafael was sending a trusted employee from his European operation and had asked Aleksey to show his hospitality and a good time out on the town.

Aleksey wanted to find out as much as possible about Don Rafael's future plans. What sort of business was Don Rafael doing in the UK? Who was he working with? Why was he employing someone from London? He'd banked money for Don Rafael before, but not when they were the direct result of an operation. Aleksey hoped Mr Kipper would let something slip.

Aleksey ordered another round of cognac which they downed in one gulp, and then left for a place of entertainment. Aleksey stopped abruptly outside a door and rang the bell.

"What are we doing here then my Russian friend?"

"This is a private gentleman's club," replied Aleksey.

* * *

This wasn't how Mr Kipper planned it. He thought they'd just hop into Aleksey's car and drive to the airport to collect the money. He hated having to work outside of the UK. He hated all foreigners and foreign lands. Travelling always made him feel inadequate and inferior. Just asking for a simple beverage in a café was traumatic because he couldn't speak the language. It had taken him forever to find his way to the meeting with Aleksey because of his abhorrence to using taxis. And now he was being dragged into some private club that could either be filled with raving faggots or whores on the make.

"No," he said. "I don't feel like it."

Mr Kipper turned and looked back up the road they had just walked along. He didn't like being outside, it made him nervous. He found himself constantly on the look for anyone staring in his direction, for just a second too long.

The large oak door opened and Aleksey turned to Mr Kipper and said, "This is my English friend, Madame Giselle's establishment, one of the best members -only whore-house in Paris. Come on, let's go in and have some fun. I'm paying, so try everything and anything you desire."

Mr Kipper followed Aleksey inside. It wasn't curiosity

which made him follow. He knew that he had lost control of the situation.

They walked up to the bar and sat on black leather stools. Aleksey ordered Champagne. In a booth at one end of the room four men in suits talked quietly amongst themselves. Two girls approached Mr Kipper. "We drink Champagne," they both said giggling.

"I bet you do," the Londoner replied with a snorting sound emanating from his nostrils. "You'd better ask him, he's paying." Mr Kipper pointed at Aleksey who had moved up to the other end of the bar and was in deep conversation with a tall dark muscular doorman dressed in a well-fitting black suit, who had a swarthy complexion and cropped naturally black hair. Aleksey looked back at Mr Kipper, ordered two more glasses and had the barman take them to the other end of the bar.

One of the girls wandered off, while the other sat on the stool next to Mr Kipper and introduced herself. "My name is Coreen," said the young Italian woman with auburn hair and beautiful sun-kissed skin. She brushed her body suggestively against him as she reached over for her drink.

"That feels very nice," he commented.

"You are not drinking?"

"No." replied Mr Kipper. He wanted to get out of this place, get the business finished, and get home. Aleksey looked as if he was settling in for the long haul.

"You have a very strange accent. Where are you from?"

Mr Kipper thought for a moment. "America," he replied.

"Oh how wonderful," she said giggling again.

Mr Kipper looked blankly at the attractive tart sitting next to him sipping Champagne at two-hundred Euros a bottle, his mind turning over what he should be doing right now.

"You like me?" asked Coreen.

"Yes. You're very beautiful. What man wouldn't find you desirable?" Mr Kipper knew that if he didn't talk to the girl, he would have to talk to Aleksey.

"You want to come upstairs with me? I can show you a

really good time, and I do a very unusual speciality."

"I'm sure you do and I bet you're very good," said Mr Kipper, curious at last.

"First you will lay back and watch me play with myself. Then as you become aroused, my friend will come and join me and we will pleasure each other before we both pleasure you. Of course you may do anything you desire, and I mean anything. It will be very exciting and we have many extras if you wish to indulge even further. Afterwards we will all share a bath together, and your friend can join in too if you wish. One thousand Euros is all it will cost."

"My friend will be paying, but he will definitely not be jumping into any bath that I'm in. Of that you can be certain." Mr Kipper said sharply. He cast a glance at Aleksey who was still in deep conversation.

The attractive young woman said, "Shall we go upstairs now?" and holding Mr Kippers hands, she pressed them to her small pert breasts.

"Let's go," he said standing. Aleksey looked up from his conversation and smiled. He picked up his Champagne flute and raised it towards Mr Kipper, who watched and thought no way was Aleksey getting into a bath with him and these tarts.

Mr Kipper nodded at Aleksey and indicated that he was going upstairs.

Aleksey smiled.

* * *

Mr Kipper followed Coreen into the darkened room. He turned and locked the door. He didn't want Aleksey barging in and he wasn't interested in watching two girls making out either. He sat on the edge of the bed. He had no intention of doing anything. He just wanted to be alone and wasn't interested in conversation, no matter how basic.

Coreen put on soft music, she wasn't in a hurry. Time was money. Mr Kipper watched her slowly take off her clothing. He was surprised to see that she had a hairy beaver. He couldn't take his eyes off the triangle of dark hair, as younger women always shaved these days. He was starting to feel aroused.

The memories came flooding back of his youth when getting women to oblige had been much easier. He watched between her thighs as she undressed him. It had been a long time. She placed handcuffs on his wrists and ankles and then secured each one in turn, with deliberate display and a definite pleasure. Slowly she began massaging his erect penis with warm oil, her hand slipping gently up and down his shaft. He closed his eyes.

He sighed as her soft thighs straddled him. He felt the warmth of her as their bodies merged. The arm and leg restraints only heightened his excitement. And moments later, his eyes bulged open as an explosion ripped through his abdomen and he experienced a euphoric, massive and welcome orgasm.

The tart didn't use a condom, but he didn't care. He closed his eyes and lay perfectly still as the handcuffs were released.

* * *

In a room along the hall Aleksey sat on a chair, spread his legs, and let the young French tart nestle between his knees. He cupped her pert breasts and watched Mr Kipper through the mirror. He had learned a lot about his business associates by watching them in bed. The thing about Coreen was that she had a trick. Mr Kipper would leave the room and never know he hadn't been fucked. She'd smother his penis in baby oil and guide it between her ample, clenched buttocks and hold it in place with her hand. It was an old whore's trick, but Coreen was good at it. Not many men could tell it wasn't the real thing. Aleksey smiled.

* * *

Mr Kipper had parked his hire car in a quiet corner of the airport's long-stay car park. He directed Aleksey towards it. Otherwise they had sat in silence for most of the journey since Mr Kipper reacted angrily to Aleksey's persistent questioning.

"You liked Coreen, huh?" Aleksey asked. "She's very good." He teased.

"Why don't you shut the fuck up, and mind your own business." Mr Kipper snapped. It had been long time since he'd felt like this.

"Turn left and then straight ahead to the far end and the car is on the right."

"Well you sure did tuck it in a quiet corner."

"Stop here," said Mr Kipper pointing at the small red hire car.

"You left a suitcase full of money in this car?" Aleksey asked incredulously.

"Yes," replied Mr Kipper.

"You're a crazy man. This town is full of low life criminals and crack-heads. They break into cars in car parks all the time."

"Well then, we're very lucky aren't we, because they missed the jackpot this time?"

Aleksey turned off the engine, and they both stepped out into the neon light of the multi-story car park. They walked over to the red hire car. Mr Kipper looked around. The car park was quiet, no one around or watching. He opened the boot and reached inside. Aleksey peered in. He didn't see a suitcase.

Aleksey felt a crushing blow to his kidneys. He staggered and turned to face his attacker. The blow had knocked the wind out of him and before he could recover, his legs were kicked out from under him, and he landed heavily on the tarmac.

Mr Kipper kicked Aleksey in the ribs, then seeing the head undefended he dropped his body weight down onto the Russians chest and placed one hand around his throat and the other across his nose and face and pressed down hard.

Aleksey was younger and a lot stronger than he looked. Mr Kipper knew he should have put both hands around his throat and collapsed his windpipe with a short sharp action. But right now Aleksey had hold of both his forearms and was pushing with everything he had left to survive. Mr Kipper leaned forward and head-butted Aleksey savagely, and then stood up.

This was going to be a lot messier than Mr Kipper had planned. That was one of the problems working abroad. You couldn't carry a gun when flying. He went back to the boot of the hire car and pulled out a long wooden pick axe handle, quickly moved back to where Aleksey was laying, and swung the handle at the Russian's head with all his strength. The makeshift weapon wasn't heavy, but it opened skin and crushed skull bone with ease. Aleksey's head lolled onto the ground. Blood and gore seeped across the tarmac and congealed in a viscous pool.

"Oh Shit," Mr Kipper muttered under his breath. Blood had sprayed over his jacket. He hadn't wanted any blood, and now he had a contract with head wounds, and they always bled worse of all. At least the Russian was relatively quiet.

It was time to clean up. Mr Kipper opened up the passenger door of Aleksey's Lamborghini and dragged him across the tarmac. He manhandled the body into the seat and positioned him into a limp sitting position before securing the seat belt. There was some bloody frothing around Aleksey's mouth as the body settled in the seat. He had heard that victims who should have been dead sometimes recovered. He wondered if this bugger was still alive and decided he couldn't take any chances. Mr Kipper searched the glove-box for a makeshift weapon, found a lethal stiletto dagger, which he used to cut the throat from ear to ear. Now they'd need a medium if they wanted to talk to Aleksey.

After his work was done, he slammed the car boot. Mr Kipper fastidiously inspected himself. He wrapped up his jacket and placed it inside a plastic bag and wrapped the dagger in an old cloth from the Lamborghini so that he could clean it thoroughly later. Finally, he got in the hire car, fired up the engine, and drove back to his hotel. He was flying back to Stansted first thing the next morning. Working abroad had one advantage; by the time they found the body he would be long gone. He'd left no evidence and no clues as he had no previous form in France. They would be looking for a needle in a haystack.

Chapter 5

After hearing that Nash was about to be released from prison, Martha obsessively checked the Heathrow Airport live update app. on her iPad for that day's arrivals from Hong Kong. She waited at her home on the Sandbanks peninsula. Excitement flooded, and then ebbed as each flight came and still she heard nothing.

It was four hours after the last flight from Hong Kong had landed when Martha received a call on her mobile phone from Jasper Nash, checking she was at home and able to pay the taxi fare from Heathrow to Dorset. She waited impatiently, constantly looking at her watch, waiting for the taxi to pull-up outside.

When Nash did arrive, Martha rushed down to the main entrance of the luxury apartment block. She went outside and had to take a second look at the man she hadn't seen for over eight months. He had wasted away. His suit hung badly and his face was haggard and gaunt. He appeared to be unsteady on his feet as she went down the steps, throwing her arms around him before paying the taxi and leading him back indoors.

Once inside, Nash clung to Martha for a long time without saying anything. At last he spoke. "I was wondering if you would be here when I came back?"

"Why wouldn't I be?"

"Do you remember I once told you to forget me if anything happened?"

"Yes, but I never took you seriously."

"Well, I meant it when I said it."

"It wasn't that easy to put you out of my mind."

"You couldn't have tried hard enough," he said, and laughed for the first time in a long while.

"I wrote a letter to you every week. Did you receive any of them?"

"No. The Chinese would have destroyed them."

"Was it really terrible?"

"Terrible doesn't even come close," he nodded. "But I really don't want to talk about it right now. It's far too depressing. Later maybe," he hugged her again. "You feel good enough to take to bed."

"Well I'm glad your time in Hong Kong made you a little needy for me."

He laughed, kissing her willing lips long and slowly.

"Are you pleased I'm back?"

"I'm ecstatic," she said. "I can't think of anything better than you actually being here with me."

He looked at her for a moment, "I really don't deserve you Martha."

"I thought that, but then I had a premonition about everything turning out all right."

"I'm going to turn over a new leaf, you know Martha. The only thing that matters now is that I love you very much."

Nash saw the look on Martha's face and added quickly. "I don't want you fretting about the financial side of things. I'm owed a hell of a lot of money, and invested carefully the interest should keep us in Champagne and exotic holidays for many years to come."

"I don't care about the money Jasper. I can earn enough for both of us to get by on."

"I know, and money isn't everything, I know that. But I need to know that I can look after you properly."

"We'll look after each other," she said.

"Is that a promise?"

* * *

Thirty minutes later and Martha had to call for an ambulance. Nash had collapsed and was running a fever. He was taken to Poole General Hospital and placed in an isolation room until the doctors could determine what was wrong with him. Another month in the Chinese prison would have killed him. The thought sent a shiver through her bones.

Now that Nash was back, Martha felt whole again.

She looked forward to life with him again, and remembered how lonely she had been while he had been incarcerated. She wondered if Nash was really willing to give up his old life. A life that... She decided to keep an open mind for the time being.

* * *

Dillon considered Vince Sharp as one of his closest friends and most trusted of work colleagues. Vince was everything Dillon was not. Although overweight and Australian; he had a smart intellect that seemed to work in binary code at lightning speed and he could always see the dangers of any given situation, which made him invaluable as Dillon's back-up and technical support. His voice was pitched somewhat louder than average. Not loud enough to suggest that he was hard of hearing, but loud enough for people to notice that he was there. He had an infectious smile and an uncomplicated personality that was reflected in the clothing he wore. The jackets were always too small for his big frame, and emphasised his large paunch, but he was self-confident and body happy.

Dillon knew that Vince was back from New York because he could hear his voice down the hallway. He pushed aside the files he was working on and the mail intercepts that he was reading for the moment, and walked to the computer lab. Had it been any other person, Dillon would have waited for them to come visit him, but for some inexplicable reason Vince was different and his banter was uplifting.

"How's it going mate?" said Vince, turning to face Dillon as he came through the auto-sliding door into his computer lab.

"I'm fine," answered Dillon. "How was New York?"

"I was only there two days mate. There wasn't enough time for any sightseeing and things were busy."

"So, how did it go?"

"The Americans asked London if they could send someone with first-hand experience of our old friend Professor Kirill and, in particular the programme that he had been working on in Scotland before he departed this world for the next," Vince smiled remembering how they had literally crushed both Kirill and his Chimera Code. It appears that Kirill and Ramus were not only trying to take over the world digitally, but they were also heavily involved in smuggling 'Class A' drugs on a grand scale, and this has now got the Americans all stirred up."

"Not surprising. The Americans get twitchy when a mouse farts in Washington." Both men laughed. "But it's extremely interesting I'd often wondered how they had financed themselves." Dillon spoke quietly.

"They certainly did. And get this - they used that bloody great big stealth ship to transport vast quantities of the stuff all over the world - completely undetected."

"Doesn't surprise me at all Vince; after all, Kirill and Ramus would have succeeded in their mission had it not been for a single and most disastrous of mistakes. Their quest to destroy Scorpion helped us to destroy them. That's what happens when you underestimate the individuals you're attacking!" Dillon grinned.

"But surely you could have assisted them via a secure video link, rather than flying over there in person?" Dillon added.

"I suggested that, but they wanted me in person. When I arrived, there were all and sundry coming out of the woodwork. Since the Cold War ended - it would seem that international terrorism and drug smuggling organisations are at the top of the most dangerous list. I was introduced to C.I.A. and Drug Enforcement Agency case officers, even the MOSSAD have come out to play, and giving the names of people they suspect in arms for drugs deals."

"Umm, that's very interesting. Anything we could use on the Maximilian Kane and Jasper Nash assignment?"

"Maybe, you know what it's like Jake. There's only so much cable TV a chap can take, so I decided to sniff around the mainframe at Langley."

"You are taking the piss, Vince?"

"Don't worry, I was extremely careful and diligent in covering my tracks."

"How the hell did you get past the vast array of security measures protecting their systems?"

"Oh that was easy, but I'll tell you about that when

we've got more time! The important thing is this. Jasper Nash is on their radar." The big Australian raised his eyebrows and paused just long enough for Dillon to get impatient.

"OK, I'll let you have your glory. Tell me - why is he on the C.I.A.'s radar?"

"Well, it transpires that MI6 have him as their prime suspect for selling UK military and nuclear secrets to North Korea. I couldn't find out what exactly he's been up to but it looks as if Nash is getting his information from a squealer on both sides of the pond or someone who travels freely between Whitehall and Congress!"

"And our brief is to find out who it is?" Dillon wondered if the C.I.A. would want to cooperate fully with him. But that was a big if and the Americans could be tricky when it suited them.

"I see that Customs have sent through an interesting passenger manifest that has flagged up Mark Cane..." Vince paused and looked at Dillon.

"Should I know who Mark Cane is?"

"Oh you know him alright. Mark Cane is an alias used by Maximilian Kane."

"Max Kane. Well, well there's a turn up. I wonder what he's up to in Paris - no good that's for sure." Dillon pondered this for a moment.

"He took a flight to Paris Charles de Gaulle Airport and then booked another flight three days later to Amsterdam. But here's the thing, he never took that flight."

"Which means he's either still in Paris or has flown or driven somewhere else."

"I'll look into it." Vince said.

"Good," said Dillon. "I'd really like to see that slippery snake put down for a very long time."

* * *

Maximilian Kane stepped out of his Bentley Continental. His face looked more drawn than usual. The skin over cheekbones was taut and his lips were pale. He looked up at the sky, and then stopped to retrieve his umbrella. He then locked the car and strode down the road, umbrella hooked over his arm.

He had not contacted Jasper Nash for a month after his return to the UK. It was a tactical decision. He knew from his own experience that it took time to adjust to normal life after a spell in prison, and to make plans for the future. He also knew that he had to let the dust settle after that calamitous dinner with Martha. He didn't want her poisoning Jasper's mind with thoughts of retirement. He hoped that Jasper would be on time for a change.

"It's raining again," he said on the phone, "How about taking in a gallery at noon?" He had a moment's panic that Jasper might have forgotten the coded location, but then reminded himself that Jasper had not been away for such a long time. They would have to establish a new coding protocol before they went back to work in earnest.

The wind grabbed at his jacket as he crossed the car park and entered the Harbour Heights Hotel. He felt really apprehensive about the meeting. He had a sneaking suspicion that Jasper was really contemplating retirement, and he had to draw him back into the fold. People he could trust were very thin on the ground these days. Suddenly he felt incredibly weary. It was hard work continually persuading people to work in a way that was acceptable to him. What was wrong with everyone? He gave them an opportunity to earn shed loads of money and all they gave him was problems. He had to take it easy or he'd end up with an ulcer. In the last month he had flown all over Europe and had meetings with the Colombians in South Africa. He was working harder now than he'd ever worked before and he'd had to stop using his fake passports and was travelling under his own name until he could arrange for another identity to be created.

He caught sight of Jasper sitting in a quiet corner by the window and went to join him.

"Good to have you back Jasper," he said, sitting down opposite him.

"It's good to be back Max," replied Jasper Nash.

"You're looking better than I expected. But we'll still

have to put some flesh on your body."

"I'm doing fine thanks Max. I spent four days in a hospital bed with a virus I must have picked up in that shit-hole of a Chinese prison. But I'm feeling much better now."

"Sounds like I got you out just in the nick of time."

"You did. And I'm really grateful."

"Don't mention it. You would have done exactly the same for me."

"Tell me Max, how did you manage it?"

"I'll tell you later. I want to hear what it was like." It would help Jasper to get things off his chest.

They sat drinking their coffee in silence. Outside the weather had turned decidedly nasty. Wind and rain beat against the windows of the luxury hotel. In the harbour boats swung on their moorings like boisterous dogs pulling on their leads. Kane continually scanned the lounge bar for any eavesdroppers while Jasper droned on about his experience in the Chinese prison he had been held in. He wasn't really interested. He wanted to get down to business. He watched the waiters flitting around, serving drinks and clearing tables, and all the time Kane was wondering if any of them were undercover police officers.

"See that?" said Kane, interrupting Jasper.

"What?" said Jasper, looking around.

"It doesn't matter," said Kane. He'd grabbed the initiative. "It's good to see you've put Hong Kong behind you. You don't know it, but you've come back at exactly the right time Jasper. I've been busy while you've been away."

Jasper leaned forward in the armchair and raised a hand to stop Kane. "Before you go on Max there's something I've got to tell you."

"Oh really," said Kane, looking innocent. He already knew what was coming.

"I've decided to retire. It's simply not worth the risk any more Max. I want out."

"Why Jasper, you can't be serious. It was only six months. I did at least twice that when I got put away."

"You did twelve months on remand in an open prison in Norfolk. Not six months in a shitting hell-hole. Anyway, this is not a competition. I've decided that enough is enough. Martha and I are going on a long holiday somewhere quiet and hot. And when we get back we're selling up and moving to Italy. I've promised her that I'll quit, and that's that."

"I see," said Kane thoughtfully. He hadn't thought Martha would interfere to the extent she obviously had done.

"To be honest Jasper, that's a bit of blow. I don't suppose there's much I can say or do if your mind's really made up?"

"I have no doubt you'll manage just fine Max," said Jasper. "You always do. But, I think you're taking one hell of a risk. Times have changed. I had a lot of time to think things through during the last six months." Kane began to interrupt but Jasper carried on. "No Max, let me finish. You should take a long hard look at what's going on around you. I've only been back a month and all I'm reading in the press is drug busts every other day. You're acting like an ostrich with your head stuck firmly in the sand. Don't do it! Since the dissolution of Russia and more importantly the war in Afghanistan opening up; all the security services and drug agencies have been desperately grappling for every scrap of intelligence coming out of the biggest producer of opium and cannabis on the planet. They're all trying to justify their existence. The public enemy isn't a communist any more. It's a drug smuggler and terrorist."

"But you're talking about opium," interjected Kane irritably.

"Sure. Hard drugs - if they come across some cannabis at the same time they're not exactly going to turn a blind eye. Get real, Max. You can't fight off world-wide resources. You've earned enough to live off for the rest of your life."

"Wait a minute," said Kane. "There have been developments since you were put away. Things have changed. I've made new connections. How else do you think I managed to spring you out of prison? I've moved up into the premier league Jasper, and I've got a hell of a lot of protection."

"You're deluding yourself."

"No, I'm not. Drugs are definitely here to stay. There are growers all over the world who are controlled by the cartels. The cartels use revenue generated to purchase arms that they then sell on to the South American warlords. Why do you think the cartels and the warlords are tolerated?"

"To be honest Max, I don't care why."

"Well, it's all to do with the C.I.A. who like them preserved to use for their own end. Without them they wouldn't be able to destabilise any governments who don't want to play ball with good old Uncle Sam."

"Oh come on, Max That's just a convenient interpretation."

"No, it's fact," said Kane, emphatically.

Jasper Nash shook his head. "We started this business for a bit of a laugh, Max. Hell's bells, I was a student when we did the first one. It paid the bills and for the holidays. It was never meant to become a way of life. You've been in the business longer than me. Don't you remember what it was like in those days? It was easy, and it was fun. I'll always be eternally grateful to you for including me. But it's time to quit now. You've done much better than me. At least you have your property business. You've done good Max. Don't push your luck."

"Of course, you might be right under different circumstances," said Kane finally. "You might be right, except for one thing. I wish I could quit, but I can't. The money has all but gone."

"What money?"

"I had my life savings invested in the Hong Kong consignment Jasper. Virtually everything I had - gone."

"Why on earth did you do that Max? You've never risked your own wealth before."

"Incentives - the Chinese offered a fifty percent discount for the entire payment up front."

"I would never have believed it." Jasper was aghast. "You broke the oldest rule in the book. If you pay in advance you lose your insurance policy. The supplier no longer has to honour the deal or keep his mouth shut. Come on. You know that better than anyone. That's what credit is for. I shouldn't have to lecture you of all people Max." Then the truth began to dawn on Jasper. He looked more intently at Kane. "I wondered what had gone so horribly wrong. I was very careful, Max. That consignment got popped because you got greedy."

"No," said Kane quickly. He certainly hadn't wanted Jasper to jump to that conclusion. "I kept to the usual format - pay a deposit and the rest only on delivery. At the eleventh hour the Chinese informed me that there was another buyer after the same consignment offering higher, that I would have to show the colour of my money in full if I wanted to secure the deal. I believe that I was played for a fool by the Chinese and betrayed without doubt. Afterwards, I called in a few favours from a friend of mine who is fairly well connected with the Triads in Hong Kong. I simply told him that I had been cheated out of a considerable amount of money and he obligingly hunted down the gang and tortured each and every one of them. Unfortunately I haven't seen a penny of the three million back that I paid out."

"Perhaps you should go to Hong Kong and dig a little deeper with your Triad friend. Because I'm sure the Triads aren't out of pocket? This whole mess is cock-eyed - and it definitely doesn't add up."

"There's no need to. I know exactly what happened. The Chinese organisation was infiltrated by an undercover drugs squad officer of the Hong Kong police department. They found out who this was and executed him."

Jasper ran a hand over his shaven head. "Max, I don't want to be involved with anything like that, or with those sort of people," he said. He wanted to put the business behind him. "Forget it," he reiterated. "I'm really not interested in any of it anymore. It's all history as far as I'm concerned." He walked off to the smoking area outside, struggling to light a cigarette as the wind kept blowing out the flame from his lighter . He was annoyed by what Kane had told him, and by his cavalier attitude to losing three million pounds. Kane came and stood next to Jasper and for a moment the two men were silent, gazing out across the harbour towards Brownsea Island in the distance. "There's something else you should know," he said, at last. "A word of warning Max, I was stopped when I came through Customs at Heathrow and interviewed by a spook called Jake Dillon. He told me he was going to make sure you were put behind bars."

Kane looked thoughtful for a moment. "Oh him again, there's a name from the past. It's strange how he seems to reappear from time to time."

"What's he got against you?"

"He has never forgotten that business in Cornwall all those years ago. He blames me for that girl's death. Apparently he has never forgotten that I didn't turn up for the girl's inquest and believes that I should have been charged with at least manslaughter."

"But that was years ago."

"Yes, you're right. But now he's apparently part of some clandestine organisation who works alongside the security services. His reputation is frightening."

"Well, I wouldn't take his warning lightly then," said Jasper.

Kane said nothing. He appeared to be thinking about it. He wasn't. He didn't give a toss about some Government lackey with a long memory. He'd put him in his place if he got too close. Anyway, he had that angle covered. There were more important things to deal with. "I don't want you thinking I'm to blame for what happened in Hong Kong."

"It doesn't matter whose fault it was. I had a good run for my money. And talking of money, I'm going to need the rest of what you owe me very soon."

Kane stared out across the water from their elevated position. He didn't want to look Jasper in the eye. "I'm afraid that will be a problem, Nash." Max always called Jasper by his surname when he was feeling uncooperative.

"Problem?" echoed Jasper. He didn't like the sound of that. And when Kane called him Nash, there was always something unpleasant in the background. He had two hundred and fifty thousand which Kane had banked for him. When Kane mentioned problems, they were invariably financial.

"Getting you out of that high security prison in Hong Kong wasn't cheap. It cost just a tad over one hundred thousand pounds, by the time everyone was paid off. That leaves about one hundred and forty, but it's tied up in what I lost on the

Hong Kong deal. You've still got the power cruiser that we bought from the proceeds of the Dutch deal a couple of years ago, that's worth around ninety-five thousand. I'll sign it over to you and take it off the bill."

"Whoa, wait on a minute, that's what it cost. It's definitely not what it's worth today."

"What's it worth then?"

"I'd say that a third hand forty-foot Princess of that age is worth around no more that forty to fifty thousand. However on this market, I'd be lucky to get twenty-five."

"Well, there you are. Let's call it thirty thousand."

"No, Max. The boat is a joint asset. Half is mine anyway. So we're talking about fifteen thousand off the bill."

Kane thought for a moment. "Expensive business, boating," he commented. "We should take a close look at our investment. We could go out on her when the weather picks up." He suddenly hesitated. He'd remembered something. "No. Don't sell it. I'll buy your share." Jasper raised his eyebrows, but Kane didn't explain his change of heart, and Jasper didn't want to know the reason for it. Kane had a feeling that the boat might come in useful should he need to get out fast. In a high risk business he needed to keep as many options open as possible. "Where is the boat now?" Kane asked.

"It's somewhere safe and discreet where it won't attract any unwanted attention."

"Good," said Kane.

"Let's get back to business," said Jasper. "The money you owe me Max?"

"Jasper, Jasper. You don't have to worry about that. It's guaranteed by the property I own. It might take a little time to convert it to hard currency with the market as it is at the moment, but I've put the entire portfolio up for auction. I've also put a low reserve on everything, so it should sell, even in these times of austerity."

Jasper shivered. He had barely enough money to buy a house let alone start a business. His plans for retirement were already looking decidedly dodgy.

Kane read Jasper's expression. "Let's have a bite to eat.

I've booked a table here in the hotel to celebrate your freedom," he paused. "I want to talk to you about something. It could solve all our problems. "He wondered if he'd said enough, then added, "I'm sure we can work things out."

Chapter 6

Dillon steeled himself for the Monday morning meeting with his stalwart boss, Edward Levenson-Jones. He had come to various conclusions over the past few days. Maximilian Kane was definitely up to no good, and almost certainly planning something new, but this time his modus operandi was different. Dillon had received a photograph by email from a Metropolitan Police surveillance unit which was watching two known underworld enforcers who were believed to have been involved in murder, smuggling, trafficking and just about anything else that was illegal, immoral and highly profitable. The police had sent over the image hoping that the third man, whom they did not know, would be identified. The first two men were Ryan Edwards, known as Razor, and Conner Hawkins, known as Cracker. Dillon magnified the image on his iPad where the third man was positioned. It was definitely Maximilian Kane. However the police, with their inherent mistrust of intelligence departments were unwilling to tell Dillon the exact nature of their investigation, and only begrudgingly imparting the picture on the direct order of the Home Secretary's personal secretary Dunstan Havelock.

So far as Dillon knew, this was the first time Kane had been in contact with the hard-boiled criminal underworld fraternity. Judging from the expressions on their faces, it wasn't a coincidence that the three men were photographed together.

It was time to reacquaint himself with Maximilian Kane. Dillon wanted to place a Ferran & Cardini surveillance team on him. He also wanted a phone tap on his land line and mobile numbers. He knew he would have to fight for the resources and hoped that Edward Levenson-Jones would be in a good mood. He prayed that no strange requests had filtered down from the Partner's or the Home Office requesting new priorities, because they were always guaranteed to irritate the hell out of LJ.

He knocked on his boss's door at precisely nine-thirty. He opened the door in response to the bark from within. Edward Levenson-Jones was approaching retirement. His personality reminded Dillon of a silver back gorilla he'd once seen at Jersey Zoo, appearing quiet and good natured, sometimes behaving brusque, but always dangerous. He appeared placid, but he was cantankerous if taken away from his routines. The many mugs of strong black coffee that he ritualistically drank each and every day was complimented by the Slim Panatela cigars that he smoked. This was one of the many things that irritated him, having to go all the way up to the roof to the designated smoking area. After forty years in the intelligence services, little if anything surprised him. Dillon refused the offered double espresso coffee because he had once accepted a cup and had regretted it when he smoked more cigarettes and couldn't relax for the rest of that day. He noticed the many Cuban cigars inside the humidor and remembered that LJ had been to Cuba at the end of the previous week.

"How was Havana?" he asked casually.

"Havana old son, was exactly as it always is. On the one hand the food is spectacular, the people are delightfully friendly and the cigars are just perfect. On the other hand the C.I.A. is still dishing out bullshit, misdirection and has no conscience about wasting my bloody time. Their definition of controlling the global drug smuggling cartels is to know what routes their shipping takes from Colombia. They ignore the problems when it suits them and like to mention the lax attitude of European Governments as if their own administration were whiter than white. Then it's off to the brothels on Friday night, party all weekend, and then all the bullshit starts again on Monday morning. So everything was exactly as it's always been, old son."

"Oh, pretty much a waste of time then?" Dillon smiled inwardly at the thought of his boss kicking his heels in a country renowned for its unique blend of colour, vibrancy and exceptional hospitality. And to think that there wouldn't have been a steak and kidney pie or ham and cucumber sandwich in sight.

"Pretty much old son, pretty much," LJ said looking over the top of his gold wire framed spectacles. "So, to business then, what have you got for me?"

"Maximilian Kane." Dillon said placing the file on the desk.

"Let me guess. This file came from Dunstan Havelock?"

"Yes."

"No resources available old son," responded LJ, brusquely.

"The Home Secretary wants Kane and his sidekick Nash placed under intense surveillance. One or both of them have been obtaining highly classified military secrets, and selling them to the North Koreans. Kane has been monitored flying all over Europe like a blue-arsed fly."

"Old son, it might have passed you by, but the entire world is in deep recession. Money is tight and Government money is so tight it hurts. The Partners have been told that there is no extra funding for additional manpower hours. We simply can't throw very expensive human resources at an assignment on one of your hunches, or whims, or whatever you call them these days. We must have more than that."

"Is selling highly classified military nuclear secrets to North Korea not a good enough reason for extra resources?"

"The last time Dunstan Havelock got us involved with an assignment involving the Home Office you ran up a bill of over three and a half million pounds of taxpayer's money, old son. The Partners were not pleased - and if my memory serves me, you had to take a year's sabbatical leave, or the C.I.A. and MI6 would have had you put away for twenty years."

"That's the problem with the Intelligence Service today!"

"And what might that be?"

"They're not gracious in defeat and never say thank you when you save their ass from a public enquiry."

"That's the way it is and how it will always be."

"So, we need guaranteed results."

"Yes, but you've got something personal against Kane. A field officer without a grudge would let it go and not let it consume him. If you can give me something concrete old son, then I'll make sure the Partners are able to authorise as much money as you think you'll need to throw at Maximilian Kane and bury him forever."

"I wasn't thinking of a full scale surveillance job. I reckon we'd only need a small team of three working on a shift rota for no more than a week."

"I need results. As you know I intend to retire within the year and would like to leave with a one hundred percent success rate. Who is this Kane chap after all? Some small-time drug smuggler, well the world's moved on since then old son. We are here to track down, apprehend and bring to book, terrorists - serious organised criminals - traitors and megalomaniacs. Does Mr Kane fit into any of these categories?"

Dillon remained quiet for a brief moment and smiled before saying, "He fits into all of them!"

"We have a number of high priority assignments running at the moment for both the British Security Service and the C.I.A. and I know Dunstan Havelock wants you to take control of this one personally, but the order has come all the way down from the top of the Treasury Department that the Home Secretary's budget is tight and the taxpayer is under enough strain as it is, without you racking up a huge bill because you've left a wake of dead bodies behind you."

"Oh, come on. They're only dead if they've tried to kill me. Max Kane is not only a major cocaine smuggler, but he is a possible traitor to this country. The reason why we are involved with Dunstan once again is because the Government wants this dealt with quickly, and resolved effectively without any official fuss. Kane will almost certainly make a mistake before too long and we'll be there to snap him up along with his sidekick Jasper Nash, who, to my mind is potentially the one we need to keep a very close eye on."

"OK, perhaps the proof will drop into your lap. And, I admit you are the luckiest man I know. However, that still doesn't alter the fact that I think we should not be involved with this matter at all."

"So I'll deal with this quietly and without incurring

additional expenditure. That'll keep everyone happy and we'll still get the job done."

"Still the same Dillon, aren't you? OK, I'll talk to the Partners and get their approval for the assignment. You're one of the best field officers in the business, but don't fuck this up for the sake of your own ego or some age old grudge you might be harbouring." LJ stared at Dillon, watching for a reaction. None came.

Dillon never liked being talked to as if he were a naughty school boy, but he remained silent even though he wanted to say something sarcastic back at his boss. The silence in the room made him feel a little uncomfortable. He stood up to leave.

"There's one other thing old son," LJ spoke without looking up from signing the papers on his desk. "You already know that you'll be working with Vince Sharp on this assignment, and that he will be your technical support. But you will also be joined by a Swedish officer from Interpol who will be working alongside you both."

The tiny hairs on the back of Dillon's neck prickled and he suddenly felt very angry with Levenson-Jones. "Why?"

"Why what, old son?" LJ said in a tired voice.

"Why am I being lumbered with an officer from Interpol?"

"Lumbered old son, you will benefit greatly from Miss Lindberg's expertise in the field of narcotics smuggling. She was part of the team investigating a particularly gruesome murder on Dutch soil, which they believe has something to do with someone on this side of the North Sea. Needless to say, but I'll say it anyway; you will afford Miss Lindberg every assistance and courtesy while she is with us."

"Any idea what she's like?"

"No idea. But she arrives on Wednesday so you'll find out then. Miss Lindberg's office will email my assistant prior to departure, and we'll need to arrange accommodation for her both here in London and down in Dorset as her time will be split between the two locations. Nothing too flash, say a small bed and breakfast or public house. You know the sort of thing old son."

"You know how I hate working with people I know nothing about."

"Yes, but on this occasion you are going to overlook this and try your very best to be nice. Interpol needs to know how we operate and the Partner's feel that it is very important to build personal relationships with our counterparts across the Channel."

"OK, I'll try. But if she gets in my way, she will be told to take the next ferry back to wherever it was she came from."

"Jake, from now on we'll be working more closely with our counterparts on the Continent whether we like it or not."

"OK, I hear what you're saying. Have you got any good news for me?"

"There's always good news - it's Monday morning and another week begins."

Dillon waited until he was outside the office and the door was fully closed before he hissed, "Bollocks!"

It didn't make him feel any better. So he walked back to his office and focused his thoughts on Miss Lindberg and what he was going to do with her.

* * *

Jasper and Martha stepped out of the Mercedes and looked at the Georgian country house. This was the fourth one they had viewed in as many days. Martha was surprised at how willingly Jasper had agreed to move to the country. This property was the best prospect so far. It was set amongst the rolling west Dorset countryside on the outskirts of what the estate agents termed a - picturesque village setting - just forty minutes from Poole and the Sandbanks peninsula. It was built from traditional Portland stone under a slate tiled roof and much larger than Jasper had expected. Martha put her hand on his shoulder and said. "It's just perfect."

"We'd better take a closer look inside," he replied.

The estate agent had given them the keys and told them they could view on their own. They walked all around the outside of the impressive four storey building, peering in through windows at the large rooms. No one had lived there for about three years. A few items of wicker furniture remained on the veranda and the formal gardens were neglected, but nothing that couldn't be put right. "Well, there's plenty to do," smiled Martha.

Jasper looked around the courtyard at the back of the house. There was an archway leading into the cobbled yard. This was the place where originally tradesmen and deliveries would have been received out of sight of the main house.

"Martha, there's a lifetime of work here," said Jasper looking skywards. Thinking what a good place it was to stash cocaine, but reminded himself that he was not getting involved with the drug thing anymore. Selling military secrets was a far easier way of making serious money.

Martha put the key in the lock and pushed open the door. They stood just outside on the large weathered flagstone step breathing in the musty atmosphere. She looked around, her eyes taking in every detail. "It's wonderful," she said as they entered the main kitchen. "Oh and look at this Jasper; this is how the family would have summoned the servants to answer their needs by way of this mechanical call bell system. It's so cool that it's operated by wires and pulleys from the first-through to fourth-floor rooms. And each room has its own bell so that the staff would know exactly where to go, so surreal. "

They explored the kitchens, sculleries, cold rooms and larders below stairs before making their way up the wide stone staircase to the main reception floor. Jasper looked up in awe of the fine detail and original architecture that had survived for over three hundred years. "We can strip out these rooms and knock down a wall or two to create an open-plan feel and then artex - yeah, artex the lot. "

Martha gave him a sideward glance and said. "You Jasper - are a Troglodyte."

Jasper found it hard to visualise. He walked around in circles trying to imagine them both living in this enormous mansion. "I think it's far too big for just the two of us Martha."

"I was hoping you'd notice," she said with a mischievous smile. "My idea is to have a home and income in one. Wouldn't this make a marvellous bed and breakfast and as a bonus, we'd have our very own established market garden thrown in as it's a dream." Her enthusiasm was undiminished by the wary look on Jaspers face.

"It's hellish expensive for the amount of restoration required."

"We'll make the agent an offer," said Martha confidently. Jasper followed her through the vast reception hall into ornate drawing rooms with high ceilings and fine open fireplaces, and watched and listened to her with growing admiration. He never realised how much she knew, or how good she was an interior designer. She had a natural flair for colour. As an artist she was good and never out of work.

Martha looked in cupboards and up chimneys, "Jasper, this house is fantastic, let's go upstairs."

They wandered through the rooms, imagining how they might look when restored. "Of course some of these features would have been added at different periods during the lifetime of the house, but from what I've seen so far they don't look bad and will most likely stay during the restoration." Martha opened the windows in the master bedroom. The view was the best Jasper had ever seen, spreading across the apple orchard to the rolling landscape of west Dorset beyond.

It would be virtually impossible for anyone to get to the main house undetected, thought Jasper.

Martha leaned tentatively against a large dressing table. She looked seductively at Jasper. "I want you, Jasper," she said a little breathlessly. "I want you now!"

Jasper Nash turned and looked at her, startled for a moment. With growing anticipation he watched her slowly take off her clothes, run her hands over her breasts, her nipples hardening under her own light caress. His hands fell to his belt buckle. They stood apart, never losing eye contact. Martha slowly unzipped her skirt and let it fall to the floor revealing smooth bare legs. With a surge of excitement Jasper realised that she was not wearing knickers. He took a slow step towards her, releasing himself from his jeans. He lifted her gently on to the dressing table, her legs naturally wrapping around his waist, she leaned back on one hand and with the other guided him inside her.

"Now this is definitely our room..." she whispered, then stopped, as a moan took over as he slowly pushed himself inside and slowly pulled out, repeatedly.

"That feels so good," she moaned, leaning forward and pulling up his shirt and pressing her breasts against his chest.

He gripped her tightly, pushing himself deeper inside her, with urgency and increased desire. The dressing table creaked and swayed. "Christ," thought Jasper, "don't let this fucking old piece of furniture give way now." They moved frantically together and then simultaneously shuddered in crescendo of physical and emotional release that they both clung on to for a long moment as it rushed through their bodies, Martha exhaled loudly and the room fell silent again. Jasper held onto Martha for a while. When he opened his eyes he looked beyond the flaking white paint and out to the orchard.

"Yes," he said. "This is where we will live and bring up a family." He kissed Martha's cheek.

He stepped backwards and she released him.

"Do you think our relationship is just sexual?" Martha asked with a smirk.

He smiled. "No. But it's a very good foundation."

Jasper pulled up his trousers.

"Why do you always dress so quickly?" She asked.

"Because it's difficult to run with your trousers around your ankles that's why!"

Martha picked up her skirt and slowly dressed. "So you're happy for us to make an offer?" She asked.

"Of course we should make an offer. If you can arrange the mortgage then I can pay for the restoration in cash."

"Sounds like the basis of a deal," said Martha. She buttoned up her blouse and tinkered with her hair and then stood up. No one would ever have guessed she had been making love.

"I do love you Martha." Jasper said.

"You're not going all soft on me, are you, Nash?" Martha laughed and reached out for his hand.

On the way back to Sandbanks Martha began to have

her doubts about Jasper's commitment. He seemed to be distant. She tried to find out what was wrong.

"I'm worried about the finances Martha," he said finally.

"Don't be. My business is doing really well and I know that I can afford the mortgage. Now you're going to make an honest living you'll soon realise what a good thing it was that I started my company."

"Yes, I suppose you're right," he replied, without enthusiasm.

Martha remembered how quarrelsome he had been when she first suggested it. He thought she was being absurd. He earned more than enough money for both of them. She told him it was just a matter of money; her self-respect was at stake. She didn't want his money. She didn't want to be a kept woman, owned by him and his money. She wanted independence and security and if they separated, or something happened to him, she wanted to be able to carry on with life unhindered. He finally accepted that she was determined and offered to finance her, but she refused; if she wanted money she would go to the bank. She knew that for some time he felt an irrational jealously. She was no longer available to go out and play whenever he felt like it.

Perhaps, in some curious way, his pride was hurt. But that was ridiculous. Life was too short, and she was lucky to have him back again.

* * *

Dillon was late arriving for the Air France flight at Terminal Four. He had intended to collect the Swedish Interpol officer as she passed through immigration and then get her out of the terminal through a staff exit, bypassing immigration completely, but he had got snarled up in a two mile traffic jam on the M25. Now he was over an hour late. He searched his pockets for the printed email which contained the Swedish woman's name, and then found it in the first pocket he'd checked. He scanned it quickly and went straight to the airport's information desk to ask for an announcement for Miss

Lindberg arriving from Paris. He waited for her to turn up. Dillon had one more night in London and then he would return to Dorset, which would soon hopefully reap him rewards with the arrival of Jasper Nash back into the UK.

Dillon became aware of the official at the information desk trying to attract his attention. He noticed a slender Scandinavian blonde woman smiling back at him as he stepped forward, and immediately realised that Inger Lindberg was naturally very beautiful. She was probably somewhere in her late twenties to early thirties. She was tall, at least five eleven, and he looked down to confirm that she was wearing heels.

"This might just be OK having Miss Lindberg tagging along for a while," he thought, immediately disappointed for having such a stereotypical male thought.

She spoke with a slight accent, the ubiquitous American tinge that continentals seem to acquire when they learn to speak English. "Hello. I am Inger Lindberg."

"Hi, I'm Jake Dillon." He extended his arm. Her hand felt cool in his. "I'm very sorry I'm late. I got stuck in a traffic jam on the motorway."

"Please, don't apologise. My flight was late anyway."

Dillon picked up her luggage. He noticed that it was considerably travel worn.

"No problems coming through immigration?"

"You know they actually searched me and my entire luggage."

"What?"

"Your immigration officials searched me, thoroughly!"

"Didn't you tell them who you were?"

"No. I wanted to see how thorough your border security was. And I must say it is very impressive if not a little over zealous."

"Well, sorry about that. Welcome to the UK anyway."

"I'm pleased to be here. I've heard a lot about you Mr Dillon." She smiled.

"Just Dillon will do, and I'm sure it's all bad, no matter who you've been talking to."

"Mostly, but according to your Mr Levenson-Jones

you're misunderstood." She laughed, showing her perfect white teeth.

"OK, we're staying in London tonight. I'll get someone in the office to arrange your accommodation. I have to monitor the close of an assignment."

"Naturally," said Inger.

Dillon led her through the throngs of people and out to the car park.

"What a stunning car Jake. What is it?"

Dillon remotely unlocked the doors. "It's the new Porsche Panamera S Hybrid."

"I drive something much less impressive and very old. Mine is VW Polo, and the colour is a very dirty red."

"Oh, I'm not trying to be flash. I'm what some call a petrol-head, love cars, always have. My last was a Porsche 911 Turbo until it was blown up. You know how it is."

They both got in to the luxury vehicle and Dillon made his way out of the car park and onto the link road that would take them to the M25 motorway.

"Where are we going?" Inger asked.

"Ferran & Cardini International HQ in the heart of London Docklands. You've arrived just in time to watch the final play-out of an intelligence operation that we've been assisting a number of law enforcement agencies with. Including; MI5, SOCA, the Drugs Squad and HM Customs." His first impression of Inger was that she had a really easy going personality. He had to remind himself that this stunning Swedish blonde woman was not a blind date, but a highly trained intelligence officer with a master's degree in psychology and another in criminology.

"The operation has been running for around nine months. We've been onto this firm for some time, and hopefully tonight will mark their demise and an end to the misery they've been peddling in for so long. But as organised criminals go; this team is extremely professional and very careful with it. Their mules carry cocaine for the firm who report back to the cartel in Colombia. They use small fast private jets to fly the cocaine out of Bogota in Colombia to Haiti in the Caribbean. You know that Haiti turns a blind eye to private aircraft landing on their soil for the right price?" He hesitated for a moment to see if Inger would comment, but she ignored it. "The shipment is then passed to the mule in line, re-packaged and he or she then gets on a scheduled flight bound for Florida. When this flight touches down, there is usually a member of the ground crew who will ensure that the luggage is monitored during the customs check with sniffer dogs during the transfer to the London bound aircraft. The luggage used is made to special order by highly skilled craftsmen using sophisticated materials that are lightweight, airtight and tough, making detection of the cocaine inside by a sniffer dog or electronic devices virtually impossible - but there's always the chance that a really good dog will sniff out the case. Once the flight from Florida lands at Heathrow that's when the real game starts."

"Presumably the intelligence is solid enough to allow your border guards to stop them before the drugs leave the airport?"

"Not that simple. Don't forget, they are operating a multi-level scam with at least three identical pieces of luggage - each with a courier - one getting on the aircraft at Haiti and then two more boarding in Florida. Ever come across that one?"

"Yes." Inger replied. Dillon consciously glanced away from her lips. "The multi-courier and luggage scam works like this. There are a minimum of three couriers involved. And as I said before, one courier boards the aircraft in Haiti. The other two join the flight in Florida. They all have identical suitcases. But the cocaine is in the suitcase which originated in Haiti. On the flight to London they all swap keys. They arrive at Heathrow. Two of the couriers take the luggage without the cocaine..."

Inger interrupted. "How do they know which suitcase? All three are identical."

"They are all identical, except the one which has a barely noticeable mark. Now all three suitcases are taken from the aircraft's hold and the baggage handlers deliver them to the arrivals baggage claim hall. The two cases without the cocaine are collected by the couriers and they go through to customs.

The third case is not collected by the courier who originally boarded the aircraft in Haiti. This courier exits the airport through customs with only hand luggage. The unclaimed suitcase is then collected by a security guard, who is also on the payroll of the firm. Once he has it in his possession then it's a simple matter of getting it through to a location where it can be picked up later. And that's how one version of the suitcase scam works. More often than not the couriers and the cocaine get through without hindrance."

"How strange," Inger said with a smile on her face and a hint of disbelief in her voice. "Are you telling me that your border agency knows about this scam and yet it works time and time again?"

"This is intelligence work. It's only the tip of a Titanic-sinking size iceberg."

"You know, in Holland and Sweden we have a very different problem. A drugs operation of this nature could involve at least ten couriers and sometimes twenty, so quite big and complex by your standards here in the UK."

Dillon was mildly irritated by her apparent competitiveness but said nothing except, "sounds pretty big." It wasn't a bloody competition between England and Sweden. "The thing is Inger, these couriers or mules are often pathetic people taking enormous chances out of desperation or coercion. Customs once found a kilo of cocaine that had been surgically implanted beneath the skin of a very, and I mean very overweight woman."

Inger shivered. She continued to be surprised, hearing about the things that people do to themselves in desperation.

Dillon drove down the ramp and into the underground car park of Ferran & Cardini International and parked the Panamera in his reserved space. "Let's go," he said leading the way towards the Special Projects department. Inside the secure facility Dillon looked at the information streaming down the screen and saw that the flight was on schedule. He stood at the large rectangular shaped island unit and drew his fingertips over the glass top. Instantly, the wall mounted screens lit up with live cam links. Inger looked around in awe at the multi-million pound equipment. Dillon studied the screens for a moment and then said, "Would you like a coffee or perhaps a tea?"

"A black coffee would be good, thank you."

Dillon walked over to the Jura Impressa coffee machine that LJ had insisted on having brought over from America. He stood in front of the machine and wondered which button to press first, placed a trendy glass mug under the one of the spout, and pressed a button, and a moment later black coffee appeared, repeated the process and then went back to where Inger was standing.

Inger sipped the black liquid, "Umm, this is definitely not how I remember English coffee." She said with a smile.

"Oh, I'm pleased you like it." Dillon had to admit the three thousand pound coffee machine did make a spectacular cup of Colombian dry roasted. He was enjoying it as it were his last cup ever.

"What's happening now?" Said Inger pointing at one of the large flat screens on the wall.

They were watching two small groups of men, all heavily armed with automatic weapons, apparently having a meeting. The covert webcams recorded both vision and sound. And then the two groups dispersed and the scene was quiet.

"Sorry about that," he turned to Inger. "It sometimes ends up like that; the Colombians work with the Armenians to traffic cocaine all over the world. Catch these guys and we take out a major league cocaine producer - like a house of cards, if you pull out the right one, the whole lot comes tumbling down."

They drove into the city through heavy traffic and Dillon delivered Inger to her hotel. He stopped for a quick drink with her, and was glad for the chance to talk to her away from the office and out of working hours. There were things he wanted to say which would be difficult in the office with the others around. He felt that LJ should not have thrust an outsider upon him and this latest assignment, and while he wanted her to be aware of that, he didn't want her to feel that she was being excluded. Above all, he didn't want her to get in his way.

It was some time later before they settled down in the

bar. As was usual in London, they had to hunt for a parking space and then walk the short distance back to the hotel. Inger ordered a Bombay Sapphire and tonic water, and immediately changed her mind in favour of a mineral water. Dillon hoped this indecision over her drink was not a recurring characteristic, because otherwise she'd be better off staying back in the department's office.

There was an awkward silence. Inger crossed her legs. She had slender ankles. Dillon looked away.

"I understand that you have your own agenda," said Dillon bluntly.

"And what agenda would that be Mr Dillon?" The Swedish lady's tone was questioning.

"There is a case that you are involved with in Paris and you've come over to the UK to continue your investigation here."

"Yes."

"Well, I hope we will be able to help you. Apart from that I understand you expect to be working alongside my team on our assignment so you can learn how we operate."

"That is correct Mr Dillon."

"Please, Jake or just Dillon."

"Jake."

"Well in that case I think it would be a good idea if we discussed how we're going to work together." Dillon studied her face for a brief moment.

Inger guessed what was coming. The Special Projects department of Ferran & Cardini International was very busy. They were all busy. Not much time for explanations. She was starting to think that her main role while seconded to them was to run errands. Making coffee and fetching sandwiches. Of course they were busy. They were working for the British Government and waging war on terrorists, organised crime syndicates and drug traffickers.

"Yes." She eventually answered with a demure smile.

"Something you must know is that I do not expect anyone in my team to do anything which I'm not prepared to do myself. That's everything including the most mundane of filing

and report writing - before, during, and after an assignment."
He hoped that she hadn't noticed his barefaced lie. He hated
paperwork, and he detested writing reports and he especially
disliked having to babysit during an important assignment. He
was sure that she had already read his file and would have read
this from the unclassified data within it. But she had remained
obligingly quiet. Dillon smiled self-consciously, and darted
a quick look at her, his green-brown eyes glinting under the
bright lights of the bar.

Inger nodded. She was about to say something but he
continued. "This said, I put the fieldwork side of any assignment
first and the paperwork on the back burner. And I want to
apologise in advance if I'm sometimes aggressive or overly rude
towards anyone and everyone, but working with other people
always brings out the worst in me."

"I have no problem with mucking-in, Jake. And, I'll
try not to give you cause for agitation during my time here."
Her brilliant blue eyes seemed to have turned a steely grey. He
looked away.

"Just one thing, though. Would you have had this little
pep-talk with me had I been a man?"

Dillon was slightly taken aback. Inger Lindberg hadn't
given the impression of being a feminist. "Whoa - of course I
would. Ask anyone who works with me and they'll tell you
that, what you see is what you get."

"Perhaps I will." Inger stood up. "Thank you for the
drink." She picked up her room key off the bar and pulling her
case walked towards the lifts.

Dillon followed her. They weren't getting off to a great
start. "Hey Inger," he said. She turned and glared at him.
"You've misunderstood."

"I do not think so, Jake." The lift doors opened and
she stepped inside, turned to face him and said. "I'll see you
tomorrow."

"I'll pick you up."

"No need, I can make my own way thank you." She
said as the lift doors closed.

Dillon sighed. "Damnation." All of a sudden he felt

tired. He'd been lumbered with someone who had something to prove.

* * *

Nearly seven weeks had passed since Jasper had returned, and Martha was growing impatient with him. She knew he was having nightmares about his experience in Hong Kong. She knew he was owed a considerable amount of money by Max Kane. He didn't seem to have turned over a new leaf though, and he was still having frequent meetings with his old associates, although he claimed they were to clear up loose ends. She really didn't give a damn about Kane having to sell a number of his properties to pay back Jasper. She had her life to live and Jasper was the man she wanted to share it with. She didn't want Kane lurking in the shadows.

"I have to sort out my finances," he said. "I think that's more important than looking for work, don't you?"

"If you're worrying about buying the house, let's not do it," retorted Martha.

"I'm owed a lot of money Martha, and I want it back," replied Jasper irritably.

Martha guessed that wasn't the whole reason for his indifference. She asked him what was wrong. But he fobbed her off with vague answers. Jasper had a dilemma. At first he hoped Martha would guess the agonising decision he had to make. He didn't dare tell her. He knew what her answer would be. He'd promised her that he would get out of the smuggling game for good, but that was before he had discovered he didn't have enough money to support himself, let alone both of them and a huge loan. That was before he looked realistically at his limited potential for conventional employment. That was before he became involved in some dilapidated manor house in the country. He had precious few options and now Kane was offering him a solution. It would solve his problems for a lifetime. The operation would be over within ten days. He would earn a minimum of one and a half million pounds sterling without having to take any undue risks. He simply couldn't refuse Kane. When it was all over he would tell Martha. If he

99

told her before that, she wouldn't believe it was for the very last time.

He looked back on the last thirteen years and despised himself. He reckoned he had squandered well over three million pounds, but there wasn't any point in having regrets. He'd spent the money on too many things to worry about it now. He should have saved it for a rainy day. Like a spoilt child he had to do things impatiently. He travelled to the most exotic parts of the world not once but many times. He learned to fly a helicopter and had rented one for a while, and had thought about smuggling dope across the Channel in it, but soon abandoned the idea as far too risky. He bought a string of expensive sports cars; his favourite had been the Aston Martin Vantage which he had raced for a season. It had been professionally prepared and race tuned by his own mechanic before each race; and all he had to show for that folly was the memory of exhilaration as he drove the elite sports car at high speed around some of the finest Formula One race circuits in Europe. It wasn't hard to spend two or three hundred thousand a year with a few five star holidays to far flung locations travelling first class. He never wanted to be an old man living in a cold bedsit saying. "If only I'd been more frugal. If only."

The moment the offer on the Georgian manor house was accepted Jasper Nash knew he was going back to work again. As soon as he made the decision he felt as if a heavy lead weight had been lifted off his shoulders. He felt the adrenaline rushing. He was back in a world he understood. He felt whole again, in a world where cunning and survival were freedom and failure was incarceration. It was a world where luck simply didn't exist. All that knowledge, gained over many years, came flooding back. He was good because he'd never stopped learning. He had always liked to study criminals as well as the police. He was always careful and unlike so many criminals varied his routines constantly. That's how they were usually caught. They always went to the same pubs. They were lazy because they were complacent, like so many humans. They always went to the same travel agent in the high street to book their two weeks in the sun. They couldn't resist driving their flash cars to meetings instead of using public transport. They wore the same clothes. Drank the same drinks, and they even used their own personal mobile phones instead of going out and buying an unregistered pay-as-you-go handset. The police knew who they were and always made a point of pulling them over and asking questions. They complained but it never got past the desk sergeant at the local nick. Most criminals were gamblers, but they never looked at the odds on a roulette wheel. Most criminals were lucky if they didn't get caught.

When Jasper took Martha out to dinner to celebrate the acceptance of their offer on the manor house, he told her of his plans to start a luxury power yacht brokerage. She didn't guess that he was up to his tricks. The business would provide him with the necessary cover for his meetings and trips away. Of course he would go to the auctions and run a few advertisements here and there as well as creating a website. Martha would want to accompany him when he travelled abroad because it helped with her painting, gave her inspiration and invigorated her soul. He could work from home negating the overhead of a flash office. Visit the marinas to inspect any of the boats for sale. Most importantly, this would make it much easier to disappear for periods of time without any awkward questions or having to explain why he was going out at odd times of the day and night.

Martha responded to Jasper's change in mood. He was upbeat and positive again. He was like his old self. "Let's go home to bed," she said, taking the brandy glass from him and placing it on the table. They left the restaurant and Martha drove back to the luxury peninsula property they shared. She felt this was a new beginning - a second chance.

They turned out the lights and undressed each other slowly in the muted light coming through the bedroom window. Outside the moon perched high in a clear sky, shimmering down onto a calm sea. She pushed him gently on to the bed and then straddled him.

"I think you'll have to let me make love to you." Martha said running her hands over his chest.

"I love you."

"I love you too," she answered, quietly. "I love you for what you are, not what you pretend to be." He tensed for a moment and wondered how she could have guessed...

He slept a restless sweaty sleep, and woke early the next morning feeling ashamed. The sadness he felt was the lie he was telling her. He hadn't the strength to tell her the truth. He did not know if he was frightened because he might lose her. He clung tightly to her and kissed the soft skin on her shoulder, but she didn't stir. He felt a loneliness envelop him.

Chapter 7

It was the beginning of April, and the world's second largest natural harbour was transformed by the first really warm sunshine of the year, which seemed to herald spring. Maximilian Kane did not care for spring and the sudden appearance of copious numbers of power boat riffraff and old school yachties on the water, as well as the increase in foot and vehicular traffic. As he walked along the seafront he noticed things like the number of pedestrians. How many cars were parked? How many people were in the cars? Three people in a car suggested an undercover surveillance operation by the police or perhaps one of the other law enforcement agencies. Were there too many taxis in the rank, and were there any eyes making quick glances in his direction from the tables of the peninsula café. He wondered if he told anyone he would be at that particular spot at that precise time. There were other reasons why he didn't care for spring. He suffered from hay-fever, inflamed sinuses and an allergy to bee stings.

Nevertheless Kane was more cheerful than usual that morning. He was on his way to lunch with Jasper and he guessed he was about to hear some good news. After all, Jasper wouldn't have called him if he didn't have something to tell him. He had booked a table at the Haven Hotel on the peninsula. It was important to remind Jasper of those little pleasures he might be relinquishing if he was thinking of retirement. He was looking forward to the 1983 Dom Perignon which he had pre-ordered. There wouldn't be much change from a grand. He'd pay in cash as always, because it left no traces.

He wouldn't tell Jasper he had liquidated his property development company for a little over six million pounds in case he wanted to take what he was owed and decide not to return to work after all. Things were falling into place perfectly. In view of the sluggish property market no one would suspect the real reasons for the folding of the company. Least of all Jasper and no one would guess he was pulling out of the UK because it was too hot with coppers for a legitimate criminal to live in peace anymore. From now on he would work out of hotel rooms and live in the Bahamas. He'd fly into the UK to arrange the deals, and fly out when they were under way.

Kane found Jasper Nash waiting for him in the hotel's lounge bar. They were shown to their table, and as a matter of course Kane requested another table on the other side of the room: there was always the slender possibility that the table was bugged. They sat down. Kane looked across the table at Nash who placed a slender black box upon the pristine white tablecloth that had two antennas projecting from one end.

"Is that what I think it is?" Kane asked casually.

"Got it a couple of days ago, and it's the latest model." Nash switched the device on. This Max, is the Profinder 1207i and is one of a new class of counter surveillance bug sweeping devices which is the most reliable tool for tracing different digital transmissions such as GSM, bluetooth, WiFi, etc. So if the police or anyone within a one hundred feet of us using a covert spy camera or listening to us talking - then we'll know about it!"

"Back to your old self I see Jasper, and I'm very glad to have my old friend back with me. But isn't that box of tricks a little too high-tech and over the top, even for you?" Kane took out his handkerchief, blew his nose, and asked the waiter to remove the vase of fresh flowers. He looked around to satisfy himself that everything else was to his liking and turned to Jasper. "Have you made your decision yet?" he asked.

"Yes."

"So what have you decided?"

"I'm in, but there are a few conditions."

Kane smiled. "I'm sure we can accommodate those." He paused and felt a warm glow of satisfaction. "It's good to have you back on board again, Jasper." He meant what he said. Planning a smuggling operation was an arduous affair. There was the absolute need for total secrecy, and having a partner with whom to talk it over with was reassuring. "I always have the feeling nothing's going to go wrong when you're working with me."

"I'm surprised you still think that way after the fiasco in Hong Kong."

"Ah yes," said Kane. "That doesn't count." They both smiled. It was like old times, making light of adversity. "I guess we could put that down to experience."

"Experience seems to be the name everyone gives to their mistakes," said Nash bitterly. The memory of prison remained vivid. Rich food still made him feel queasy. "Going to Hong Kong was a mistake. I broke one of my own rules. Never work abroad because you don't know the landscape. You don't know what the policemen look like. You don't know where danger might be lurking. I really should not have gone there. We should have listened to our own gut feeling. We should have left all the arrangements to the supplier."

"It's easy to say that now," said Kane. "At the time we thought we needed someone to oversee quality control, otherwise we could have ended up with four tons of baking powder at this end."

"You'd still have lost that couple of million because the problem came from another quarter."

"What?" Kane said, suddenly baffled. He'd only lost two hundred and fifty thousand.

"You'd still have lost a shed load of money," elaborated Nash.

Then Kane remembered. "Oh yes. Yes I would, wouldn't I?" He finished his Champagne quickly. That was the trouble with telling a lie. You had to be on the ball forever afterwards. He had to remember that as far as Jasper was concerned he was broke. Relatively broke. The bill for this lunch would rather cause confusion and stymie the suggestion of bankruptcy.

"Sorry. I was thinking about something else. Let's order. Have you chosen?" He glossed over the indiscretion.

They summoned the waiter and ordered. They chose from the à la carte menu and while enjoying each of the four courses talked about the mechanics of the new operation.

"This gig is going to make us more money than all of

the others put together," said Kane.

"I really don't see how, Max. We've done some big trades in the past. The only way we'd make more money was if we wholesaled 'smack' to the European market place; and you know I'm not willing to touch that vile stuff."

"Agreed," said Kane. You know that I am not interested in the heroin market. But listen to this." He began his explanation.

With their pudding, Kane ordered two glasses of Marco Cecchini Picolit dessert wine. Jasper had to admit he was impressed by Kane's planning. Despite his previous reservations he already felt excited. Once again he was being seduced by the thrill of danger. He felt a certain admiration for Kane's to the pursuit of extreme riches.

"When will you stop Max?" Nash asked.

Kane sipped his wine and then placed his glass gently onto the table cloth. "When I have my own island in the Caribbean," he lifted his glass by the stem and held it up to the light. "This really is a splendid dessert wine, you know. The way its light bouquet fills one's nostrils; and the subtle flavour dances on the taste buds, is simply magnificent. Like a delicate violin passage."

Jasper didn't like to say that he knew nothing about wine except that this one was far too sweet.

"We've come a long way since those early days," said Kane.

"I'm not sure whether we're any better off."

"We weren't paid anywhere near enough for the risks we ran."

"That might be so, but the money was worth far more in those days."

"No it wasn't," said Kane. "We didn't have so much of it. Speaking of money, by the way, I've managed to scrape together forty grand. I've got four envelopes about me each containing ten grand. I will go to the cloakroom in a moment and leave them locked inside the cubical at the far end. When I return you excuse yourself and go to collect them. This way should there be anyone watching covertly all they'll see two blokes going to the cloakroom separately to take a leak after a boozy lunch. You'll need to ensure that you've got some change on you to unlock the Cubical door with the emergency release. That should keep you going for a couple of weeks or so, and pay for a few expenses along the way."

"Thank you, Max," said Nash, wondering why he was thanking Kane for returning a small portion of money he was owed.

Kane went off to the cloakroom, returning a few moments later. The two men exchanged a few pleasantries, and then Nash excused himself and went off to the cloakroom. When he returned they lapsed into silence, each of them thinking about the past. Nash remembered sitting up for nights on end studying flight and train timetables, as well as the times of ferry crossings. He came up with permutations of classic, and not so classic scenarios, covering every eventually. He used software that would allow him to track aircraft flying from Australia to Hong Kong, Dubai to Paris, Geneva to Amsterdam, and thousands of other flights. What Nash was looking for was convergence. He was looking for a stop-off destination where the passengers would be changing flights for the final leg of their journey and have access to their luggage. He would choose specific flights and then run the programme to find out which of these were arriving at Gatwick or Heathrow airport. The key was to find a minimum of two flights arriving at either airport at exactly the same time, and then they were onto a winner. Certain airports made a mistake, allowing transit passengers to collect their suitcases and then mingle and discreetly swap luggage with direct flight passengers in the departure lounge. The British Customs and Excise never suspected passengers arriving from Switzerland to be smuggling a suitcase full of best quality Hawaiian Black hashish sealed into airtight, lead lined and sniffer dog proof secret compartments. Kane would say, "Getting a little low on cash Jasper." And ten days later they would be twenty thousand pounds better off.

Unfortunately airport security tightened with the continual threat of terrorist bomb attacks and the flight schedules changed. This made planning a nightmare and Max declared that he was fed up with only making pocket change anyway. He decided to turn to much bigger things, and started hauling only premium Pakistani Black marijuana. And as Max said, "Why import twenty kilos when you can import two to three hundred kilos?" They learned about haulage, freight, trucks, container ships and fishing vessels.

"By the way," said Kane suddenly. "I've changed my mind about the boat. I want you to sell it after all. Put the word out and keep the price competitive."

"Why?"

"I had an idea, but it's not going to work out."

"Fine," said Jasper. He hadn't been to see the boat yet. He wondered what sort of shape she would be in. The batteries would certainly be dead, and he hoped it wasn't full of water. They'd learned their lesson with boats. They were hard on the nerves and the weather was never reliable. Air freight made a lot more sense now they had the right connections. In any event he could do with the cash if Martha's offer for the Georgian manor house was accepted.

Kane smiled. "I anticipated a celebration," he replied blandly.

* * *

Inger arrived at the Ferran & Cardini Head Quarters punctually at nine on her first morning. Neither she nor Dillon referred to the previous night and their abrupt parting. Dillon decided that they had reached a convenient stand-off, and he was no longer under an obligation to be more than courteous and friendly. If she wanted someone to show her the sights of London then he was definitely off the hook. Nevertheless, she did waft some fresh Nordic air into the department. No one, not even Tatiana, had ever worn Lycra leggings, an expensive designer mini skirt and matching hacking jacket with velvet collar to work before. The other women in the department looked on with envy tainted with a hint of disdain, and the younger men showed more interest than was healthy. Dillon enjoyed showing her around and introducing her. Vince made no secret of looking her up and down, and wasn't even embarrassed when he was caught staring at her pert breasts shown off to perfection under a white almost see-through blouse under her jacket. He liked what he saw, and smiled. Inger ignored him, and Vince bristled with envy that Dillon had her attention. Dillon was amused...

The three of them stood awkwardly in Vince's IT lab, and then Dillon initiated a full tour around the public areas of the building. On the roof terrace Dillon lit a cigarette; Vince leaned on the stainless steel railing and gazed out across the impressive Docklands landscape.

"So Inger, do you have any questions?"

"No," she answered. "But, you can tell me what your current assignment involves. I do not want to cause undue problems."

"Well, you've turned up just as we get started on a new assignment. This one should prove interesting and will show you something of how we work," said Vince.

Inger stared at Vince. She was obviously uncertain of the big Australian.

Vince wondered if she would like to spend the afternoon with him in the IT lab. That would give her an insight or two into the technical side of a field assignment. Every now and again he caught the swathe outline of her breasts beneath the white blouse; they weren't too small and they weren't supported.

"It's difficult," said Dillon. "The surveillance on this job is going to be difficult and will require a thorough knowledge of the area we'll be working in. Our options are somewhat dictated by what the other agencies can achieve within the law. Although without these restrictions we should be able to achieve our objective!" Dillon smiled, "However, I would point out that the police will lock us up at a moment's notice if they get half a chance."

Vince looked at Dillon and then Inger, "What have you got in mind Jake?"

"LJ and the Partners are dead against all of it," warned Dillon.

"I suppose you told them you had a gut-feeling about this assignment?"

"We have to go by our instincts. If we always did things their way we'd never get anywhere with these investigations," Dillon said.

"Sounds like we're in for a roller-coaster ride again then."

"Remember Maximilian Kane and Jasper Nash?"

Vince frowned. "Sorry, Jake," he said. "I promised I'd have the latest intel. on those two. Sorry, I forgot. I'll get right onto it."

"Thanks'," said Dillon, thinking it was unlike Vince to forget.

"Which one of them are we going for?" Vince asked.

Dillon nodded, swerving away from the question. He turned to Inger, and explained. "For about fourteen years Kane and Nash have been smuggling cocaine and marijuana. The Custom and Excise boys managed to catch Kane in possession of a large sum of money a few years ago. They gathered their evidence and even got him as far as a court room, but his obscenely expensive lawyers spun a good yarn and the jury found him not guilty. He has carried on smuggling but they don't quite have him back on the radar yet. However, he's become a little careless of late, and a number of incidents have raised a few alarm bells in various quarters. His right hand man, Jasper Nash, was imprisoned in Hong Kong for ten years, but was released about eight weeks ago. I'd put a bet on, that Kane paid a large bribe to spring him." Dillon stubbed out the cigarette and said, "Come on. Let's go back down to the department and I'll show you what we've got so far."

Dillon led the others into the op's room and brought up onto the screens the intelligence file of Jasper Nash. He dragged his fingertips over the glass screen in front of him and a photograph appeared. "This is Jasper Nash. I took this image at Heathrow airport on his return from Hong Kong. Meanwhile, Kane was spotted travelling to Paris and Switzerland. He's been seen with two known criminals who specialise in armed robbery and murder, and who are under surveillance by the Serious Organised Crime Agency. It was Interpol who followed him to a hotel in Paris where he met with a man identified as

Aleksey, no one has ever been able to discover his surname. He is a Russian drug baron."

"How do you know about the movements of this man Kane?" Inger asked.

"We have access to virtually all Government, law enforcement, immigration, airline and shipping databases, and we have the unauthorised cooperation of intelligence agencies across Europe, America and Asia. I'm surprised you didn't know that," said Vince from the other side of the room.

"I know that," snapped Inger. "I asked, because you might have obtained this information by illicit means, or there might be an existing surveillance operation in progress."

"Furtive imagination or what - if we had Kane under surveillance already, then we wouldn't be having this conversation now, would we?" Vince said, superciliously.

Inger controlled her irritation.

"No," Dillon said to Inger. "There has been no other agency involved."

"So where did the intel. originate from about Kane and the two rough looking men he's been seen associating with?" Vince asked.

Dillon scrolled through to info. "What the big Australian means Inger is where we got our info from." Although he enjoyed Vince's thrusts at Inger, he felt he should remain impartial. She might realise how unreasonable she had been the previous night. He turned back to Vince. "The SOCA guys thought we might know who he is and emailed this image over to us. As you can see, it shows Kane with the two men they've identified. They wondered if we could take a look and make any suggestions as to what these three have in common." Dillon increased the size if the image on one of the large screens.

Vince looked at the image quickly. It showed three men standing beside a black Range Rover. This was a typical surveillance photograph, a long lens shot, indicating that the police photographer was concealed some distance away. The three men looked surreptitious. One was opening the luxury 4x4's door. The other was walking around the back of the vehicle. Kane was talking to the first man, but his attention was caught by something out of shot. That was what made Kane look suspicious. A criminal's eye wandered, watching in case he was being observed, when he told his secrets.

"It's circumstantial at best," said Vince finally. "Those crafty boys over at the Serious Organised Crime Agency have sent over nothing more than a tantalising morsel to whet our appetite. There's nothing definite to go on. I really don't want us to get egg on face if we go any further with this assignment and find out that Kane really is doing nothing illegal."

For a brief moment Dillon was baffled. Vince had encouraged him to ignore LJ's concerns and take this assignment as it had come from Dunstan Havelock's office, and now he was pulling back. He still thought that there were reasonable grounds to proceed with the assignment because he knew Kane, and knew that he would still be smuggling drugs. As for Jasper Nash, he had been sworn to secrecy by Havelock not to disclose anything to anyone about him. Dillon was the only one who knew that Nash was the real target and that selling top secret classified information to the North Koreans made him the number one enemy of the state.

"I'm still going to run with it for a while," said Dillon.

Inger leaned forward and studied the image on the high definition screen.

"It sounds like you've got something personal against Mr Kane," said Inger. "Am I right, Jake?" She paused. "We all have our crosses to bear, but you've no proof that this man was the cause of your friend Anna Westcott's death."

Dillon shot the Swedish lady a cold look that told her not to go any further.

"Sorry. Before I came over to the UK I read your personnel file."

"Standard procedure I suppose. You will have seen then, that Max Kane was the last person to see Anna aboard his ocean going yacht Freebase II. But like you say, we all have our crosses to bear."

Dillon wondered whether Inger might be right. It was possible to interpret evidence in a myriad of different ways.

"I am sure that I have seen this man, Maximilian

Kane.," said Inger. The op's room was suddenly silent. They could hear their own breathing. At that moment Dillon forgave Inger everything. He turned his attention to her. "I have seen a photograph of this man maybe two to three weeks ago."

"How can you be sure?" said Vince, for no good reason. Inger ignored him. She was excited. "Jake, you remember I was telling you how there was a murder in Paris of a Russian drug baron called Aleksey?" Dillon nodded.

"Interpol was making enquiries in France and Holland. They have been watching Aleksey for many months, and have images of many people he is meeting. This man you call Max Kane was meeting Aleksey. The surveillance team have a witness. It is Aleksey's girlfriend. She has been identifying these people for us. Aleksey saw this man. We are paying for her to stay in a central Paris hotel until our enquiries finish. You see, we take murder very seriously."

"What do you think about it now?" Dillon asked Vince.

"We should send this up to the Partners and copy in LJ as well."

"OK, do it." Dillon remarked.

"I will obtain the file from Interpol that relates to Max Kane." Inger said.

"So we all know what we're doing and are agreed about where we go from here on?" Said Dillon, Vince nodded.

"We'll do a little investigating of our own for the next few days until we hear from Interpol. We'll keep it low profile and between ourselves for the time being. No official records at the moment." Dillon turned to Inger. "Can you request the whole file on Aleksey? There might be something that we can use in it."

"Yes."

"Next, we've got to find out what Kane was doing, with what looks like, a couple of east London thugs."

"I don't think Inger will be much help there. She wouldn't understand how these roughnecks fit into this game," said Vince.

Dillon winced, and darted a glance at Inger. Vince had finally attracted her attention. "This is too much," said Inger.

"You are being deliberately rude to me."

Vince raised his eyebrows, and turned to look at her. He smiled. "Not at all, I'm only being realistic."

"Then explain this to me."

"OK," said Vince. He sat on the edge of a workstation.

"I don't know what your thoughts are, but here we have two very different types of drug smuggler. The first are small time dealers who cut costs by smuggling small quantities of cocaine, marijuana, and pills. These middle class chancers run much higher risks and invariably get caught when they become greedy. The second type is organised criminals who keep clear of the main drug traffic. They smuggle very large amounts of cocaine and heroin, usually anything from half a ton up to two or three tons of the stuff. They tend to copy the South American drug barons preferred methods of shipping." He noticed the quizzical look on Inger's face. "Oh, they dissolve the cocaine in petrol, making it easy to ship in tankers all over the planet. When it arrives at the other end they simply reverse the process to extract the drugs again. Very shrewd because they not only get to sell the drugs but also have the fuel as a free bonus as well. Now, this second type of smuggler operates a simple system of need to know and nobody knows anybody else." Vince stopped abruptly. "So there you are. The lesson is over. Unfortunately, you probably won't be here long enough to learn anything useful about how we operate against these elusive criminals."

"Thank you," replied Inger. "It's not so different in Sweden, I have to tell you. We have organised crime there too. We also have small-time drug peddlers. So let me ask you something. You wish to know why this man Kane is talking with two roughnecks from east London."

"That's right," said Dillon.

"Is it not obvious that these criminals are doing business with him? They have money from their own illegal activities and they must invest it. No? Do I miss something?"

"No. I think you're right on the nose with that," said Dillon.

"Good. Because I was thinking maybe Vince has some

problem to make this connection." Dillon looked at Vince, who raised his eyebrows, and scratched his head. He was beginning to enjoy this relationship. Inger opened the door. "I will email a request to my superior officer at Interpol and ask him for information about Aleksey to be sent to your secure servers here in London."

"Any chance of a coffee, luv?" Vince asked. She looked at him, and then ignored the remark. She closed the door gently behind her.

"Do you think she'll be any good?" Vince asked.

"I think she might give us a surprise or two."

"Seems like she might have an authority issue," Vince grinned.

"The Swedes are not known for their humour," said Dillon grimly.

"OK", said Vince. "I'll give the girl a chance." He picked up a folder lying on one of the workstations. "The most important thing is to find out where Kane is now. I'll run a check through all of the agency databases and surveillance camera links. It'll take a bit of time but if he's been captured on camera, then my new face recognition programme that I've written will pick him out in an instant."

Five minutes later Inger returned to the op's room. In one hand she held a mug of what was unmistakably dark roast Colombian coffee. There was only one place she could have found it, and that was in Edward Levenson-Jones office. Dillon looked vacant. He wondered if she had said anything to LJ about the assignment. Inger interrupted his look, and smiled. "No. I did not say anything to him. He called me into his office when he spotted me looking for a coffee machine. I smell this divine coffee coming from Mr Levenson-Jones office. He gave me this cup thinking that it was for me. We had a good conversation, and he welcomes me to the department. He tells me you are very good field officers and that I could not be working with any better." She looked directly at Dillon, and smiled. It was a private joke. He grinned back. He guessed he was forgiven. "So, if you would open up your main email server I have the answer to my question already."

Dillon typed quickly, and a moment later the email appeared on screen in front of them.

The reply was in Swedish, Vince spoke a command and the screen text changed to English. There was no further information on Kane, but there was plenty on Aleksey, and Interpol were interested in anything more they could find out. Aleksey was killed by an unknown assassin. It was assumed that it was a drug related killing. He was found inside the luggage compartment of his sports car with his arms and legs broken to make him fit in the smallish space. The car was reported stolen by Aleksey's girlfriend and eventually found at Charles de Gaulle in the airport's long stay car park ten days later. In 2003 Aleksey was suspected of killing an associate, and ordering the assassination of four rivals. He had been under periodic surveillance since that time. It was possible that his own death had taken place as a reprisal for the killings he had ordered. Kane had been seen leaving the Hotel Des Grandes Ecoles after a meeting some two weeks previously. It was not known what had been discussed at the time nor had Kane been identified. Aleksey's operations were large and he was known to have imported at least fifteen tons of Panama Red Marijuana a year into France for distribution to locations across Europe.

"Do you think that Maximilian Kane was involved with Aleksey?" Inger asked.

"Definitely, if they were seen together," said Dillon. "He didn't fly to Paris for a cup of afternoon tea with an old chum. We know he flew to Switzerland shortly after that meeting. I'll bet that means he went there to conduct banking business. Perhaps he had struck a deal with Aleksey."

"Do you think Kane is having something to do with this killing?" Inger asked.

"It's not his form," said Dillon. "There's no evidence that he is violent. On one occasion we heard he was ripped off and he actually advocated not going after those who had done it to him. Violence attracts the attention of the police. The smart career villain like Kane knows that. It's the criminals who are violent." Dillon paused. "No. It's not really Kane's game at all."

"You've got a good memory," commented Edward Levenson-Jones, as he walked into the op's room.

"Hello boss." Vince said.

"You're completely wrong Jake," said LJ, sharply. "He's most certainly capable of it. He's ruthless."

Vince shot Dillon a glance. There was an awkward silence. Inger broke it. "I do not know what you mean. You make a difference between these words, career villain and criminal."

"I know. It's a class distinction. In the UK it's hard to see anything outside of a status context which is very much still with us. Kane is a career villain because he's been around the block a few times, had a few run-ins with the law, and made a huge amount of money from his illicit activities in the process. Whereas, the term criminal covers a wide spectrum of law breaking and these individuals usually get caught. They're often opportunistic, reactionary, and largely stupid without the skill or organisation to plan a caper properly. However, they take pride in serving time and they're getting themselves educated at the same time. Most of them come out with new skills that they've learnt off other inmates. Consequently, crime is a habitual occupation," said Dillon.

"It is a very strange thing this. From where I come from a criminal is a criminal!" Inger stated, "So what can you tell me about these two individuals, or criminals, who are with Kane?" Inger walked up to the screen and tapped her finger on the image.

"The men are convicted armed robbers," said Dillon, rolling a pointer over the image of one of the men. "They are both hardened criminals. The one by the open car door is called Razor; he got that name by carving his initials into the foreheads of his victims when they didn't pay their weekly protection money. Like I say, some of these people are just plain stupid. The other man is Conner Hawkins, also known as Cracker."

"Why is he called Cracker?" Inger asked.

"He likes to blow safes. He has a schizophrenic personality and his unpredictable behaviour makes him very dangerous." Vince commented.

"Is there anything else?" Inger asked.

"That's all the information there is on their record sheets, which is precious little. I have a feeling the Metropolitan Police will be reluctant to tell us much more."

"Why? You must know what they are doing if it is connected to the assignment you are working," said Inger.

"There's a lot of competition between Ferran & Cardini and SOCA If they have spent weeks watching someone and then we suddenly come on the scene with our own agenda, they get a little pissed off when we get all the credit for a successful outcome on the back of all their hard work. When we are assigned to a case the police are working on; it's not by chance, it's with the full authority of the Home Secretary. Our involvement with an active police investigation only happens if there is reliable intelligence that the involved parties are connected to a threat to national security, and only then is there a complete exchange of information. But to be honest, we don't like co-operating with the police. Their security is not as good as ours, and operations have a tendency of going wrong when they're involved."

"You know what I am thinking?" Inger said. "There's something odd about putting Aleksey's body in the small boot-space of a car when it could have simply been dragged and rolled under the vehicle."

"It's not surprising, although in this instance maybe a little unusual to be so thorough that this particular killer went to so much trouble to conceal the body in a space so small. I mean to say, the victims arms and legs were broken to get him inside. It would have taken both skill and strength to do this, and presumably only done to enable the perpetrator sufficient time to get as far away as possible." LJ said from the far end of the op's room.

"I've only seen this once before," commented Dillon.

"Where was that, old son?" LJ asked.

"About five years ago. Remember that assignment we were on with MI5, involving the contract killing of those four London gangland bosses. One of them had been shot through the head and was then forced into the boot of his Aston Martin

118

after having both his arms and legs broken in exactly the same way as Aleksey's had been snapped."

"So maybe that is what happened. Perhaps Aleksey was not killed by a Russian or Frenchman. But by an English contract killer." Inger said.

"I still can't see Kane being involved," repeated Dillon, looking up from the file he was now reading.

"We'll find out soon enough," said LJ confidently.

* * *

It was time for Kane to introduce Jasper Nash to Razor and Cracker Conner. He was apprehensive about the meeting, anticipating Jasper's reluctance to work with unknown people; and consequently he was usually flippant. "Make sure you're not seen with them, Jasper. They're not our sort. They wear designer hoodies and expensive bling jewellery after they've done a job. They drink too much and flash their cash to celebrate, but there are simply some things, in particular breeding, that you cannot buy, however much money you have."

"Max, you're becoming a right old snob in your middle age," responded Jasper.

Kane felt reassured by the remark. Perhaps Jasper wouldn't react to them. "Their bark is much worse than their bite," he concluded.

But even Max was beginning to have his doubts about Razor's ability to fix things. It was too late to start looking for someone else, and, anyway, Razor was too involved now. He was the linchpin of the operation. Kane was learning to his dismay that Razor's attention to detail left much to be desired. When Don Rafael wanted someone to deal with Aleksey, Kane only had one person he knew could undertake such a job, but he was in Australia. He mentioned it to Razor who took the problem off his hands. In retrospect, Kane realised it was a mistake; he was beginning to hear rumours that Aleksey's death had left some messy details which needed further attention. He would have to give Razor a lecture.

Kane had arranged to meet them in the Russell-Cotes museum on the East Cliff of Bournemouth, and therefore took the psychological advantage by placing them on unfamiliar territory. Razor and Cracker Conner looked insecure as they waited for Kane to arrive, surrounded by cultural exhibits and incomprehensible chit-chat.

* * *

Kane watched them standing in the relative safety of the museum, just inside the main entrance. "The one on the right is Razor. The other's Cracker Conner."

"It was a bit unfair meeting them at a place like this," commented Jasper.

"We're not going to discuss anything here. The idea was to encourage them to become a little more discreet. Widen their horizons. Make them security conscious. Right now they probably think they're in the middle of a senior citizens' day centre."

Jasper looked at Kane. "I'm not sure you're allowed to call them that anymore."

"Call who what?"

"Older people, that's who," Jasper said.

"Oh, well I didn't mean any offence by it."

Jasper turned his attention towards the main entrance of the museum. He looked at them. Razor wore a worn brown leather bomber jacket. He had a wiry build, and stood with a boxer's stance that would enable him to stand his ground. He had a viscous looking half-moon scar around his right eye which made his eyelid twitch every now and again. He appeared to be the dominant personality, but Cracker looked more sinister. Razor was obviously nervous whereas Cracker betrayed no discomfort.

It was Cracker who absorbed Jasper's attention. There was a threatening air about him. His face was lightly tanned and angular, almost chiselled and without expression. The features were all there, a thin nose, strong cheek bones, cropped blonde hair that gave him the hard cold look of a young man without feeling. His eyes darted, devoid of reaction. He wore a three quarter length black overcoat, and he kept his hands firmly in the pockets. Razor pulled out a silver hip flask and knocked back a good swig of whatever alcohol it held, but Cracker drank nothing, he simply looked at the entrance.

"We had better join them," said Kane. They both walked across the road and through the main entrance. Kane went over to the museum's donation box and pushed a folded fifty pound note into the narrow slot.

Razor immediately registered Kane's arrival and barged through the many people milling, past the displays towards him. Their presence was spreading dismay and consternation among the art and artefact fanciers, especially as every eye was on them.

"When you say three o'clock I understand three. Sharp!" Razor was evidently not pleased. "Next time - one minute late and I'll be gone. Perhaps you'd like to synchronise watches?" He pulled up his sleeve and flashed his Breitling watch.

Kane glanced at Jasper. There was the hint of a smile. "I don't think that will be necessary. I usually synchronise my watch with the BBC news time. By the way, this is the friend I was telling you about. Jack."

"All right, Jack?" Razor said by way of a greeting, ignoring Jasper's outstretched arm. "Don't worry; I won't be calling you nothing because I know that ain't your real name. But I know Maxi here. We did a little time together in the Scrubs. Didn't we, me old twinkle?" Kane winced at the remark.

As Razor spoke, his torso moved from side to side and his head swayed ever so slightly, most likely from too many heavy bare knuckle blows in the past.

"Excuse me," said a bald man in a beige rain coat, butting into their conversation, "Can you please let me through. Thank you."

Razor turned round on the red faced man and glowered at him.

"What is that you've got in your mouth mate? Oh, it's a bloody plum." Razor said sneeringly at the bald man who was withdrawing hastily in the direction that he had just come from.

"The things you see and hear when you haven't got a gun," commented Cracker, coldly.

Jasper looked at Cracker, and realised that he was serious.

"You've had a right laugh here, haven't you Maxi boy," growled Razor. "Next time we meet, I'll pick a time and a venue. Let's get out of this old people's place. It gives me the creeps, and fancy meeting in the middle of a lot of old Q-tips."

He started for the door and they followed. One or two of the Q-tips stared at them as they left through the main entrance.

"What are Q-tips? Kane asked quizzically.

Razor stopped and turned to face Kane. "A Q-tip, Maxi, is a very old white haired person. They usually come with Zimmer frames and life support units which they carry over their shoulders in a satchel bag." Razor grinned and then walked on.

They wandered around Bournemouth for ten minutes and poked their heads into a pub which proved completely unsuitable for conducting a conversation about a serious criminal venture. Everyone in the bar looked about twelve years old and the noise level was unbearable. "I don't like this place," said Razor and walked out. "Don't you have any decent boozers round here?" He complained. "Next time we meet on our turf."

Finally they tried The Moon in the Square where they found a table near the back of the bar. Cracker looked around while they waited for their drinks to arrive. "Don't mind this place," Razor commented at last. "There are some nice girls in here! No scrubbers. If you know what I mean?"

Jasper turned and looked at a pretty leggy brunette. Youthfulness oozed out of her.

"I bet she moves great in bed," remarked Razor.

Kane looked across at the roughneck with disdain. He then turned to Cracker and said, "What about you Cracker. I wonder, is she to your liking?"

"Nah, I prefer men, thanks." Cracker said and leaned back in his seat taking a sip of his gin and tonic. Kane looked across at Jasper and raised an eyebrow.

"Let's talk business," said Razor, and leaned forward

conspiratorially. "The first consignment from the Colombians is due to arrive at the end of next week. We don't have the day yet, but as soon as I'm reliably informed I'll give you the nod Maxi. Then he can tell you Jack." Jasper didn't comment. "The thing is where to meet up."

There was a moment's silence. Jasper suggested. "There's a burger-bar in the car park at Baiter slipway. Vans and cars are always parked there during the day."

"Fair enough," said Razor. "I'll check it out. You bring a van, and make it a big one. Get there about eight in the morning and give me the keys. Cracker will come with me and we'll rendezvous with the driver picking up the container from the docks on a flat-bed trailer. We go straight to the warehouse we've rented on a nearby trading estate, cut open the rear panel of the container and load the van with the candy. We're gone two hours at most. We come back and give you the van. You got any problems with that?"

"Well for starters, it sounds far too simple for my liking!" Jasper said matter of factly. "Do you really expect to load a consignment of class 'A' drugs weighing one ton into a van in broad daylight, without being collared by Customs?"

"That's exactly what I expect to do, Jack my old mate. And, I have it all taken care of." Razor said smugly.

"I very much doubt it. There's always something that's overlooked or forgotten! Tell me, how many people at the docks know what you're up to?"

"Two. There's the dockyard supervisor and a bent Customs officer with a very bad gambling habit. How does that sound?"

"Sounds like you might actually know what you're doing. You definitely talk the talk. But how do you know that these characters won't sell us all out? Eh…"

"Oh that's simple. I have every conversation I've ever had with them recorded with high definition video and sound. Now does that answer all of your smart-assed questions, Jack?" Razor sneered as he spoke the last word.

"Yes." Jasper kept his voice calm and expressionless.

"The van!" said Razor, turning his eyes on Jasper. "I

don't want some scrap heap. It's got to be clean and unmarked. Definitely no van hire and no writing on it. Don't want it more than a year old in case the old bill stops us and asks for documents. You got that?"

"Oh yes," said Jasper. At least these two London wide-boys understood the importance of having a vehicle that looked respectable. Razor kept staring at Jasper. One of his eyes was twitching. It was hard to hold the stare without laughing out loud.

"We'll meet you one week later to collect our share of the dosh," said Razor. "Make that ten in the evening at some boozer."

"No," said Jasper. "We meet at six-thirty. As it's just after rush-hour there's less risk of being followed."

"What's your problem? This ain't a job for the feint hearted who are scared of the old bill?"

"Well, it's your money," said Jasper. "And if you want to take chances with it then that's your prerogative."

"I don't really give a toss when we meet. Make it six-thirty then." Razor glared at Jasper.

"Where?" said Jasper.

"Bournemouth Central train station," suggested Kane. "There are plenty of people around."

"There are plenty of armed police around too." Said Cracker out of the blue, and surprising the others with his sudden entry into the conversation.

"So, are there any other suggestions?" Razor snapped.

"Poole Greyhound Stadium, at that time it'll be manic with people wanting to get through the gate. The car park will be full and there's a large central police station right on the doorstep. What better than to meet right under the nose of the local police force?" Jasper said, grinning for the first time that day.

"Very funny," said Razor, derisorily. "The stadium sounds good. But you make sure you're right on bloody time. Bring the money in a nondescript holdall with grip handles as well as a shoulder strap."

"OK," said Jasper.

"Why don't you go and order me another pint of lager? I want to have a quiet word with Maxi," ordered Razor.

Jasper glanced across at Kane, and then got up and walked out of the bar and went down into the Square for a look around. Ten minutes later he saw Razor and Cracker leaving the pub and returned to Kane.

"So what do you think of my two little jailbirds?" Kane asked cheerfully.

"They're definitely a liability," said Jasper matter of factly.

"Of course you are quite right Jasper." Kane said thoughtfully. "We certainly don't want to be seen with them. They're common and uneducated, with form as long as your arm. I'm not joking. If the police see you with them you can kiss goodbye to your liberty. They're not our sort Jasper. They drive cars that are ostentatious and crass that anyone with an ounce of good taste wouldn't be seen dead in, for God's sake. I know they're both like loose cannons, but they are in fact quite pliable. Which means I can manipulate them anyway I want even though they both carry semi-automatic handguns."

"Max, I'm not joking. These two are bad news and go completely against our rule. We do not work with ex-cons."

"Well, that counts us out," Kane laughed at his own joke. "This is different. We need these two for the shipping of the freight. They have contacts and they come highly recommended by people we both know and trust. You let me handle them. I know what floats their boat, but I also know which stick to wield to keep them in line."

"Max, we've always tried to avoid working with criminals of this type. These characters carry weapons and I have no doubt about whether they would use them." Kane thought he'd defuse the atmosphere. He didn't want Jasper to get skittish. "Listen Jasper, these two are all front. I'll tell you a story about Razor when he was still doing the armed robberies. He used to go into a petrol station or one of these mini-supermarkets and let off a sawn-off shotgun into the ceiling to show he was serious. One time he slipped on a wet floor and almost took his foot off. His mates had to carry him out blubbing his eyes out and abandon the raid."

"That's exactly my point," said Jasper. "Do you really want to work with a couple of assholes like that?"

"Don't worry about it. They're voices on the edge of the real action. They think they're hard. Sure they have connections, but then they don't have the expertise to put things together. They couldn't smuggle a bar of chocolate into the country without my help or contacts."

"Well, so long as you're happy with the situation, Max."

"I wouldn't say I was happy. After all they know my real name. I'm taking all the risks. But at least I didn't waste my time in prison. I made some very useful new contacts."

"You know what they say, Max? Prison is the ultimate old-boys networking club."

"Bollocks," retorted Kane. He thought of himself as a self-made man and amongst those who dragged themselves up from the gutter. He most definitely was not an 'old boy'.

"Listen, I've got to fly," said Jasper. "Martha's waiting for me."

"I thought we might have dinner together," said Kane, feeling somewhat rejected.

"I don't want to meet again until this deal is done and dusted, Max." Jasper delved into his jacket pocket for something and pulled out two small mobile phones, he passed one of them to Kane.

"These are unregistered mobile phones. They are virtually untraceable and are programmed to only call or receive from each other, but so as to be doubly sure of not being GPS tagged by any monitoring unit, I will only switch mine on for five minutes every morning at precisely ten thirty and again every evening at exactly seven o'clock. If you want to contact me - do it only then. But don't bother trying at any other time because the phone will be switched off and the battery taken out. I suggest you do the same."

Jasper stood up to leave. Kane walked with him as far as the bar where he ordered another drink.

* * *

It was just after three-thirty in the afternoon. A cold wind was blowing off the sea, and the weather forecast even hinted at the possibility of heavy rainstorms overnight. At the side of the road just off Bournemouth town centre, an unmarked police car was parked on double yellow lines; its bonnet lifted and hazard warning lights flashing. Sitting in the front of car were Detective Constable Steve Harvey and Detective Sergeant Rosie Trent of the Metropolitan Police, seconded to the local force on a surveillance operation. They had an excellent view of The Moon in the Square. He was looking forward to some traffic cop trying to ticket them for a parking violation. Even better if a truck was sent to tow their Ford Focus off to the pound.

He fancied a little confrontation to alleviate the boredom. They had been sitting in silence for the last ten minutes as every topic of conversation from the general to the personal had been talked about over the last three hours. DC Harvey was huddled in the passenger seat with his quilted jacket pulled tight around him. He was feeling cold and irritable, and at thirty-seven years of age he detested being cramped up in a car and having to wait for a couple of second rate criminals to turn up. But he only ever thought it, he was damned if he would allow SOCA to trample all over their investigation, as they'd been following Razor and Cracker for the last four weeks. DS Trent was also feeling the ill effects of being stuck in a confined space with an aging bachelor who had a farting problem because he ate a curry the night before. She looked over at her subordinate and gave him a look of disdain, while lowering her electric side window.

Sooner or later these two reprobates would make a mistake and he would be there to collar them both, and a promotion to Detective Sergeant in the process.

Harvey wiped the condensation off the inside of the windscreen and peered up the street at the pub entrance. SOCA knew nothing about what was going on in Dorset. They didn't even know where Kane lived. They'd asked him earlier in the day. He wouldn't tell them even if he knew. If they wanted information, they would have to turn over something to benefit his case. Kane had nothing to do with armed robberies at supermarkets and petrol stations. Right now Razor and Cracker were meeting some new bloke whom he hadn't yet identified, but he'd find out before the day was over. Best thing would be if Razor and Cracker went back to planning armed robberies and SOCA could get on with pursuing Kane.

Harvey knew a few things after fifteen years in this game. Razor wasn't about to commit some crime. This sort of thing was social. Since when did Razor go to museums or visit trendy south coast holiday towns? It just wasn't his style and more importantly he never left London, unless it was of the upmost importance. Bloody Razor was getting ideas way above his station. He'd be learning how to speak properly next. Harvey knew how Razor and Cracker worked all right, and it wasn't like this. He'd been about to treat the entire day as a complete waste of time, that the two young criminals were just out on a jolly for the day, when Kane turned up with the unknown bloke who looked like he worked for an accountant. Maybe Razor was looking for help with his tax return.

Twenty minutes later; Harvey spotted Razor and Cracker come out of the pub and saunter across the road just behind the Ford Focus on their way to their BMW six series coupe. Trent let them go. There wasn't any need to follow this time round; there would plenty of opportunities in the coming days. They were really easy to track because they were arrogant and had a belief that they were untouchable. What she wanted was more information about Kane's friend. Harvey opened the car door and got out; stretched his arms above his head and felt the blood start to circulate again after being cramped up for so long. Trent remained in the car while he made his way into the pubic house.

As Harvey entered the bar area he passed Kane's friend leaving. He cursed under his breath. Turned around and walked straight back to the car. Trent had already closed the bonnet with the engine running, and as he slipped into the passenger seat beside her, gently pulled away to follow Kane's friend as he walked away from them past the bus stops towards Westover Road.

Chapter 8

Martha was furious. Jasper couldn't expect her to believe that he was not up to his old tricks, when he was out all day and came back late into the evening. She'd suspected it for the past week and hoped it wasn't true. She felt used, and she didn't like the feeling. She looked at her watch. It was nine-thirty. She was allowing her life to be ruled by him. She had been happier and better off when he had been away. At least she had been in control of her social life. Now all she did was to wait for him to come home. She worked and she did the shopping, as well as all of the cleaning. Meanwhile he treated their luxury home like a hotel.

Nash returned home at nine forty-five. "You told me you were going to be back at eight. I've cooked your dinner," said Martha.

Nash followed Martha into the kitchen, sheepishly. "What is it?" He asked.

"Thai green curry on a bed of jasmine rice, which is now congealing on the plate." She took the plate out of the oven and placed it on the granite work surface. "Yep, congealed and ruined because you couldn't be bothered to come home when you said you would." Martha said coldly, and walked out of the kitchen.

"What's wrong?" Nash asked, stupidly.

"You are wrong, mister. I want the truth and you'd better tell it."

"Of course I will," said Nash. He knew what was coming.

"Are you hanging around with Max Kane again?" Martha stared at him. Nash held her gaze, but he hesitated just a fraction too long before replying. "Give me a straight answer - yes or no."

"Martha, it's not as simple as that," said Nash.

"Then the answer is yes. You've lied to me. You said you were retiring."

"I am. But it's really not that easy. There is unfinished business to clear up."

"Now you're just deluding yourself Jasper. It really is quite simple. You quit." Then she added. "Or I quit."

"Please listen, Martha."

Martha Interrupted. "What to, more lies?"

"No, not lies. Give me a break. I'm trying to pick up my life. I haven't done anything yet. Sure, Max would like me to do a few things."

"So you're thinking about it then?"

"I don't have much choice. I have to get the money I'm owed."

"Forget the money, Jasper. Grow up. Can't you see what Maximilian Kane is? He's narcissistic. He doesn't give a damn about anyone else. And he never has done. What did he do for you, while you were rotting in that Chinese prison?"

"Martha, he got me out. That's what Max did."

"He got you out!" Martha said sarcastically. "He got you out because he felt guilty and had the cash to bribe the right people. You didn't have a decent lawyer arranged, did you? Why not? Did you ever stop to think it through? Either he forgot you, or he was too bloody scared he might get himself implicated."

"Martha, you really don't understand."

"Why don't you bloody well open your blinkered eyes for once? Your friend Max isn't the man you knew when you lived in Paris. He's turned into a megalomaniac. He's got about as much respect for you as he has for the rest of humanity and that isn't saying much. I know. Believe me. I know, because I'm a woman. I didn't tell you, but I had dinner at the Chewton Glen with him because I wanted to know what had happened to you. But he didn't say a word about you in Hong Kong. No. He was far more interested in trying to get me into his bed. That's your friend Max. Nice sleazy Maxi who wants to fuck Martha because he wants to fuck Jasper."

"Martha, this isn't fair. I don't believe you. I think

130

you've misinterpreted Max's intentions."

"Fair!" shouted Martha. "Don't you dare talk to me about fair! Is it fair that I have to share you with Max Kane? Is it fair that I have to continuously lie to everyone for you, waiting for the day to come when they lock you up in a high security prison? It's not fair, and I don't want you staying here until you feel you can make some kind of commitment to this relationship. The fact is Jasper - it's me or Max."

"I'm not prepared to make a trade-off like that."

"Well, you know what you can do!"

"I'm tired Martha. My head's spinning with all this. I love you, but I can't stand all this. Please, bear with me a little longer."

"No. You've run out of time. You go away and think about it. When you've made up your mind, come back and let me know." Jasper looked baffled. "That means now, you fuck off and think about it. Go and talk to Max. See what advice he offers you."

Jasper picked up the car keys off the breakfast bar and walked to the door. He turned to look at Martha. Neither of them said anything. She stood with her arms crossed and held his gaze. A moment later he walked out.

Harvey was surprised to see the suspect walk out of the luxury apartment on Banks Road. He had just received details of the car which the suspect was driving. It was registered to Martha Hamilton at the address opposite. She was probably the suspect's girlfriend. But the night wasn't over yet. The suspect was back in the car and was now driving away.

"Are we going to follow," Harvey said to Detective Sergeant Rosie Trent sitting next to him in the passenger seat. As the suspect drove off along the one-way road Harvey pulled out and followed him down towards the chain link ferry, around to the right and onto Panama Road, Trent cautioned the Detective Constable. "Back off a little. He might have spotted us already."

Jasper stopped the car suddenly outside a pub. He'd been driving aimlessly around for half an hour, feeling numb. Inside the pub he was relieved to find it was not crowded. He ordered a large Jack Daniel's, drained it in one gulp, and ordered

131

another. He found an empty table at the back of the bar and sat down. He felt hurt and rejected by Martha's reaction. She didn't understand. He was going to work for both of them, and their future security. Now she had given him an ultimatum.

He imagined a life without Martha. She would always be there, just as she was now, watching him from another table nearby; except that she would be with another man. She would be dressed to impress. Always to impress, and talking just a little too loudly, making exaggerated gestures to illustrate just how important her conversation was. Her dark eyes would ignore him sitting in a darkened corner, slowly getting drunk until his face went numb and his brain became incoherent. She would stretch her hand out to lead the man out of the pub, to take him home. Jasper's imagination followed Martha until she was in bed with that other man. He imagined those intimate moments, savoured the pain he felt, and drained his drink.

He went to the bar and ordered a refill. He was not going to lose Martha. They had been together for over six years. She had taught him how to feel, and not to be afraid of those feelings. She had drawn him out of loneliness and given him something he was afraid of losing.

His thoughts switched to Max Kane. It was strange how people changed. Especially old friends, they seemed to change imperceptibly. Over the years their priorities shifted. Although Maximilian behaved abominably at times, Jasper kept an image of him from their early days. Friendships were based on memory, not on reality. Jasper found it hard to put his finger on exactly when it was that his relationship with Max had altered. But Max had been there for him when it had mattered. Max had got him out of jail. Whatever Martha said, if it hadn't been for Max he would still be in there.

All the same he was not prepared to dump someone he had known for over fifteen years, on someone else's whim. He'd shared his formative years with Max. They were bonded by their experiences. They'd been a good team. Max had the ideas and he had put them into practice. They'd had some great adventures. He wasn't going to throw all those memories away because he was having an argument with Martha. He felt calmer now. The pub was closing. He'd stay in a hotel for the night, and see if Martha was more reasonable in the morning. If necessary he'd tell her the truth, and then move out of the flat until the job was over. If not, he might introduce Max to someone who could do the work for him. He'd take a percentage for the introduction to keep a finger in the pie. Yes, that was the best solution he thought. His smart phone vibrated on the table and the screen lit up with incoming mail. He looked at the short message reading it carefully before wording a reply. When he'd finished he placed the smart phone in his jacket pocket, finished his drink and walked casually out of the pub. He crossed the road to find the nearest public telephone box and make a call to a private number in Westminster.

* * *

Outside, the cold air sobered him immediately. He looked around the Square and up the road towards the Bournemouth International Centre, all the time looking for anything suspicious such as cars parked where they shouldn't be and people looking out through café windows, supposedly watching the world go by. But Jasper Nash knew better, he had been evading the police surveillance teams for years. After a short walk through the pleasure gardens he found a telephone box at the top of a flight of steps that led to the road above. He checked that it hadn't been vandalised, and then opened the door and went inside the cramped space. He quickly inserted a tiny digital earpiece into his right ear canal before dialling the London number he had been sent. The earpiece had been purchased on-line from a specialist security and surveillance products company. It enabled every word spoken to be recorded on his smart phone. It was also Jasper's insurance policy should things go wrong. A moment passed before the person being called answered their phone. Jasper listened carefully to the digitally altered voice that spoke without interruption for just over two minutes and then disconnected without preamble. Jasper replaced the receiver on its cradle. As he stood outside, he thought about catching a taxi and then remembered Martha would need the car in the morning. He walked off along

Westover Road towards the Pavilion Theatre where he'd parked the car. He got in and pulled away from the parking space. He waited for the car in front of him to pull out onto Exeter Road and then moved forward, indicated right and pulled out into the evening traffic. He'd only driven one hundred metres before he was being waved into a layby and vehicle access point for the beach front, by a Police motorcycle officer. He stopped by the kerb and the uniformed officer came and stood in front of the car. Jasper noticed a woman standing on the pavement and a man approaching him from the road side. He wound down his window and heard the words 'Police officers'. He switched off the engine and stepped out.

"May I see your driving license, sir?"

Jasper took his licence out of his pocket and handed it over.

"You were pulled over because we have reason to believe that you have been drinking. Mr Nash. If you wouldn't mind getting into my vehicle, so that I can give you a breath test?"

"That doesn't look like a police car and you don't look like a plain-clothes policeman," said Jasper bluntly. "I'd like to see your identity card." There was no point making things easy for them.

"By all means," said the policeman, pulling out his card.

"Thank you, Detective Constable Harvey," said Jasper.

He sat on the back seat of the unmarked police car and blew into the machine, and watched the light turn predictably red. It came as no surprise to him. It had been that kind of day.

"We must ask you to accompany us to the police station, where we will take another reading."

Jasper remained seated in the back of the police car. It was a short drive across town to the police station at Madeira Road. Jasper guessed he had a long wait. It looked as if there had been a crime wave that night from the number of people waiting to be processed. The two coppers disappeared. In due course the desk sergeant asked him to blow into the breathalyser machine, and again it registered positive. He was asked if he wanted to give a blood or urine sample. He opted for the latter;

134

the mere thought of needles made him feel nauseous.

Harvey returned and escorted Jasper downstairs and passed him a sample bottle. They were alone. Jasper felt the large wad of cash inside his jacket pocket. There was around two thousand pounds in fifties. He looked at Harvey. He was somewhere in his late thirties or early forties with fair hair and a pallid complexion. There was the start of a belly about to expand, and he had little if any dress sense or style. He looked a man of a certain age and rank who had few prospects and little money.

"Can I talk to you off the record?" Jasper said.

It was some time since Harvey had heard anyone use that expression. He knew what it meant. It meant that he was about to be offered a bribe.

"Maybe," said Harvey.

"Have you been drinking alcohol, Detective Constable Harvey?" Jasper asked. He knew he was taking one almighty gamble.

"I've just worked a twelve hour shift, why?"

Jasper took out the wad of crisp new fifty pound notes.

"What's that for?" Harvey asked. There was the smallest flicker of interest in his eyes. Things were taking a surprising turn.

"It's for you to piss into this jar."

Harvey looked at Jasper Nash. This was turning out to be a strange affair. He wanted to find out more about this one, and now he was being paid for his trouble. There was a moment's hesitation before he stepped towards the urinal. He stretched out his hand for the money. Jasper passed him the sample jar. He took it, and then held out his hand again for the money. Jasper gave it to him. He looked at the notes, considering whether to count them. "How much is here?"

"There's two thousand there," replied Jasper.

Harvey stuffed the notes into his jacket pocket.

Jasper guessed he had a right to watch since he was paying. There was something indecorous about the way he fumbled with his flies. Perhaps he was worried about another officer walking in on them. The policeman spilled some of the urine down the side of the jar and onto his shoes.

Harvey buttoned up and wiped his hand down the leg of his trousers.

"Never done that before," he said.

"Well, there's a first time for everything," said Jasper.

Cheeky bastard, thought Harvey, but what I'm going to tell him now is going to cost him a lot more than two thousand quid.

"Mr Nash, this little charade was incidental. I wanted to have a quiet word with you in private. I've got a message for you to deliver to your friend Max Kane. I've got some information for him and it'll cost him seven thousand pounds."

"Why don't you tell him yourself?"

"He's a little bit elusive these days, and I wouldn't want to make him nervous by looking for him."

Harvey opened the door. He turned round, and said, "I'll meet you at that pub tomorrow lunchtime. Let's say twelve sharp."

"Since I got back from Hong Kong, I really don't see much of Kane these days." Jasper covered himself. "I don't know if I can contact him that quickly."

"OK. Make it the day after tomorrow. But be warned. You make sure he's there, or I'll come knocking on your flash front door," threatened Harvey.

Jasper followed Harvey back to the desk sergeant and completed the formalities under his suspicious gaze.

Outside the police station, Jasper hailed a taxi. It was one o'clock in the morning. He'd had too many surprises for one day. He decided not to stay at a hotel. Back home, he found Martha in bed.

"I thought you'd really gone," she said sleepily.

"No," said Jasper. "Not yet."

"I'm glad."

"We'll talk about it," said Jasper. He squeezed her hand.

"In the morning," said Martha. "Come to bed now. I'm really sorry about this evening."

* * *

When Jasper woke, Martha was standing by the bed. She was dressed. She must have woken him. He stretched out his hand fumbling for the clock and saw that it was half past nine. She was just getting ready to go out. There was an hour until he had to phone Max. He rolled over.

"Where's the car?" She asked.

The previous night came flooding back. "Oh, I left it in Bournemouth. I had too much to drink. I'll go and collect it later this morning."

"OK, it's not a problem. I've been asked over to a gallery in Lymington to discuss the possibility of holding an exhibition of my watercolours there."

"Sounds interesting," Jasper said stretching his arms above his head and yawning.

"It is, they're not just thinking about taking some of my paintings for their forthcoming exhibition next month, they're talking about all of them and the exhibition would only feature my work."

"That's marvellous Martha." Jasper was genuinely pleased for her. "How are you getting there?" he asked casually.

"Taxi into Poole and then I'll train it to their front door in Lymington." There was the sound of a car horn from outside. "There's my taxi, got to go. Now don't forget, we're having lunch at Jenkins & Sons in Penn Hill at one-thirty." Martha's words wafted over her shoulder as she walked to the front door. After she had left, Jasper flopped back down into the comfy warm bed and stared up at the sun streaking the ceiling with its morning glow.

* * *

Vince Sharp opened the door to the department and was unprepared for the chaos which confronted him. The office was buzzing with activity; men and women talking into telephone handsets, computer screens alive with script and images, and Dillon ransacking his office. Dillon looked up and stopped rummaging through drawers and turned to face him.

"Where the hell have you been?" Dillon snapped.

"I have been at Legoland for best part of the day being

given the run around by our friends over there."

"And how are our friends at MI6 these days?" Dillon asked.

"Paranoid. They've picked up some chatter from Westminster that has set them all of a twitch," Vince watched Dillon continue to search around the office for whatever it was he had lost. "Can I help you find whatever it is you've lost?"

"I've misplaced that image of Kane which I printed off yesterday."

"I'm sure I left it on your desk."

"Are you sure Inger Lindberg didn't take it with her?" Vince said shifting some of the papers on the untidy desk top.

"No, she had her own print out."

"Maybe LJ has it."

"Oh, that's an idea. Never thought of the boss, all he had to do was download it from your files; he has full access after all. Although, possibly not since he told me that Kane wasn't worth pursuing and was deemed very low priority." Dillon thought for a moment. "Anyway, what would he be doing in here?"

Vince didn't bother to answer the question. "So what's your problem, mate? I'll just make you another hard copy."

"Yeah, I know that. But it's really weird that it's gone missing, don't you think? Wait. Did you say chatter from Westminster - to where?"

"A public telephone box in Bournemouth. And I can tell you it's got them all stirred up."

"A call box in Bournemouth, now that is interesting. Well it looks like we're going to Dorset sooner than we expected then."

"What about the image of Kane?"

"Oh, I'm sure it'll turn up." Dillon looked around Vince's office in disgust at the mess he had caused.

"You're right," he said, finally resigned to the loss of the picture. "Email me another image of Kane."

"Where's Inger?" Vince asked.

"She's gone to the Dutch Embassy for something or other."

"Any idea when she'll be back?"

"Before six, I hope. I want her to make a few enquiries for me."

"I might see if she wants a bite to eat tonight," said Vince. "I thought it might be a friendly gesture."

"Good Idea," said Dillon, curtly; he didn't want Vince getting too friendly with the lady from Interpol.

Dillon set about clearing up the mess he had so effectively created. He was now impatient to start the assignment into Jasper Nash and Maximilian Kane. It was always the same before an assignment. The waiting, and the confirmation that authority had been granted for Ferran & Cardini to legally pursue the suspects on behalf of the security service. Tonight he would spend drinking the finest single malt whiskey. Waiting - always waiting - for the Partners to give their seal of approval after assessing every conceivable element that could go wrong with any given situation.

"Oh, and next time mate," said Vince. "I'd be grateful if you'd stay out of my office until I'm there to ensure you don't ransack the place."

Dillon remained quiet and carried on putting everything straight again, every now and then taking a sneak look at the paperwork in more detail.

* * *

For the fifth time Max Kane glanced down at his Rolex. He was sitting on a bench overlooking the East Cliff in Bournemouth, waiting until the designated time to ring Jasper on the mobile phone he had given him. He pulled out of his pocket a black box, about the size of a cigarette packet, with three stubby antennas screwed into one end. He pushed the switch to turn the solid-state device on and the red light glowed. He smiled and thought how clever technology was today. He turned the portable Mobile Phone Signal Blocker in his hand, as long as he remained within a metre and half of the device it would allow him to make and receive calls while shielding him from anyone attempting to listen in or locate him using GPS triangulation software. He was five minutes early.

The wind was bitterly cold, blowing off the English Channel; he stood up and walked towards the cliff top looking out across the watery landscape. He turned and casually looked along the road in both directions. Just in case there were any cars with occupants who weren't of retirement age and would almost certainly be plain clothes police surveillance officers. Sitting back down, Kane pulled the collar of the heavy black overcoat he was wearing, up around his neck. All of these precautions were necessary to his survival. He had made it his business to stay abreast of developments. He knew that there were a number of spy satellites over the Atlantic and each was capable of monitoring infinite amounts of virtual computer traffic as well as mobile voice and text. There were now law enforcement agency computers generating data from these satellites so powerful that they could pick up a single key word, monitoring words at a speed of six million characters a second. They could read an entire book before a person could say the title. It was for this reason that Kane had got hold of the unregistered mobile phones and would dispose of them once the job was done.

In Paris, Aleksey habitually used his mobile phone at home and consequently his security had been terrible. He should never have been in partnership with Aleksey. Russian dealers were surprisingly aggrieved when they were busted but they didn't have the right to complain. They only ever had their wrists slapped and a minimal suspended sentence in exchange for a substantial pay-off to the right officials.

Kane never mentioned names, dates, times or places specifically over the phone. Cryptic remarks sufficed and he limited his call time to a maximum of two minutes and thirty seconds.

He glanced at his watch. It was exactly ten-thirty. He pushed the call button and waited for Jasper to pick the call up. Kane was irritated by Jasper's over zealousness with the cloak and dagger stuff this early in the deal. The problem was that he always insisted things were done his way.

Hangover or no hangover, Jasper reached over and picked up the ringing mobile phone. "Good morning," said

Kane.

"I need to meet you." Jasper's tone was brusque. Kane didn't take kindly to anyone dictating to him.

"I'm a bit busy at present," said Kane. He had a number of calls to make. The air charter operation was proving to be a nightmare. He was finding that it was easy getting the cocaine onto the aircraft while inside the private hangers, but getting it off was a completely different matter. Each time there was a problem he had to consult Razor.

"It is rather Urgent," he heard Jasper say. He hoped that Jasper wasn't having a change of heart. He would be particularly annoyed if Jasper was going to drop out of the operation at this point.

"I heard you," he said. "In forty-five minutes. How about having breakfast?"

"See you there," said Jasper, and pushed the end call button.

Breakfast, was a mobile burger bar located in the car park at Whitecliff on Sandbanks Road, overlooking the Harbourside Park and South Deep beyond. Kane got up from the bench, and walked back along the Overcliff Drive towards the town. After a short distance, he took the road that leads down to the pier, constantly looking over his shoulder to make sure he wasn't being followed. Satisfied that there was no one tailing him, he took a path on the right that took him all the way to the warmth and comfort of the four-star Royal Bath Hotel. He had a few calls to make and he liked to be in comfortable surroundings with a pot of freshly ground coffee served in the finest of cups. He'd hardly been able to hear Jasper over the noise of the traffic and the howling wind. It would have been impossible to conduct an international call.

There were moments when Kane looked on his life with a degree of self-pity. This was a lonely occupation. There was no one in whom he could confide with safely. He always seemed to be wandering around the foyers of hotels waiting for a phone call or a man with a suitcase full of money. It was lonelier than the life of a movie spy - without glamour and without recognition. At least spies had support networks and voices in high places who could arrange a trade-off. Unlike his job where there were no heroes, win or lose.

Kane shivered at the thought of ever truly being caught and sent to prison for the rest of his natural life. Perhaps he should take Dillon a little bit more seriously. He knew that he was treading on thin ice. But with one big advantage over others who had been in a similar situation to him; he was intellectually more capable than any other criminal he'd ever met. And, his natural survival instincts were at their peak when he was under pressure. Anyway, Jasper would shield him from all of that, and insulate him from the risks. If anything did go wrong, a few individuals in secret places would ensure things didn't get too hot because they wanted to be paid; a quarter of a million bought a lot of loyalty.

He looked around the Royal Bath's foyer. Everything looked normal. De Vere Hotels were similar the world over. De Vere customers didn't like surprises. Neither did Kane.

* * *

Jasper could tell from the way Martha was sitting opposite him in the restaurant that she had made up her mind. He guessed she had worked out her terms and nothing would change her mind. That was how she operated. She liked certainties. She picked up the menu, looked at it briefly and laid it back down.

"That was quick. Have you chosen?" Jasper asked.

"Yes," she replied. Her tone was a little tense. Food was not on the agenda.

Jasper spent longer deciding what to order and knew that his indecision was irritating her. Nevertheless, the menu provided a safe place to hide. Finally he chose. He wondered if he heard a sigh of relief from Martha.

"So, have you thought about it?" Martha asked.

Jasper assumed she was referring to her ultimatum of the previous night. Of course he had thought about it. They'd agreed to have lunch together to discuss it.

"Shall we order?" Jasper suggested.

Martha didn't reply. She immediately recognised

Jasper's stalling tactics. She watched him signal the waitress. She waited patiently for the waitress to finish serving a party of six middle aged women and then appear at their table. They ordered lunch. She decided on the wine. She waited until they were alone again. "So have you thought about it?" She repeated.

"Of course," said Jasper. "I suppose you want to know whether I've chosen you or Max."

"You got it in one."

"It's not much of a competition. If you put it like that, I have to choose you."

"So you won't see him again?" Martha insisted.

"That wasn't the deal. You can't expect me not to see my oldest friend"

"If you see him, how do I know that you're not working with him?"

"You'll have to trust me, Martha."

"I already tried. Admit it Jasper. You can't be trusted."

There was a long awkward pause. Jasper perceived that the discussion wouldn't be constructive if it carried on along these lines.

"Do you still want to continue the relationship with me?" He asked.

"Yes."

"Well at least we have a starting point," he said. He wondered in which direction to develop the conversation now.

Martha took the initiative. "You don't seem to understand. If I'm living with you, then what you do affects me. Indirectly it affects everything and everyone else around us."

"I understand that, Martha. Believe me. I'm not stupid. I'm concerned for us both. I want to make enough money so that we can have a secure life."

"Jasper, you are so full of bullshit," said Martha with sudden vehemence.

"Why do you think I'm doing it?" Jasper asked in an aggrieved voice.

"Because you're afraid of giving up and having to rely on making an honest day's living. You'll have to stop taking your lead from Max."

"You're not giving me much credit for self-determination. Why do you dislike him so much?"

"I've never met anyone who's so egocentric."

"He's really not as bad as you think. He's got a good heart." Martha didn't comment. "He's done some good things in his time. He paid for clean water and sanitation to be installed throughout an entire village in Africa. That's an altruistic gesture. He probably saved the lives of many children."

"One good deed doesn't make him a saint," commented Martha, intransigently. Then warming to a theme she continued. "After all, he was only playing at God. A role he obviously feels comfortable with." Jasper said nothing. Martha downed a glass of water. "Yes, I remember now, you told me that rather endearing story once before. You were very impressed by his gesture. I was disappointed in you, if the truth be told. If he paid all the taxes he owes, then a lot of people much closer to home would benefit also."

"Martha, we're not getting anywhere, are we?" Jasper said pragmatically. "What if I say I won't work with Max? I'll see him from time to time, for a drink, but I won't work."

"Well, if you really mean it this time."

"OK," said Jasper, "I mean it. But so there are no misunderstandings, I'll have to see Max a few times to introduce him to people who can take over from me. I can't very well leave him completely in the lurch. It'll take a couple of meetings, and then it'll be over."

"I hope you're not taking me for a fool, Jasper. Because if you break your word. That will be the end of us."

"I won't Martha, I promise, and for the record, I haven't broken it yet. I might have been tempted but I would have told you. I'm not guilty." He smiled.

Martha looked stern. "Good," she said.

"Bloody hell!" thought Jasper. He was shocked by his ability to lie. "I'll speak to Max this evening," he said.

* * *

Early on Monday morning the street cleaners were clearing rubbish on the Rue Jean-Baptiste Pigalle in the heart of the Paris red-light district. Despite the city council's attempts to get the hookers off the streets, the junkies tended to gravitate there to score deals and indulge in 'speedballing', to shoot up or smoke a mixture of cocaine and heroin; ecstasy mixed with ketamine; the simultaneous use of a stimulant with a depressant.

In a quiet side street, under a pile of cardboard, the street cleaners found a body, and called the police.

The body turned out to be that of a healthy woman in her mid to late forties. She had auburn coloured hair. Her hands had been tied behind her back with a nylon cable-tie. She was wearing what had been an expensive designer dress which had been partially torn at the neck line to expose soft skin as pale and as fine as porcelain. She was wearing handmade Italian patent leather evening shoes. Her black brassiere had been pulled above her breasts.

She had been garrotted with a fine wire. There were cuts and abrasions to both knees and there was bruising to the forehead. There were rope burns around both ankles and her underwear had been discarded. The woman had been sexually assaulted in the most disturbing way.

By the following day the body had been identified as that of Natalya Varennikov. She was the girlfriend of the murdered Russian drug baron Aleksey, and had been on the French witness protection programme. There was a mass of forensic clues, but no indication of who her killer might be. It was assumed that the murder was connected to that of Aleksey.

Chapter 9

Twenty-four hours after Inger had emailed the photos of Max Kane to Interpol, Edward Levenson-Jones summoned Dillon to his office.

"I've had a request from the French. They want to interview Kane," said LJ. "Did you have anything to do with this?"

"Sorry, not getting your drift." Dillon said, innocently.

"I hope this is a genuine assignment, and not one you've put them up to through Miss Lindberg."

"No way," said Dillon. "It was Inger who saw the image by chance. A Metropolitan police surveillance team took it, and then had to pass it across to us at the insistence of Dunstan Havelock for us to confirm that it was actually Kane."

"I'm pleased that you're on first name terms with Miss Lindberg," said LJ, and nodded, suggesting he we reading something into the fact. Dillon didn't react. LJ continued. "I suppose you had better track down Kane for an interview with Miss Lindberg."

"It won't be as easy as that. If you remember, no one really knows where Kane is living at the moment. If we pick him up I doubt he'll want to talk to us before speaking to his solicitor. And if he speaks to a solicitor he'll be gone within minutes."

"I'm not sure if Kane is worth all the effort, Jake." LJ commented wearily.

"Well, the police and Interpol seem to think he is worth the effort. But our brief is with Kane's sidekick, Jasper Nash. He is Ferran & Cardini's primary target, and my number one priority."

"Very well, then," said LJ. "This is what I propose. We put together a six man team to locate Kane. We allow seventy-two hours for this part of the assignment. If we don't find him, then we leave it to the police. His last known whereabouts was Bournemouth in Dorset. That will leave you, Vince and Miss Lindberg to concentrate on Nash. I've already sanctioned the rental of a house in Sandbanks for your use. Now I know you have your own property there, but it really is too dangerous to use it. Much better you keep the location of that a secret. However, if we do find him we review what we've discovered before we move in on him."

"I think the policy is too cautious, and we need more than seventy-two hours to get anywhere with this slippery snake."

"Seventy-two hours," said LJ firmly. "Tell the team there will be a briefing in the op's room at six o'clock prompt. In the meantime I want you to tell me everything you know about Kane and Nash. I don't want any nasty little surprises later."

"There is just one more thing, LJ."

"What is it, old son?"

"I'll be going out with the surveillance team for a day"

"Why on earth would you want to do that, it's way down the scale for you to get involved with."

"Nothing is too far down the scale for me. I have my reasons. I know these two criminals, and I know what they're really like. I might be able to add value to the team with my insight of them. I also think that it might be useful for Inger to see how we go about these things."

"To be honest Jake, your considerable expertise could be put to far better use if you were to concentrate on coordinating the assignment, instead of your insatiable appetite for rolling up your sleeves and getting in the thick of it all." He stood up to indicate that the meeting was now over.

"I'll take that into consideration when I'm up to my neck in the shit that inevitably goes with this type of assignment." Dillon turned and left the room before LJ started lecturing him.

At six o'clock, there were nine Ferran & Cardini special field officers including; Dillon, Inger Lindberg and Vince Sharp, all waiting for Edward Levenson-Jones to arrive in the op's room. The atmosphere was informal, as always within the department, but each member could feel the excitement spreading around the room. It was always like that when an assignment was about to take off. After many weeks of research and planning, they were going to get to grips with the real business of seeking out the targets and bringing them down - hard.

The room fell silent as LJ entered the room. Over the years Dillon had learned that he tended to become a short-tempered diva late in the day. The blame was generally attached to the amount of coffee and Slim Panatela cigars he consumed, along with a lack of nutritious food intake during the day.

"Good afternoon," began LJ. "I apologise for holding this briefing so late in the day, but I realise that some of you are already working on other assignments. So I'll try and make this as brief as possible. This operation is code named 'Quisling'. No doubt you'll all be wondering why I chose that particular word." He paused. He always liked the team to know why he had chosen a particular code name. "Well, a quisling is a traitor, more specifically a traitor who collaborates with the enemy to promote occupation and suppression of a native people. This word is of Norwegian origin, making it one of the few Norwegian terms to enter the English language. And this assignment is not only about busting open a cocaine smuggling operation, but about hunting down a traitor of the British Realm who is selling highly sensitive military secrets to North Korea." He paused for added impact, before continuing. "Now then, back to the nuts and bolts. We are informed by customs that they believe there is a conspiracy to import a large quantity of pure Colombian cocaine in to the UK, very soon. As some of you are aware the two main suspects, Maximilian Kane and Jasper Nash, have been under investigation, on and off, for the last four to five years. But since Nash was caught red-handed in Hong Kong, certain things have come to light that have started the ball rolling again. Things are soon to come to a head. The police are conducting their own enquiries, as are customs, into the cocaine smuggling. But we have the full authority of the Home Secretary to investigate and move freely across all agencies in our quest to track down the 'Quisling'."

Dillon was surprised. He hadn't expected LJ to give the assignment such a high profile. He realised that he continually underestimated him, even after all the years of working with him. The man was a communicator and he was conveying, on the basis of very little information, the impression that this was a major operation. On the other hand, LJ had to account for the department's resources and this would read well if there was ever an enquiry.

"I want to emphasise that we must be very careful. These people are very good at their craft. They've been honing their skills over many years, since their time at university together. This incidentally was where they first met. They are extremely difficult to follow and they are constantly on high alert. What we have on our side is the psychological factor. They will be very loathed to give up an operation that they might have been planning for many months or even a year or more. They will be only too happy to persuade themselves that they are not being watched. Nevertheless, any field officer who makes the mistake of showing him or herself will be removed from the team. Do I make myself clear?"

There was a murmur of agreement from around the op's room. LJ continued. "Do not underestimate the organisational skills of these two men. We have a report from Interpol that at least one dealer has met a sticky end, and this may be closely connected to the investigation that we are being asked to conduct. Furthermore, we are investigating what I like to call organised crime. If we take a look at the characters involved, that will become perfectly clear."

He opened the folder in front of him and placed it on the flat screen of the workstation. The image immediately appeared on the wall monitors. "This is a photograph of Jasper Nash. He is the reason for our involvement with this assignment. He's one very slippery customer. MI5 and MI6 have had him under their watchful eyes for some time, but unfortunately he has a brilliant lawyer who always has him released within six hours of any arrest taking place. He is the right-hand man for this character; another image appeared on the monitor screen. His name is Maximilian Kane. He is also known by a number of alias names, although I am told that we do not have all of them on our files. He is extremely well connected within the underworld and is thought to be behind some of the larger cocaine shipments entering the UK over the last three years. By big I'm talking about a minimum of one ton, but more often than not upwards of five tons. Kane doesn't work for less than a million pound arrangement fee."

"He's been a busy chap." Dillon ran a hand through his thick dark hair, walked around and stood next to LJ, and then continued. "But so have I. The check I asked Vince to carry out involved the Border Agency database." LJ's head snapped round and he shot Dillon one of his, oh no not again, looks.

"It would seem that's he's been clocking up a considerable amount of air-miles recently." A series of maps appeared on the wall screens. "Places of interest include, the Middle East, France, Switzerland, Holland, and Colombia, to mention a few of the - how shall we say - more suspect ones. What's a lot more suspicious is that when he travels he employs a number of little tricks to smokescreen his movements. He has used an alias under the name of Cane. It could be the slip of the typist's finger, but which serves to disguise him from the system and any on-going enquiries."

"You will each be given a file, the contents of which you will memorise and then hand back to me before you leave this department. I would hate for any of you to go into action not knowing who the stars of the show are." LJ peered at his attentive audience properly for the first time since he had entered the room. He seemed to be taking stock of the individuals. He removed the image of Max Kane and pointed to the one of Jasper Nash. "For about six months Nash was imprisoned in a high security prison in Hong Kong having been caught in possession of one ton of cocaine. He has had a close association with Kane for many years. He came to the security service's attention a little over three years ago, but the level his activity was such that he must have spent some years building his contacts. Nash is a particularly tricky customer. He only speaks on unregistered mobile phones when he communicates with Kane and one other person - as yet unidentified - in London.

He is virtually impossible to follow, as you will find out. We believe he will be project managing the next cocaine shipment into the UK, and it was for this reason that only someone with an immense amount of money and contacts at the highest level managed to have him sprung from the Hong Kong prison. This person we are almost sure was Maximilian Kane." LJ pulled two more photos from the file and placed them down on the glass screen top. "Finally, we have these two convicted armed robbers who have recently been seen in the company of Kane and Nash in Dorset."

Dillon studied the two rough looking faces staring back at him from the screen on the wall. He wanted to know when and where LJ had obtained the two pictures. And why had he not shown Dillon before this briefing.

LJ continued, "We do not know the precise nature of their involvement. However, they are presently under surveillance by the Metropolitan and Bournemouth police units. The last thing I want is a complaint that Ferran & Cardini field operatives have in any way interfered with these active operations. To date, the police have indicated that they are prepared to hand over any information which might be relevant to our assignment. We will of course, reciprocate when and where appropriate."

LJ paused. "Are there any questions?" He asked, but there were none. "Good. Those of you working the surveillance shifts will meet up at the garage tomorrow morning at five-thirty. It's an early start, I know, but it can't be helped."

As the Ferran & Cardini officers each picked up the file in front of them and stood chatting in the op's room. LJ slipped towards the door. He liked to take a stroll along the Embankment and then drop into his club before he headed home.

"What is it Jake?" LJ said turning towards Dillon.

"I want to know when you obtained those two pictures."

"Which two pictures would that be, Jake?"

"The pictures of Razor and Cracker Conner," elucidated Dillon patiently.

"They were already in the file, old son," said LJ without further explanation, and strode off down the corridor.

"No," Dillon said aloud, but no one was there to hear him. He was sure that they were not already in the file. He wondered where they had been and why they were suddenly re-introduced.

* * *

"Fuck Jasper!" Kane thought. "Why the hell can't he keep his bloody woman under control?" It was hard enough being in this business without having their lines of communication disrupted. He looked with contemptuous distaste at the mobile phone that Jasper had provided him with and told him to only call at set times each day. Martha had to be bloody good in bed to put him under virtual house arrest, he'd show her the door.

Kane watched as people came into the pub. He assessed each of them to see if they might include Harvey. The phone call on his private mobile phone had come as a nasty little surprise, but it couldn't all be bad. A meeting at a busy pub was much more interesting than one in a police interview room at Madeira Road. It was typical of Jasper to get himself into a fix and then expect him to sort the problem out. What if the policeman was wearing a wire or a covert camera? He would have to be very careful of what he said. He'd find out if the copper was on the level. He'd play it by ear and make sure the conversation went at a pace that he was controlling. Something would come to him. It always did. The first thing he'd do was insist they left the pub and throw off the surveillance.

It didn't take much effort to spot Detective Constable Harvey. He stood out like a sore thumb amongst a pub full of university students. Wearing such a badly fitting suit he could only be a policeman. He wouldn't fit into it if he lived to be ninety. The unpleasant thing was that Harvey identified him immediately.

"Where's your mate?" Harvey asked without preamble.

"Keeping an eye open outside," replied Kane. There was no harm in pretending that he was taking a few basic precautions. He finished his drink.

"Let's go," he said, and then casually added. "We'll find somewhere a little more quiet, where we can talk."

Outside Kane hailed a taxi. "Winton Banks," he instructed the driver. He sat on the jump seat opposite Harvey and looked at the traffic behind. He couldn't see any obvious signs of surveillance.

"I hear you have plot of land to sell."

"Yeah," replied Harvey.

"It sounds expensive," remarked Kane.

"It's a prime location," replied Harvey. "You'll be surprised how good it is."

"We'll see."

Ten minutes later having crossed Bournemouth town centre, the taxi entered Wimborne Road, and Kane ordered the driver to stop. They stepped out. Kane paid. He watched to see if any cars had followed, but he was confident they were alone. They were standing in the centre of a busy high street, cars and vans nose to tail at the traffic lights, exhaust fumes filling the air. He quickly turned left and walked off along Talbot Road. Harvey followed, his rubber soles making no noise. Within thirty seconds Kane had hailed another taxi, and two minutes later they entered a quiet suburban residential road where the properties were impressive and the driveways filled with luxury cars. He told the driver to pull over and again he paid the fare. Kane stood for a second on the pavement looking around as he had done previously, before turning around and quickly walking across the car park of the exclusive health and sports club.

"Nice," said Harvey. He was impressed.

"That was just for starters," said Kane.

"Where are we going now?"

"Where do you think," commented Kane as he entered the health club, and signed Harvey in.

"You're a suspicious bastard aren't you?" Harvey commented.

Kane nodded. When it came to doing deals like this he became a paranoid schizophrenic. They were going to take a sauna together. He'd be damn sure then that Harvey wasn't wearing a wire.

Once they were ensconced in the sauna Kane felt much

153

safer.

"What are you selling?" Kane's voice was blunt.

"What I'm offering is information."

"What is it?"

"The money?" asked Harvey.

"I've got it here in the building." Harvey looked sceptical. "You'll have to believe me." Kane wasn't lying. He always kept a few grand in his locker in case of emergencies.

"You're connected with a couple of London thugs called Razor and Cracker Conner?" Kane didn't answer. He didn't know if Harvey was ferreting for information. "OK. Maybe you call them Razor and Cracker. But I know you're involved with them because they're under surveillance by the Met. I'm seconded to the Bournemouth end of the investigation with my sergeant. I've been following those two for over a month."

Kane was glad they were in the sauna. He felt faint. He could hardly bring himself to ask, "Why are you watching them?"

"I hope you're not trying to pull one over on me?" warned Harvey.

"Why should I?" replied Kane.

"They're planning something big down here. We know they've been working for one of the firms in the Eastend of London and that they have been involved with a couple of big robberies on their behalf over in Canford Cliffs recently. We got a tip-off they were planning something much more ambitious."

"So what's that got to do with me?" asked Kane. "You must have checked me out. Blagging isn't my game."

"I hear that Her Majesty's Customs are very interested in you."

"You hear right."

"You mean, you know?" asked Harvey incredulously.

"I know a lot of people."

"As from first thing tomorrow morning your friend Jasper Nash will be under police surveillance."

"So what's new? You're wasting my time, Detective Constable. Unless you've got something real to say, I'm walking." Kane started to get up off the wooden bench they were seated on.

"Wait. There is something that you won't know."

"What is it?"

"There's something unusual about the surveillance on your friend Nash."

"Go on." Kane sat back down again.

"There's something going on with Nash and he's attracted interest from the highest level in Whitehall."

"OK. You've regained my attention. What else have you got?"

"It's not only police surveillance. I saw the case notes and there's a firm on the case as well."

"And what firm might that be?" Kane asked, his tone remaining casual.

"Ferran & Cardini International, the bloke heading up their team is called Jake Dillon."

"What is the basis for their involvement?"

"I don't have that information. Everything about this firm seems to be a bit shadowy. I think they might be spooks or something bloody like it."

Bad news, thought Kane. He felt that he was sweating somewhat profusely. "Why are you telling me all of this, apart from the small matter of a cash payment?"

"I want Razor and Cracker. I'll get a promotion if I nick those two little thugs. So I don't want my mates in the Met or this other firm messing up my case. One of the houses they burgled down here belongs to our Chief Constable."

"You realise that you're taking a mighty big chance, talking to me. After all, I am under surveillance, aren't I?"

"Not really. What you going to do? Call up my D.I. and tell him? It's your word against mine."

Kane stood up and chucked some more water on the charcoal. It was time to turn up the heat. He had an idea. He settled back on the bench. "Would you be interested in earning a little more than five grand?" It was a ridiculous question, but one had to observe the niceties.

"What sort of sums are you talking?" Harvey said, keeping what he hoped was a cautious note.

"Starting around thirty and rising to fifty grand."

"Maybe," Harvey said. He squirmed on the bench. His white skin had turned red raw with the heat. "What's the deal?"

"I'd like you to ease off Razor for a day or two. Maybe you could lose him, make up your report. I'd let you know what I had in mind. There will be an occasion or two when it would be very useful to have people think Razor was somewhere else. Do you get my drift?"

"It couldn't be for too long. I've got to get a result in the next few days or I'll be thrown off the case." Harvey squirmed on the wooden bench.

"No. It wouldn't be for too long. Say a thirty grand retainer for the first eight weeks. From time to time you could leave a document open on your computer that might contain information of an enlightening nature. This could be seen by one of your colleagues and more than likely passed onto your superiors in the Met squad along with Ferran & Cardini International. I don't want the police or this firm meddling in and possibly messing up my operation." Kane thought about some of the old scores he would like to settle.

"I'm not going to jeopardise my pitch. But what you're suggesting is possible." Harvey was thinking about the money. He had a moment's concern. "What are you up to?"

"That would be telling," said Kane. He threw more water on the coals.

"It's not a bank robbery is it?"

"No," said Kane. "You know from my file that's not my style."

"Good," said Harvey. His few reservations evaporated. "It could be embarrassing for me if it were armed robbery of any kind."

* * *

Inger lay on the bed in her hotel room and idly watched the television. The hotel was in need of refurbishment and it made her feel depressed, and she wondered if she could find somewhere more salubrious. She could afford the best hotel in Stockholm for what this dump was costing. Beneath the surface

England was a clapped out, overcrowded and thoroughly mixed up country. No wonder there was such a bloody big drugs problem. The predominantly immigrant hotel staff took no pride in their work. And why should they, working all hours for minimum wages and no thanks. She was shocked when she heard how much rent they had to pay for even the smallest one room accommodation. She hoped that Dillon was not late. She contemplated waiting for him in the bar, but couldn't face the thought of any more overweight businessmen engaging her in conversation and hoping for a quick one-night stand with a blonde Swedish girl. Five minutes of conversation and they were talking about how sexually liberated Scandinavian women were, and then there was no doubt what they had in their frustrated smutty little minds.

Inger wondered where Dillon would take her to dinner. He had asked her on her second day and she had thought she'd blown it by flatly turning him down. But he had surprised her by asking again. Although she hoped he wasn't going to take her to an Italian bistro. That was always embarrassing, more so when the tables were candlelit and the background music all lovey dovey, which never failed to make her cringe.

The bedside phone rang at precisely seven forty-five. Dillon was waiting in the foyer. Inger stood up and looked at herself in the full length mirror. She decided to apply some lipstick. She looked at herself again, pursed her lips irritably and took off her blouse and jeans. She rummaged in the wardrobe for a tight black cocktail dress. She chose a simple white gold bracelet with a matching necklace. She slipped her slender feet into a pair of Jimmy Choo high heels, stood in front of the mirror again and admired the look.

Inger realised the high heels were the right choice as Dillon stood up to greet her. He was at least six foot two inches, and as she looked at him, he smiled and raised his eyebrows admiringly at what she was wearing, his eyes lingering on her black dress that clung to her exceptional figure. He was wearing a suit which had obviously been made for him and fitted perfectly; the only thing that her trained eye observed was the way the jacket hung under his right arm. He obviously carried his Glock pistol in a shoulder holster. "Let's go," he said. He seemed to be in a hurry to leave the hotel.

He walked briskly to where the Porsche Panamera was parked and held opened the passenger door for Inger to climb in. Dillon slipped into the driver's seat.

"So Mr Dillon, where are you taking me?" She asked.

"First we're going to the theatre." He gave her a sideward glance.

"Oh. And what is playing at the theatre?"

"You'll see. I think you'll like it."

Dillon drove the Porsche through evening traffic across London to the theatre that he had purchased and renovated three years previously for underprivileged youngsters. He drove past the main entrance and found a parking space a little way up the road. A shiver ran up his spine as he remembered the bomb blast that had almost killed him and others working on the renovation at that time.

"Do you go to the theatre much Inger?"

"No," she said with a smile.

"Oh," he said, and the subsequent silence became a little surreal for Dillon as they walked into the main foyer of the theatre.

A man in his mid-twenties wearing a dinner suit greeted them. "Jake Dillon. It's so good to see you."

"And it's good to see you too, Richard." Dillon shook hands warmly with the theatre's young creative director. He introduced Inger and they were escorted to a private box inside the auditorium.

"Please excuse the pun, but do you come here often Jake?"

"As often as I can. Tonight they're putting on a production that was written by the youngsters who are performing this evening. I watched the rehearsals at the beginning of the week, and thought how talented they all are. So it should be a good show."

"I don't understand. You don't strike me as someone who would be interested in all of this." Inger said, gesturing with her hand around the theatre.

"It's always dangerous to assume, Inger."

"I'm sorry, Jake."

"No need to be. It's a pretty reasonable assumption really, given what I do for a day job."

"So, are you going to enlighten me?"

"Well, a few years back I came across this run down building that required total renovation. So I decided to buy it as a way to unwind after each assignment. I wanted something manual and creative, something that was good for the soul. Obviously that was never going to happen with my work schedule. Instead, I had a builder carry out the work and here is the end result. I still own the theatre and I'm also the benefactor of the performing arts theatre company that resides in this magnificent building. And because this project is all about encouraging talented youngsters from underprivileged backgrounds, it's got to be at the top of the list of things I'm really proud of."

"I'm impressed." Inger was taken aback by Dillon's revelation and a little embarrassed by having pressed him on the subject.

The lights dimmed and the musicians started to play, and for the next forty-five minutes the capacity audience were entertained by an energetic performance by the cast of players.

"I've booked a table at The Ivy. I hope you're still hungry?"

"Yes. But how did you get a table at such short notice?"

"Oh, I know the Maître d' there. He and I go way back and over the years I've helped him out with one or two little problems he's encountered."

Inger knew exactly the type of help Dillon would have given.

"I thought you might like this restaurant. It is one of the best. Normally I go to gastro pubs when I'm in town, but when we go to down to Sandbanks I'll take you somewhere special. There's an array of excellent restaurants around the area, where the people are friendly and the head chefs are simply culinary artists." Dillon pulled up outside the exclusive West End restaurant. He left the Panamera at the kerbside and they went into the restaurant, he handed the keys to the Maître d', who nodded and greeted Dillon warmly. He snapped his fingers and a valet appeared straightaway to go and park the Porsche.

As soon as Inger entered the restaurant she felt the cloying presence of a class-ridden society. They were shown to their table. The waiters were obsequiously servile. She wanted to tell Dillon that this restaurant was not for her, but curiosity kept her there. The sommelier came over and placed the wine list on the table. "We'd like a drink before dinner," said Dillon, and gestured to Inger to order. She ordered a dry Martini. He ordered a single malt whisky and when it arrived he gulped it down, and ordered another, with ice this time. "I'm feeling the warmth."

He was either nervous, or was he an alcoholic, thought Inger. They sat facing each other at the table and made small talk while Dillon constantly watched the other diners. "Have you always lived in Stockholm?" Dillon asked suddenly.

"No. I was born in a small village to the north. My father was the local mayor. What about you, where did you grow up?"

The sommelier returned and Dillon ordered a bottle of Dom Pérignon 2003.

"Cornwall. I grew up in a small coastal village where everyone knew everyone else and life was simple."

"So very similar to the village I grew up in. And here we are today chasing criminals and risking our lives daily. So tell me. Why do you do it, Jake?"

Dillon was saved from answering her by the appearance of the sommelier at the table. He showed the bottle to Dillon who nodded his approval. The cork was expertly pulled; Dillon sipped the Champagne costing over two hundred pounds per bottle. He nodded his approval again, and allowed the waiter to pour them both a glass.

"You haven't answered my question Mr Dillon." Inger pressed.

"No I haven't, have I?" Dillon studied her beauty, the way her skin glowed with a youthful vibrancy. "It's the only thing I know how to do," he said, and immediately changed the subject. "Is this your first visit to the UK?"

"It's my first visit as an Interpol observer. But I studied and attained my degree in criminology at Oxford."

"Impressive. Now, shall we order?" Dillon picked up his menu.

The waiter came over and took Inger's order first. "I'll start with the Mediterranean fish soup, followed by the Thai-baked sea bass."

"And what would sir like?"

"Sir would like you - not to call him, sir!" Dillon looked up at the young, embarrassed man, and smiled. "I will start with the kingfish sashimi, followed by the Bannockburn rib steak."

"How would you like your steak cooked?"

"I'd like it rare please."

The waiter nodded his understanding and went off to place their order with the kitchen.

Dillon took a sip of his Champagne and then asked, "Why did you join Interpol?"

"I think it was because of my father. Also because the work is interesting, there are not many women doing this in Sweden."

"Don't you ever get fed up and frustrated when you work on a case for months on end and then it all falls apart in a courtroom, when a smart ass lawyer gets to rip your case apart on some inconsistency or something?"

"We have a different attitude towards this, that's true. The English have far more problems than we do in Europe. You have far too many archaic and ambiguous laws that allow even the most incompetent of lawyers to keep their criminal clients on the street. Interpol have virtually limitless resources available to them from across the entire European law enforcement community. We know who the big players are, and we want to keep this drugs problem under control. One of the best ways to do this is to keep it above the ground and in sight. When we catch these criminals we treat them very differently. You send them to prison for ten to fifteen years. However, I believe you would like to kill them, Mr Dillon. That is not very humane. We have a higher social conscience."

"I agree with you."

"You do?"

"Sure I do. But only on one point, you understand."

"And what might that be?" Inger said with a slight frown.

"I agree with your belief that I would kill them. I would happily kill all the scum who are involved with the trafficking of drugs. Society needs protecting from criminals. Especially serious organised criminal gangs."

"Yes. There are many ways of doing this. Here your police and customs agencies spend inordinate amounts of time and tax payer's money chasing around the countryside after shadows like this Maximilian Kane. And, if they should be lucky enough to bring him to book, then he will have top-flight lawyers who will get him off with a minimal sentence. Why don't they use their resources to get to the very core of the evil, the criminal overlords who deal at the highest level and are seemingly untouchable?"

"Nice thought. But not a hope in hell of ever happening - because as you quite rightly say, they are connected at the highest level. Forget the justice system for these guys. A bullet in the head is the only thing that genuinely deals with the problem. It might not be considered morally right, or politically correct. But it would certainly go a long way to cleaning the planet up." Dillon sipped his Champagne and then smiled across the table at the Swedish lady from Interpol.

"Your outwardly aggressive stance on this problem is merely a smoke screen, isn't it? I would say that underneath that hard exterior is a pussycat that is genuinely passionate about bringing these criminals to book in front of a judge."

"Really - you are making this assumption on what basis?"

"On the basis, that would you really be working for an organisation, which is committed, by oath, to protecting the Realm and the people who reside within it. Correct?"

"Perhaps I'm a psychopath with a higher than average IQ who is able to hide his lust for murdering bad people."

"As stated. You're a pussycat."

"I think you're toying with me Miss Lindberg, but I'm enjoying the banter."

They ate, talked and laughed throughout the evening. Dillon found Inger to be good company, some of his humour went straight over her head, but she laughed politely anyway.

After the table was cleared, the waiter served coffee and liqueurs. Dillon waited a moment for the waiter to pour the coffee and leave them. "I hope I haven't bored you too much this evening."

"I've had a wonderful evening Jake. The theatre was just perfect and this restaurant certainly lives up to its reputation. Thank you."

"You're welcome, and I would like to say what lovely company you are."

Inger blushed, "It's getting late and we have an early start tomorrow."

"You're right, we should be going; I'll drop you off at your hotel."

On the drive across town Inger watched Dillon as he told her that he had once had a girlfriend who had drowned, and that he thought he knew who had been responsible. His only regret was for not pursuing that person. For the briefest moment she wanted to hug him, and teach him to like himself more. She checked herself. He was a loner, and anyway they had only just met.

It was just after two in the morning before she was back in the hotel.

* * *

When Detective Constable Steve Harvey reached his Bournemouth hotel that night he was a changed man. He had suddenly acquired a renewed zest for his job and ambition that he had never really thought about. For years he had protected property and upheld the law to the letter, and all he had to show for it was a dilapidated rented flat located in a seedy run-down suburb of inner London. He paid into a pension fund, but that would hardly keep him in hookers, which he had a particular penchant for. The rest of his savings had diminished from twenty grand down to seven grand overnight because of poor judgement and investments on stock markets. He was lucky, he supposed, that he still had a job with all of the redundancies made throughout the force and especially in the Met.

Now the tide was turning. He stared at the uninspiring corporate furniture scheme in the hotel room and kicked off his shoes. He switched on the wall mounted flat screen TV and went into the bathroom. He took the envelope with Nash's two thousand pounds in and the other containing the seven thousand pounds that Kane had given him, and stood on the toilet seat. He lifted one of the suspended ceiling panels and slipped them both behind it. Replaced the panel carefully, making sure it was in the exact same place as before, and stepped down off the toilet seat. He stared up at the ceiling for a short time thinking the nine grand for one day's work was more to his liking. Nine grand, with another thirty grand over the next eight weeks; he might decide to stay on Kane's payroll for a little longer than that. He opened the fridge and pulled out a cold bottle of beer from the mini-bar and flopped down on to the bed. First thing in the morning he would go and locate a safety deposit box. The cash would be safe there until he decided he had enough to disappear forever.

He was going to put in some overtime tomorrow down at the local station, and he didn't give a fuck if Detective Sergeant Rosie Trent liked it or not. He'd boot up a spare computer terminal and carry out a little research. He would have to be very careful as he'd have to key in his personal code to access the information he was looking for. Sometime in the future he would be asked by a police auditor why he had made those enquiries, especially if anything went wrong. Damn it. He had a legitimate right to find out all he could about Kane, because it touched on his investigation into Razor and Cracker. He wasn't so sure about checking out Jasper Nash. There was something not quite right about him. Something that Harvey couldn't as yet put his finger on, but he was sure it would only bring grief if he started snooping around him. The more he knew about Maximilian Kane the more indispensable he would become, and the more money he would make. He would try and obtain another officer's computer code. Someone whom he wasn't associated with and would ensure that any internal enquiries didn't come knocking at his door.

Harvey peeled open another cold beer from the mini-bar and downed half of it in one gulp, then wiped the froth from his lips with the back of his hand. He'd looked at the membership rates for Kane's health club. He'd need a bank loan to afford joining such a place. Kane wasn't short of the folding stuff that was for sure. He might be putting as much as five million a year in his back pocket. It would be worth trying for a percentage. He finished his beer and dropped the can down the side of the bed. He shimmied himself into a sitting position and looked at the hole in his sock where his big toe was poking through. Tomorrow was another day and he was no longer happy with a two week package holiday to Portugal. He wanted a villa with a pool and a large bank account. He thought of his bundle of cash and moving it from the hiding place behind the suspended ceiling. What if the hotel caught fire? He got off the bed and padded back into the bathroom and reached up and scrabbled behind the ceiling panel again.

Chapter 10

"So how do you feel?" Inger asked Dillon. It was four-fifteen in the morning. They had barely slept for three and a half hours. Dillon regretted having offered to pick her up from the hotel.

"At this ungodly hour I always feel like returning to my home in the Scottish highlands. A place where there are few people and life saunters along at a sedate pace and I could resume my life as a recluse once again. That's how I feel."

"Oh."

After Dillon's little rant they drove across town to Docklands in silence where they met the rest of the team in the underground garage of Ferran & Cardini International. LJ had done well. There was an assortment of vehicles lined up, various makes and age that would blend in and be just another vehicle on the road. There was also a fully licenced black cab which tended to be popular, especially as it could get away with parking virtually anywhere. The vehicles were uniformly anonymous, chosen by the practised eye of a former policeman who had spent twenty years on traffic duty.

The field officers knew which roles they were playing and had dressed accordingly so they wouldn't look out of place driving their allotted vehicles. The black taxi, one Ford Focus, a Citron DS3, two motorcycles and two white Mercedes Sprinter vans left the underground garage at six-fifteen and made their way out of London towards the M25 motorway in the early morning rush hour. They would all be on station in Dorset by eight-thirty. The field officers knew it would probably be at least a two hour wait before the mark appeared at his front door. Criminals were rarely early risers.

The two vans had been carefully adapted for surveillance operations. Discreet HD observation cameras and long range directional microphones had been fitted in and outside of the van giving a three hundred and sixty degree viewing area, and sound recording at up to three hundred feet. The interiors were fully fitted with monitor screens and an array of hard drives that stored and relayed every piece of information straight back to Ferran & Cardini in London, in real-time. The vans would be parked at suitable vantage points and left for a day. The field officers in the back would remain there until the drivers returned and picked them up. The space they were working in had air-conditioning, a fridge filled with bottles of chilled water, sandwiches and a portable camping toilet in case of emergency.

The use of the surveillance vans was used as a short-term measure to establish the practicality of watching the suspect's property. If Nash did not operate or entertain business associates at home, then the vans would be discarded and sent back to London.

Dillon parked the Panamera around the corner from Jasper Nash's apartment block. He drew up behind an Aston Martin convertible in a quiet side street, and having checked in with the van crews, walked to the nearest café. He was wearing a concealed radio earpiece linked by Bluetooth to his Ferran & Cardini mobile smart phone that would connect incoming calls automatically. They sat down at a table near to a window overlooking the bay. Dillon ordered a full English breakfast and Inger decided on croissants with a large pot of coffee for them both. Dillon looked at the morning's headlines on his iPad.

"I'm very pleased to be away from London and that hotel." Inger said suddenly.

"Oh?" Dillon replied, lifting his eyes slowly from the news article he was reading. "Why?"

"The hotel is not very good and I can't go to the bar or the dining room without men hitting on me. What is wrong with the English? If they see a woman who is on her own, they must ask her if she would like a drink. It is making me crazy."

"I'm sorry to hear that," said Dillon. He thought for a moment or two. "It might be possible for LJ to sort you out with one of the firm's apartments for the remainder of your stay. I'll see what can be arranged."

"You know, I think it is because a woman on her own

is deemed, how do you say, free sport for every Tom, Dick and Harry." Inger smiled at her own humour.

"You might be right there," said Dillon. He didn't want to discuss the subject so early in the morning. A moment later he decided the remark deserved more respect. "I've never really thought about it - and it must be really irritating."

"Yes. It is," said Inger sternly. "Worse than that, you have no time for your own thoughts, even in public places. Men are always trying to catch your attention."

That's the price you have to pay for being so damned attractive, thought Dillon. He knew better than to say anything, though. He picked up his iPad and wrote out an email to LJ. "I've asked the boss to have alternative accommodation arranged for you by the time we return to London, and to have your things at the hotel collected. How does that sound?"

"Thank you, Jake. That sounds just fine."

"You're welcome Inger."

Dillon's full English breakfast arrived. It did look appetising. He ate with enthusiasm, while Inger picked gingerly at the croissants on the plate in front of her. When he had finished, he looked at his watch. It was nine o'clock. He guessed Nash would be just about thinking about getting up.

He listened through the tiny wireless earpiece as the voice at the other end gave him an update. "Let's go," he said to Inger. Outside, he called the field officer in charge of unit-one, the lead surveillance van. "This is Dillon."

"Nash is leaving his apartment building and proceeding on foot along Banks Road towards you."

"Is unit-two in position?" Dillon spoke quietly to the other man.

"Yes. Unit-two is in position."

"OK. Ensure that both units are in readiness to go mobile should the need arise." Dillon broke the connection.

"Is that phone linked to a network provider?" Inger asked.

"No. Ferran & Cardini have satellite space with a few close friends. If you know what I mean, this is a secure comms link that doesn't exist and cannot be traced or tracked."

Inger tapped Dillon on the arm as Nash came into sight and they both walked across the road and into the shadows of one of the buildings. They stood in front of a newsagent's window. "I hope Nash is simply coming to get his morning paper and then off for a coffee at the Haven Hotel. That would be really convenient." Dillon said. "I'm just hoping that we're not wasting our time down here in Dorset waiting for him to lead us to Kane and ultimately, but I'm not holding my breath, to whoever it is feeding him military secrets. Bring back the bad old days. There was a time when we could have picked a traitor like this up, taken him somewhere quiet and tortured him until he talked. But today that wouldn't be morally or politically correct; and it would be an infringement of his human rights of course." Dillon said. "So we watch and we wait and at the end of the day, we might just get lucky."

Dillon saw Nash emerge at the end of Ferry Road and start to walk straight towards where they were standing. Without warning or hesitation, Dillon pulled Inger to him, turned his back to the road and kissed her. Nash strolled on by without as much as a glance at them. Dillon glanced over his shoulder and then apologised for his sudden action. He was pleasantly surprised when Inger told him that there was no need to apologise given the circumstances.

They watched Nash walk to the seafront and take a seat on one of the empty benches. The chain-link ferry had just left on its way across the channel between Sandbanks to Shell Bay, its chains rattling as the large diesel engines powered the fully laden craft through the water. Nash pulled out his mobile phone; it was exactly ten twenty-nine. Was he making or receiving a call?

"He's definitely up to something," said Dillon. "No one leaves home to make a phone call. I'll bet that phone is unregistered and that he's carrying a GPS and 3G signal blocker. I'll get Vince to start running a trace programme to locate the handset from the co-ordinates that I'll give him in a moment, you never know, we might get lucky, and if anyone can find it, Vince can." Dillon immediately sent Vince an email with their co-ordinates.

Nash finished his conversation and replaced the mobile phone in his jacket pocket. He looked at his watch. Dillon glanced at his own Omega Seamaster. It was ten forty-five.

"We've struck gold. Vince has already located and loaded the tracking and surveillance bug software into Nash's phone."

"How did he manage that so quickly?"

"A genius programme that he wrote that is impervious to a signal blocker and uses grid references to search out every handset that is switched on and in use within a fifty metre radius of the centre point. When it finds the anonymous handset it uses the nearest GPS satellite overhead to hack into the handset's processor."

"But what if there's more than one anonymous handset?"

"Ah, well that's the really clever bit. Because of the lightning speed at which it covertly searches millions of data files, it cross references and recognises voice patterns that are held on file. If you've ever been interviewed by a law enforcement agency, then your voice pattern is stored somewhere in a national archive."

Dillon and Inger were too far away to hear Nash's phone ring in his pocket. It was a brief conversation lasting no more than twenty seconds. Nash got up from the bench and started to walk back towards them. Dillon turned and walked inside the newsagents that they had been standing in front of, Inger followed staying just inside the doorway so that she still had a view of Nash as he walked past. Dillon purchased two bottles of water and they went back outside.

"Have you got a visual yet?" Dillon waited for a response from the surveillance vans.

"Unit-one, affirmative - we have the target in sight. He's walking back to his apartment block. Wait. He's bloody well stopped, and would you believe it, he's looking straight at us."

"Remember, this one is observant and streetwise. He will have noticed the van on his way out and now he's most likely memorising the number plate. Stay calm, there's nothing outwardly visible for him to get suspicious about." Dillon held his breath, and then heard the man's voice in his earpiece.

"He's on the move again and now entering the apartment block."

"Unit-one. Hold your position. Unit-two, move your location and park near to the shops at Café Shore on Banks Road. Hold this position until further notice. I want every vehicle number plate scanned, and stay alert; Kane might just come onto the peninsula in a car other than his own and in disguise."

"Understood."

Five minutes later Nash came out of the apartment buildings underground garage behind the wheel of his Mercedes, turned left onto Banks Road and drove off along the one way system towards Panorama Road. He went past unit-one who immediately informed Dillon, and a minute later unit-two picked him up on their camera too.

"Both surveillance units hold your current position. Mobile-one, stay with him and keep your distance. Mobile-two, as you're on a bike you take up position with Mobile-one."

Nash was almost immediately picked up by mobile-one; the ford focus tailed him to Canford Cliffs village, followed him into a newsagent, watched him making another phone call from his mobile phone, and finally observed him drinking a coffee at a nearby bistro. All seemed well.

It was twelve-thirty before Nash returned home. The white van of with unit-one had departed and been replaced with Mobile-three, a motorcycle messenger who was tinkering with the bike's engine at the roadside. Half an hour later Nash emerged from his home got back into his car and sped off.

"We have a go situation, I repeat a go situation." Mobile-three barked over his radio link.

"I've got him," said Dillon, catching sight of the Mercedes. He started the Panamera and began to tail Nash.

The five mobile units took up positions in Lilliput and Canford Cliffs and joined the random pursuit. Sometimes a vehicle would be a long way in front of Nash's car and then have to double back when he took an unpredictable turn. All of the drivers were highly trained and very good at their jobs, tailing and jiggling their positions so they wouldn't be noticed. Dillon monitored the proceedings from the rear, listening to the chatter between the officers. Things were going well. For the first time that day he relaxed. "I've had an email back from LJ," he turned to Inger; "If you really can't stand the hotel they'll put you up in one the firm's safe houses, or you can use my guest room when we return to London. I mean my apartment is large and comfortable. It's also only five minutes' walk from the office. I'm not around much so you can use the place as your own, and I promise I won't get in the way if you want to entertain. It might be a quicker solution than trying to find a free property in some backwater side street."

"You are a very kind man," said Inger. "But are you sure about this?"

"I wouldn't have offered if I wasn't sure. After we're done down here in Dorset you can pop round and take a look for yourself." He made a mental note to get Mrs McGrath round to do a thorough spring clean before he got back.

"Thank you," said Inger. She wasn't sure if she liked the idea. She liked her privacy. She was relieved when Dillon started to talk to Mobile-one through his phone link and then listened as he was told that Nash had pulled into a multi-storey car park in Bournemouth. Within seconds of trying to follow him on foot they had lost him.

"Did he do this on purpose?" Dillon asked.

"Couldn't say; all we know is that he was there one moment and then vanished into thin air the next. If he had spotted us, then he's not only observant, but obviously careful about his movements."

"Stay in the car-park and wait for him to return to his car." Dillon ordered.

"OK - I'll let you know when he returns."

"Did he lose your men on purpose?" Inger asked.

"Tailing Nash is going to test us all to the limits, but the GPS tracking device I had attached to the underside of his Mercedes will help though."

* * *

Jasper Nash expected a call from Max Kane on the mobile phone he had given him at ten-thirty. He hoped that Martha would go out so he wouldn't have to lie to her. He was increasingly self-conscious about his movements, knowing that she'd be suspicious. Fortunately Martha was in the middle of a call to a client wanting to commission a painting from her at ten fifteen, so Jasper put on his jacket nonchalantly and said he was going to buy a newspaper. Martha put her hand over the receiver and said, "We need milk." Jasper slipped out.

Once outside on the pavement, Nash heaved a sigh of relief. He had a lot of arrangements to make. He prayed that Jason Villiers was still at home. If it hadn't been for Martha he would have been up around nine, but then Martha's suspicions would definitely have been aroused. He dialled Jason's number. Jason recognised his voice immediately. "Jasper!" he said. "It's good to hear you. I didn't know you were back."

"Are you doing anything today?"

"What have you in mind?" Jason asked.

"How about lunch somewhere?"

"How does your restaurant in Poole High Street sound, say around one-thirty?"

"That sounds great, see you there."

Jasper broke the connection and thought about Jason. He was dependable, always cheerful, and scrupulously honest. Not only that, but he could cook like a professional. He'd worked his way up from being a bottle washer at one of London's top hotels to owning a string of Michelin star restaurants across the south coast and in London. He was one of the best distributors. He could be given fifty kilos or a thousand kilos of pure cocaine and he could account for it to the nearest gram. He also worked quickly, distributing as far afield as Newcastle and Aberdeen. If things went well, he paid up within a week. The money arrived neatly bound up, sorted into various denominations, with the Queen's head to the right. He poured his profit back into the restaurants he owned where it was were quickly laundered. His apparent success had not spoiled him, and he had the charm of appearing baffled and humbled by the accident of success.

Jasper looked at his watch. There were a couple of

minutes until Kane's call. He decided to go and look around one or two of the marinas as the first step of the luxury yacht brokerage business. It would be a talking point over dinner and help alleviate any doubts that Martha still had, or from her jumping to conclusions. It was a sound idea. He should have started a business a long time ago. It would have laundered the money, and he wouldn't now be in this predicament. He would have to decide in what area of the market he wanted to specialise. He didn't want to end up with a load of old tat tied up alongside the quay.

The mobile phone in his hand started to vibrate. He answered it. "Oh. There you are," Kane said as if he had been trying to make the connection for some time.

"Yes Max. I'm here," said Jasper.

"Listen carefully and don't react wildly to what I'm going to say." Kane paused. "Your affairs are under close scrutiny." Jasper's heart started pounding. He hadn't seen any signs of surveillance. He immediately calculated what the charges could be. He had broken out into a cold sweat; treason was the worst and conspiracy to commit a crime at best. One carried a sentence that would mean life imprisonment with the key being thrown away and the other a slap on the wrist and a caution. He knew which one he would prefer. Kane continued.

"There's something else. Your Uncle Toby is unwell." Uncle Toby? What was Kane talking about? Suddenly Jasper realised it meant his mobile phone. Uncle Toby, Moby. "I think that Uncle Toby's illness is very likely to be contagious as he's running a fever."

"That figures," said Jasper, as calmly as he could. His home phone would most certainly be bugged.

"Meet me at the club in thirty minutes." Kane said.

"I'll be there in forty-five minutes. I have somewhere to go first," said Jasper.

"And make sure you're not followed." Kane knew he didn't have to say that but felt compelled to do so every time. Jasper broke the connection.

Jasper slipped the mobile phone into his jacket pocket. His heart pounding as he went into the local newsagents and convenience store for milk. He tried to act normally; one moment it felt like he was talking to quickly, and the next, too slowly. He noticed nothing out of the ordinary as he left the shop and started to make his way back to the apartment. He remembered the white Mercedes Van from the previous morning and the motorcycle courier kneeling down next to the bike fiddling with something by the rear wheel. But both had gone and everything in the road looked normal.

He needed time to think about the seriousness of the development. He had to be rational and think logically. The knowledge could possibly be to his advantage, although he didn't see how. If damage had been done, then it was limited. He couldn't resist seeing who it was following him. He walked on past his apartment block along Banks Road. When he reached the beach car park he turned right and headed off towards the front and the cafés. He seated himself at a table outside with a clear view of anyone coming and going. He was well practiced at waiting, and he knew that if he was being followed it wouldn't be long before two or three of the shadows appeared. He sipped coffee from the plastic cup and assumed the appearance of reading his newspaper.

After half an hour he walked home. He hadn't seen signs of surveillance, although a Ford Focus with two men did attract his attention. At home he confirmed with Martha that he would need the car to visit a few of the larger marinas in the area, as a first step to setting up his yacht brokerage. She looked at him dubiously.

"You've been gone almost an hour," she said.

He wondered if it was an accusation. "I went for a coffee down by the beach and read my newspaper."

"Did you remember the milk?"

"I put it in the fridge."

"Good boy. I'm impressed."

"I'll see you later," said Jasper, and leaned down to kiss her. She seemed a little patronising, but he hoped he was just imagining it.

Jasper drove slowly into the heart of the old town area of Poole Quay. He had no intention of letting the observers know he was aware of their presence. From time to time he thought he had identified one of the cars, but it was hard to be certain in the holiday traffic. He pulled into a multi-storey car park just off the Quay, off Old Orchard. There were three exits from the car park, and each led onto a separate road. It was child's play to lose surveillance, thought Jasper. He left the car park on foot and walked the short distance to a taxi rank, getting into the first car in line. Jasper gave the driver the sports club's address and fifteen minutes later they were pulling up along the road from the exclusive venue, where an apprehensive Kane was waiting in the sauna.

"Are you sure you weren't followed?" Kane greeted Jasper.

"Quite sure," said Jasper. "After all, if they saw me here with you it would be a prison sentence wouldn't it?"

"That's a bit melodramatic."

"How did you find out about the surveillance?" asked Jasper.

"That copper Harvey. I've put on the payroll."

"Can you trust him?"

"He sings like a nightingale when you show him the folding stuff. Did you spot the opposition?"

"Yes. I spotted at least four vehicles, but I've no idea how many there are, but enough. It's a serious operation though. Do we know which agency they're from?"

"Bad news, it's not the police or customs." commented Kane.

"Then who is it then?"

"A London firm and Harvey reckons they're not on the police register. So you know what that means don't you Jasper?"

"Haven't got a clue Max, but I'm sure you're going to tell me."

"I have been asking around some of my old associates in London. One of them told me that there is a firm he's heard of in Docklands who work undercover alongside law enforcement agencies and the security service."

"What's the name of this firm?"

176

"The name he gave me was, Ferran & Cardini International."

"Well we'd better well be bloody careful then." Jasper said calmly, and then added. "You're living in a fantasy, Max. If this comes to the top, and we get pulled, there's no way we'll ever leave prison."

"We'll have to call the shipment off," surmised Jasper.

"Can't do it," said Kane. "It's too late. The consignment is already in transit from Morocco where it was transferred from the vessel that brought it across from Colombia. We can't call it off, the cartel would not look upon that with kindness," it was true. Razor had been in Casablanca dealing with the paperwork that had accompanied the consignment from the terminal there up to its final destination at Poole docks. There was no turning back now.

"You'll have to find someone else to take over from me."

"Why?" asked Kane. "You can lose these people anytime you want. I would have thought it far better to have them where you can see them. At least we know what they're up to."

Kane looked down at his bare feet swinging over the edge of the wooden bench he was sitting on. He was worried.

"Losing this one is not an option Jasper. My neck's on the chopping block. I'm not in any sort of position to pay for the consignment if it's confiscated. I'm right out on a limb, and I lied to clinch the deal. He waited for the revelation to sink in. Then he played his trump card. "You need to know Jasper that they would shoot me for the stroke I pulled on them."

"Who are they, Razor and Cracker?"

"Oh no - they're on a no-win no-pay deal. It's the people back in Colombia."

"What about Aleksey?"

"He's retired - permanently."

"He was your partner."

"Was - is the appropriate word. He was also becoming extremely sloppy. The Colombians didn't want to deal with him anymore, and he was becoming a major liability to them."

Kane said.

"Perhaps he wanted out of the Colombians."

"Listen, Jasper. It's one quick operation. We still have everything going for us. You know very well that I can't go to market without you. You've always done the marketing. They're all your people."

"I'll give you the list of my people."

"No good, Jasper. They won't work with me." Kane complained.

"How do you know they won't?" Jasper asked suspiciously.

"While you were away, one or two small opportunities came my way. One of your contacts completely blanked me."

"Whom did you try?"

"Jason Villiers. I hadn't seen him for years."

Jasper didn't comment. He was irritated to think that Kane had the audacity to approach his prime contact, but he was gratified to hear that Jason had remained loyal.

"Come on, Jasper. It's only a couple of hours out of your life. The law won't even know you're up to anything."

"I'm not into tempting fate Max."

"I'll make it worth your while. I'll up your fee to ten million. That's double what you would normally earn for a consignment of this size and purity." Jasper didn't say anything. There was nothing to say. He knew he was going to do it. He didn't have any other options. "I don't know what else I can say that will persuade you." Kane persisted.

"Don't drive that bloody great big Bentley convertible and stay away from me until it's over," said Jasper.

Kane searched Jasper's face to make sure that he had heard correctly, and then said "Thank you" with sincerity. When this deal was over he wouldn't need Jasper any more. The very nature of this business was going to change.

"Now, let's talk about the agenda. The consignment is arriving in two days. You will meet Razor at eight-thirty in the morning with the van. Wait for him to return to the Baiter slipway parking area, and the rest is then down to you. I've got us both new phones as the others you got are most likely compromised by now. Let me know when the paperwork is ready. I'm going to use the same banker as before, so you can drop the money with him."

"What about Razor and Cracker? Are they trustworthy?"

"Yes. I've told you, I would stake my life on it. They've invested in this venture as well. They won't want to see anything go wrong."

"What do you mean invested? Are you in partnership with these two chavs?"

"No. They weren't prepared to provide the facility at the port unless they could have some of the action. I gave them a twenty percent stake. They have paid cash in advance."

"That was not only risky, but bloody reckless. You must be getting old Max. There was a time when you'd never have given in to that sort of reckless decision making."

"It didn't seem that way at the time, and it left me in a more fluid position."

"Max, I'm not going to lie to you. But I've got a really bad feeling about those two guys."

Kane ignored the remark. "Listen, there's something else. I nearly forgot. There will be ten containers. They're meticulously packaged. This was carried out to my very precise instructions and specification. The gear was vacuum packaged into slabs inside a sterile room, and then these were taken through a wet-room and thoroughly scrubbed before being placed in another area to be dried, before being laminated between two plywood timber panels to make wooden chests. Then when the chests are built, they're dowsed with a chemical that becomes extremely repugnant to dogs. When this chemical is dry, the chests are filled with Indian tea."

Jasper wondered why Kane was telling him this. These were all standard precautions.

"One container is different. It's half the size of all the others. You have to deliver this one to a man you'll meet at Poole train station at midday. You'll recognise him because he'll be carrying a copy of Enjoy magazine."

Jasper's mouth dropped open. He couldn't believe what he was hearing. Surely Kane wasn't serious. No one met strangers in this game anymore, and certainly not at train stations. He looked intently at Kane, but there was no indication on his face that he was joking.

"Whoa there Max, I'm not happy about any of this. I think that you might have gone a little crazy. Then on the other hand perhaps you're trying to determine if I'm a little crazy too. Will I do this or won't I? Is that it Max?"

Kane looked baffled by this remark. "You don't seem to understand. It wasn't easy, I had to make some concessions to set this up. The deals aren't getting any easier to negotiate. This was one of them. The supplier insisted I pass a sample of the consignment to another interested party."

"I really don't care what deals you've had to make, Max. Right now I'm having a serious problem coming to terms with how you could have been so bloody stupid as to arrange a meet with someone who could be an undercover cop carrying a copy of Enjoy! I'm expected to give him a couple of packages that I have no idea as to their contents, and I'm not going to get paid for doing that. In fact, I'm actually taking twice the risk now because every time I deliver cocaine it's a risk. Except that this time it's worse because I don't know the man and I don't even get to make money on it. If my calculations are correct, it means that I'm losing at least thirty grand."

"Put it on the bill, Jasper, but do stop whinging. I thought you wanted to do this." Kane was irritated. Here he was doing Jasper an immense favour, paying him over the odds, and all he did was find fault with the arrangements. If Jasper complained any more he had a good mind to leave everything up to Razor with all the risks that incurred.

"I have to tell you, Max. I'm glad that this is the last job. I don't think that our business relationship could take the strain anymore, and has definitely run its course."

"Let's not end on a sour note," said Kane, tight-lipped. "We'll go to Positano on the Amalfi coast, charter a yacht and celebrate in style when this is all over."

Jasper gave the thinnest of smiles and stood up. "I have to be off. We probably won't speak until it's over." He left Kane sitting on the bench seat in the sauna hunched forward with his elbows resting on his knees.

Jasper had forty minutes before his meeting with Jason Villiers.

* * *

As Jason drove the Mercedes SL63 AMG coupe to his restaurant in Poole he thought about the meeting with Jasper. Things were going well in the restaurant trade. He was overflowing with customers who clambered to book a table at any one of his south coast restaurants. He'd made a name for himself by offering a discerning public; Michelin accredited chefs, service that could not be faulted and front of house hosts who were good looking and welcoming. He didn't need the money from the deal with Jasper. He didn't know why he'd accepted it. By doing so he was breaking one of his cardinal rules. Never work with anyone who had done time. He justified his decision by telling himself that a conviction in Hong Kong didn't count, and that his past dealing with Jasper had always been trouble free. Nevertheless, aspects of Jasper's release so soon after being convicted were just a little too cosy for comfort. If people were released it usually meant that they'd made a deal with the authorities. However, it did leave a few questions unanswered.

Jasper's proposal was good. Too good to turn down, but he'd have to be careful, even though he had done business with Jasper on a few occasions he didn't socialise with him. But then he never socialised with villains. One never knew where they had come from or where they were going. It was all too easy to find yourself on the police computer as a known associate of someone who'd been arrested. Jason never wanted to hear that knock on the door in the early hours.

Jasper had been running drugs and contraband for over fifteen years without any legitimate explanation for his money. It didn't take much to open up a business with plenty of loose money. That was the first thing anyone had to do if they were going professional in the game. The Jaspers of this world were opportunist risk takers. They were grossly overpaid for the little work they put in. They didn't know what it was like at the sharp end of the market. Jason used three or four dealers. Each of them would use four or five. It was classic pyramid selling. Somewhere down the line there was a policeman trying to work his way up, infiltrating the system. Somewhere down the line there was someone who might get himself nicked because he had been careless and who might try to cut himself a deal for a lesser sentence. That was the sharp end of the drug marketing business.

He knew that Jasper had other dealers, but he also knew that he was the best in the business. He knew his credentials were impeccable, which was why Jasper had worked almost exclusively with him for the past seven years. Jason had been shocked when Kane had approached him to do some marketing while Jasper was incarcerated in Hong Kong. It wasn't the sort of loyalty he expected of a partner, and he had refused on principle. He hadn't liked Kane from the start. They had met a long time ago so that Kane could make his own mind up about granting a credit line. He had started small in those days, with a credit facility of ten kilos. Over the following years he had worked up to a thousand kilos. He had not seen Kane again until Jasper's spot of trouble, nor had he wanted to. Now and again he'd been reminded of Kane's presence in the background. He was suspicious of him. He'd read about Kane's arrest four years ago, and his subsequent acquittal. As far as he was concerned, Kane was a marked man. Jason was only working with Jasper because he trusted him to be careful.

Nevertheless there were aspects of Jasper's arrangements which he didn't like and which didn't make sense. Jasper had given him a mobile phone to contact him with at the same time every day. A reference to the Daily Echo newspaper would indicate that the operation was going ahead the following day. Any other instructions should be completely ignored, even if Jasper changed the meeting places. It was as if he expected the call to be overheard. Jason shrugged mentally. Perhaps Jasper had become overly paranoid since Hong Kong.

For the first time he was tempted to ask Jasper to supply a few details to put his mind at ease. This operation was different to the previous ones. He had gleaned that. All the same, he didn't want to know about all of the details, just some of them. If things went wrong no one could suspect him of leaking information. If, heaven forbid, he was ever arrested and interrogated then he wanted to be able to deny knowledge of events with a clear conscious.

Sourcing a van wasn't a problem. Every couple of years Jason took a driving test under a different name. He frequently opened accounts with banks using falsified passports and utility bills using those names, and by massaging the accounts he would find he was offered a credit card for a while. Accessories like that were worth at least five thousand pounds. They were invaluable for hiring vans and they didn't leave fingerprints. It was his care for the fine detail which had made him indispensable to the likes of Jasper and Kane, and naturally they favoured him, not his competitors who balked at providing transport which might be traceable.

As soon as he took possession of the consignment he'd take it to a large lock-up he rented. He'd unpack and weigh it. Only then would he contact his dealers. He didn't let anyone know there was something happening. The police relied on tip-offs like that. It gave them a head start. As he thought through the plan and sequence of what was to take place to make the deal a success, his nervousness evaporated. This was another job, and the remuneration was exceptionally good. He hoped that it was prime Colombian powder diamonds, not some white powder shit-mix from Morocco with the addition of maximum strength anti-depressants and other crap. The coke had better be good. Bad powder never sold, whatever the price.

* * *

Razor stood on the Moroccan dockside watching the container ship sail out of Casablanca Harbour with Kane's consignment safely stowed aboard. It was early evening, but still, the heat of the day remained intense causing sweat to run freely down his back and everything he was wearing to cling to his body. He cursed Kane for sending him to Morocco when he should have flown straight to Geneva, which had been the original plan. Starting the powerful Japanese motorcycle Razor rode off towards the airport and his flight to Switzerland.

By the end of the following day Razor was on another Swissair flight, this time to London Heathrow. The cabin assistant suggested Razor gave her the aluminium briefcase to put in the overhead locker.

"You'll find it more comfortable, sir," she said.

"No," he replied coldly; but he carefully folded his new leather jacket and passed it to her. The businessman in the adjacent seat eyed him suspiciously. Razor sniffed deeply through his broken nose, curled his lips in a malevolent smile and sat down. He wrestled with the briefcase and finally retrieved a book. The businessman caught a glimpse of the title - in the mind of murderers. He looked away quickly and returned to hiding behind his Financial Times. Razor opened the book and spent moments nodding in appreciation at the supporting gory images. He didn't really care for the words, he preferred the visual detail. Eventually he turned the page.

When the aircraft landed, Razor dragged the aluminium briefcase from between his legs. It was designed to be of a cabin legal size and weighed, on this trip, just less than fifteen kilos. He stood up and retrieved his leather jacket from the overhead locker, slung the case over his shoulder, and thought he should go to the gym more often as it felt like it was nearly ripping his shoulder out of its socket.

He wondered if he had been too ambitious this time. He was carrying gold inside the case and as was standard for most airlines his personal allowance was ten kilos for this kind of short haul transportation. Kane paid him well for bringing the gold back from Switzerland where it was at least fifteen percent cheaper than in the UK because it wasn't taxed. That meant there were far more profits and ten grand for an afternoon's work. Not bad at all.

He dumped the briefcase on to a luggage trolley and made his way towards the exit. The first consignment arriving by air would be coming through the airport in a couple of days. Razor had made it possible for Kane to make all of the flight arrangements and pay off the baggage handlers who would unload the private Learjet, along with the security officer who would be responsible for the safe passage of the consignment from the moment he took possession of it, all the way through to the handover outside of the airport facility. As Razor entered the green channel as a Customs Officer approached him. Razor fixed his eyes straight ahead.

* * *

From the towpath the boat didn't look as bad as Jasper had expected. She was listing slightly to starboard. There were no signs of vandalism, which was probably due to the location of the mooring and the other boats up and down stream. Their owners were suspicious at best of times, and consequently were ideal caretakers. He stepped on board. She was a forty foot Princess 368 power cruiser that in her day had been the ideal transport for running cocaine across the English Channel. Her original 300hp twin inboard diesel engines had been taken out and replaced with much larger power units and increasing her cruising speed from 24 knots to 39 knots. He slipped his fingers under the stern dive platform and felt for the keys attached underneath. They were rusty after nine months submerged in water. He jiggled them free and then went up and unclipped the stern canopy, the sliding-door slid open easily after he'd worked the lock a little. The damp air rose out of the cabin. There was going to be at least a day's hard work making this boat habitable. He entered the cabin and walked straight through to the narrow stairwell, went down the steps to the sleeping level where his foot disappeared in the water up to his ankles. First things first, he thought, climbing back up to the bridge. He started pumping the bilges dry.

Half an hour later the last of the water was out of the boat. He guessed it had come through the stern gland with the high levels of rain that had fallen over the abnormally severe winter. He went down below again and checked that all the water had indeed been pumped out, and then returned to the main control panel on the upper main deck. He checked the boat's battery power levels. They were up to charge due to them having been plugged into a mains power source on land. He turned the ignition and all systems surprisingly sprang to life. The powerful twin diesel engines were not so obliging. The warning lights were showing that there was a fuel supply error. He went below and checked the engines for any fuel-line damage or constrictions, found none, and cursed under his breath for not having squared the boat properly when he left her, but he hadn't expected to be gone for so long.

While he worked he thought about the risks he was taking. It was a shock to find he was already under surveillance. They must have clocked him when he met Razor and Cracker with Kane. The police investigation into them must have been far advanced. As he evaluated his position he became more confident. Knowing that he was under surveillance gave him an advantage and a huge adrenalin rush to keep him on his toes. It was a foregone conclusion that his home phone was tapped, but they would have to be a lot smarter to get at his mobile phones as he carried the signal blocker with him at all times. It would be easy to plant a few red herrings through the tap on his home line. This thought made him smile.

Jasper went back up to the bridge and tried cranking up the engines again. They fired on the second attempt. While they were warming up he went and completely removed the stern canopy to let the air in. Soon the air was circulating, being sucked into the cabin and through the entire boat. He boiled some water on the gas ring and started to wipe down the surfaces. For the first time he realised how big she was. Forty feet long didn't seem that big. Ten feet wide didn't seem excessive. However, the surface area to be wiped clean had suddenly turned into a daunting prospect. He worked his way forward, through the day cabin, then down to the galley and sleeping accommodation, then through the watertight bulkhead into the forward sleeping quarters. The makers of this boat had finished her to a very high standard with every fitting having stood the test of time well.

It was just getting dark when he finished. He turned off the lights and closed down the hatches. Once he was happy that the boat was secure he replaced the stern canopy and replaced the padlock. As the boat was connected to a mains supply, he left the heaters on low so that it was more hospitable the next time he came.

Chapter 11

Cracker was furious. He threw the phone across the room, and paced the small sitting room of his rented flat in Hackney. He hoped Kane had got the message on his mobile phone, but he had a nasty habit of not reading them immediately. He'd given him a small Beretta Nano as a present when they'd first started working together, but the bloke seemed more afraid of his mobile phone. Anyone would think the old bill had bugged him...

He sat down on the sofa and stared down at the oak effect laminate floor. Razor really was a crazy bastard. What was his problem, why couldn't he leave his money in an offshore account, like other criminals? Instead of shifting it all over the place, buying here and selling there. For what, a bit here and bit there, nothing more than chicken feed when all said and done.

Razor hadn't been himself since they had started working with Kane. He'd never been much of a talker, but now he hardly spoke at all. It was like he had something on his mind. That wasn't the Razor of old. Maybe someone was putting the squeeze on him; that would explain why he had risked blowing their operation with this little number. Razor wasn't thinking straight, that was for sure.

He heard the bedroom door open and turned around. Chantell was out of the shower. She was nineteen with soft rosy skin. She was wearing the expensive underwear that he'd bought her the last time he'd knocked her around. For a moment he felt excited and looked down at the black trousers he was wearing and thought about removing them briefly. They were covered in fucking cat hairs. "Shit!" He exclaimed.

"What's wrong Cracker?" Chantell asked in her east London accent. She'd learned quickly there was only one way of calming him down when he was angry. She moved across the room to him, stroking his neck and leaning forward to kiss him passionately with pouting lips. His hands came up and squeezed her ample breasts. He liked to come between them.

"That fucking cat, these trousers cost a small fortune and now they look like something the cat dragged in. I should never have given you the bleedin' thing." He paused a moment for thought. "The cat goes," he said finally.

"What's wrong?" Chantell repeated.

"I've got things on my mind and I'm very busy." Cracker said, grabbing his mobile phone from a low side table.

"Are you too busy for this?" Chantell teased wiggling her pert bottom.

"I'm too busy." Cracker said emphatically, opening the door. "It'll have to keep for later," he said with a wink.

"Where are you going?" Chantell asked. "I thought we were going shopping?"

"We'll we're not. And cover up those tits. I don't want you walking around the flat like that; you never know who might be watching from one of the other buildings."

He slammed the door behind him. Outside the front door he looked to his left and then right. He didn't see anyone who might be watching him. That fucking Kane was making him nervous with all his talk about security. He unlocked the door of the Mercedes Sprinter van and opened it.

He wasn't looking forward to the drive down to Bournemouth or his meeting with Kane. Things were not looking too good and Kane was not going to be happy about it. Razor deserved a kick in the balls. What an asshole getting pulled over by Customs. And what for - trying to get away with smuggling an extra bar of gold through Heathrow. In a couple of days he'd have been able to buy as much of the fucking stuff as he wanted. Only God knew what Kane was going to say. It was too late to stop the consignment. It was on its way. He guessed Razor had made the final arrangements in Casablanca.

Two hours later Cracker was in the pub waiting for Kane. He had been there ten minutes when Kane showed up, "Are you absolutely sure you weren't followed?" Kane greeted him.

"What do you think, that I've only just stepped off the

train from toy town?" Countered Cracker.

"My dear Cracker, we must be careful at every stage now," said Kane. It was ironic. Harvey's lot were watching Razor and Cracker and they hadn't got a clue. It was pathetic really and most of all arrogant of them to not even consider the possibility. When he finally wanted them both out of the way he only had to give Harvey the word.

Cracker frowned. Kane wasn't going to like what he was about to tell him.

"So, what was so important that you had to see me?" Kane asked. "You said it was urgent."

Cracker stuck his chin forward aggressively. "Razor has gone and got himself nicked by Customs at Heathrow. After he had sorted the paperwork for this thing, he caught a plane from Morocco to Switzerland to see a man about some gold. But instead of just carrying the legal allowance he decided to put twice the limit inside his bleeding case. When he went to go through the nothing-to-declare channel he was nicked."

The colour left Kane's face. He couldn't believe what he was hearing. He'd been promised nothing like this would happen. "How did it happen?"

"Oh no," said Cracker, realising the Kane had misunderstood. "He wasn't breaking the law, just bending it a little. He was unlucky that's all, or someone grassed him up and they were waiting for him."

The relief surged through Kane's body. It was a brief respite before the anger. "What a bloody cretin! Has he got any brains at all?"

"Mind your tongue." Cracker said defensively. "He's my mate and I'll not have you slag him off behind his back."

"Steady. I don't give a damn whose friend he is. He's on the verge of making a small fortune in one day, and he's gone and got himself nicked with his reckless behaviour. It's pathetic. He's putting at stake a multi-million pound project. He doesn't need locking up. He needs his balls cutting off."

"Well just so you know there isn't any deal until he's out."

"What do you mean?" "It's his blokes who are doing

189

the dodge at Poole docks."

"You mean to tell me if we don't get him out on bail this whole thing goes down the drain?"

"Spot on me old cock. The containers will be put in a secure warehouse. Then we've got to figure some way of lifting it out of there."

"Forget it," said Kane. "That was never mentioned when this operation was hatched. You two gentlemen said you had your end covered from every angle. I don't call this being organised. You better prey Razor gets out on bail. It won't be me you've got to worry about if this thing goes tits up."

"Are you threatening me, Mr Kane?" Cracker asked.

"Fucking right I am. I'm threatening you with the people who are going to jump up and down on my head."

"Well, they'll have to wait. Razor's got a problem with this bail thing. He's got a suspended sentence."

"I don't believe it; can this bloke get any more stupid."

"You'd better show a bit more respect to Razor."

"Really - respect has to be earned." Kane said sarcastically.

"Yeah, and you need to show the respect!"

"Is the - yeah - because you agree it has to be earned, Cracker?"

"What. I've got no idea what you're talking about. But he did arrange for your Russian friend in Paris to have a fatal accident in the parking lot near to the airport." Kane didn't react. "At the air terminal - remember? The emphasis being on terminal you understand. Get it?" Cracker laboured.

"I really don't know what you are talking about," replied Kane.

"Oh yeah, as if..."

"Then you'll have to enlighten me." Kane said calmly.

"Don't you play the innocent with me, Mr Kane? You sent that Frenchman to me so we could sort out this bloke Aleksey. You owe Razor."

"I don't owe him anything, and what he gets up to is his own lookout. If you arranged for someone to do a job for someone else, then I'm sure that someone was paid for it." It goes from bad to worse, thought Kane. There was a way out of this mess, though, and Razor and Cracker were going to pay dearly if it worked. "If I get Razor out on bail, what's it worth?"

"I don't know, four or five grand."

"Fifty grand and that's non-negotiable."

"You must be joking," responded Cracker, outraged. "A brief don't cost that much."

"You're the jokers if something goes wrong on this deal. I'm not talking about a lawyer here; I'm talking about a guarantee."

Cracker thought about it. If Kane wasn't talking about a brief then he had someone on the take in Customs. If things worked out it wasn't so much dosh. "I don't reckon we have much choice."

"You're right," said Kane. "I hope I can pull this off for your sake." He stood up. He had much work to do.

* * *

Harvey was in a good mood for a Wednesday afternoon. He had something to look forward to. Every time he spoke to Kane he made more money. He was surprised when Kane told him that Razor had been out of the country, let alone that he had been arrested at Heathrow. Now he had to make sure Razor was released on bail, and then he'd earned another fifteen grand. No problem! He put a call through to New Scotland Yard and the senior officer in charge of the surveillance operation into Razor and Cracker at the London end. They'd promised to keep the Bournemouth side of the operation up to speed with any developments, but someone up there had broken the promise. Now he would take the moral high ground, and the more grief he gave them the more pleasurable it would become.

"I hear what you are saying, sir. But surely you can't expect me to believe that you had no idea that Razor had been arrested at Heathrow?"

"I don't care what you believe, Detective Constable, and don't be so impertinent. The airport is outside of my remit, as you well know, and it couldn't be helped that the suspect was lifted at Heathrow. After all, he was smuggling more than eight kilos of gold into the country and the officers were doing their job properly. It's what the tax payer expects. The arresting officer believed that the gold was the proceeds of drug trafficking and rightly seized it."

"Of course I understand all of this, sir, but don't your London boys ever look at their computer screens? Because if they had, it would have flagged up immediately that this character was under on-going surveillance by the Met and the Dorset forces."

"Leave it with me Detective Harvey; your comments have been duly noted. I'll see what can be done and liaise with the senior officer."

The call was terminated without niceties and Harvey sat for a moment seething and thinking what an arrogant asshole he had just encountered. This desk-jockey had most likely just messed up six months of investigation and put his little arrangement with Kane in jeopardy. Harvey snarled, smashed his fist down in rage and then got up off his seat. He needed a strong black coffee and a cigarette.

The next day Harvey was back at his desk when the email that he had been waiting for came through from his boss informing him that Razor had been released on bail and was back out on the street, minus his gold.

After a moment of agreeable reflection he leaned back in his chair and grinned at the wall. Razor wouldn't know what had happened. They'd both be smoking cigarettes and drinking cocktails in one of their regular dives in Hackney. Detective Harvey would be another fifteen grand ahead of the game. Let the good times roll.

* * *

Dillon had been talking to LJ on the phone for over half an hour. When he eventually hung up his first word was, "Shit!" Inger and Vince both looked at him. His day had been going quite well up to the point when LJ had called him. He had started to see a tiny spec of light at the end of the tunnel. For the past two days he'd been running on a mixture of single malt whiskey and adrenaline. Sleep was an inconvenience he suffered for four hours a night.

"What's up mate?" asked Vince.

"That was LJ. The Home Secretary's office has called him about a problem that could jeopardise our assignment down here in Dorset."

"So what's the problem?" asked Inger.

"Kane and Nash have teamed up with a couple of East End ruffians named Razor and Cracker. Now, these two are serious career criminals who have been under investigation by the Met for over three months. I have to say, they're rap-sheet is impressive; armed robbery, extortion with menaces, running a string of brothels, human trafficking, cocaine smuggling. In fact - you name it, they're into it. So, here's the problem - they are now down here in Dorset and the local plods are on the case. Obviously they have been informed that we're working down here but they don't know who or where we are. And most importantly they don't know that we're only interested in Nash, which is why there are concerns in London that they could jeopardise our surveillance operation."

"Surely that's not our problem. Let LJ sort out the politics of it all." Vince commented.

"Ordinarily he would. But Razor went and got himself arrested by customs officers at Heathrow for bringing in gold that they believe to be the ill-gotten gains of drug smuggling."

"I don't understand. Why should this development put our assignment in jeopardy?" Vince asked.

"According to LJ, it appears that this Razor is a key part of Kane's little firm. If he is locked up, then Kane is likely to call off his operation down here in Dorset and he believes that Nash will do a disappearing act. There's something else. A detective constable Steve Harvey from the local force has been coming on strong to the Met to get him released as soon as possible."

"That's odd. Why would he do that? After all, if the two forces are working on the same case surely they would be liaising on a weekly or even a daily basis."

"You're right. It is odd and we need to know everything

about this DC Harvey. Let's get the low-down on him, pull his police personnel file, bank accounts - everything. I even want to know what he eats, when and where."

"You've got it mate." Vince went over to his laptop to do what he was best at. He typed the commands into the keyboard with speed, hacking into the police database within thirty seconds. Once he had extracted Harvey's personnel data, he saved the file and printed it off for Dillon. Five minutes later he had Harvey's bank account details along with a detailed personal profile.

"Well, well. According to the police computer logs, Harvey's name comes up far too often to be just in the line of duty when it comes to Kane and his merry band. Do you think he knows more than he's letting on?"

"I don't know and I don't care," said Dillon thoughtfully.

"If he's causing a stir about Razor being held, then he's either a conscientious copper or a bent one."

"So what do you think, how do you English say, is his game?" Inger asked.

"When I find out I'll let you know." Dillon smiled. "In the meantime we'll go off the radar. That means we only use our Ferran & Cardini smart phones on scramble and definitely no radio comms until we know where DC Harvey is leading us. I'll put one of the surveillance teams on him and let's see if that brings anything interesting."

"But Harvey isn't part of our brief." Inger said.

"No he's not. But what if he were on the take! If he is, then the question is, who from, Kane? He is the most likely of all of them. But what if it was Nash?"

"Nothing like a bent copper in your pocket if you always want to be one step ahead of the pack, or, if you want to remain elusive let's say." Vince said.

The luxury waterfront property they were using offered the latest in secure wireless networking technology. The one hundred inch plasma screen mounted on the end wall of the living room was now the main monitor for Vince's equipment and the main portal for Edward Levenson-Jones to talk to the three of them.

They all looked around and fell silent as LJ's bony angular face appeared on the plasma screen. This was unusual, especially as Dillon had only just come off the phone to him. If he wanted a video conference they invariably received an email beforehand.

"Jake, I've just come off the phone with Dunstan Havelock. He has asked what progress we are making with Jasper Nash?"

"Slow but progressing in the right direction is how I see it. Nash is street wise and cautious; he is definitely up to something with Kane who has brought in a couple of east end lads named Razor and Cracker to do the heavy work on the operation down here in Dorset. We're not sure what their roll is yet, but it's most likely for their muscle, and the distribution of the drugs. All that Nash has done so far is spoken to Kane on the phone a few times, and met briefly with him on two occasions. We also followed him to Wareham where he appears to have a power boat moored on the river. But to be honest this craft looks a bit of a dog and has obviously been neglected for some time."

"Are you sure he's not met with anyone else?"

"Not while we've been watching him. He couldn't fart without us knowing. Vince has bugged his home extensively with high-definition pin-hole cameras and we've placed a GPS tracker to the underside of his car."

The screen showed LJ pacing his office while smoking one of his Slim Panatela cigars.

"You know you shouldn't be smoking inside the building Mr Levenson-Jones." Inger blurted.

"Young woman, I admire your forthrightness, but I have no intention whatsoever of not smoking in my own office." LJ continued to pace while he thought about what he had just been told by Dillon.

"What about Nash's girlfriend, what's her name, Martha Hamilton, anything there that might be of interest?" LJ asked suddenly.

"She's a very talented artist, but that's about it. Vince is sending you the transcript of a telephone call she had with one of her close friends. She told her that if he has anything more to do with Kane then she'll kick him out. She's not naïve and doesn't believe that he's going to change his ways or lose his best friend. But true to form, Nash is lying to her all the way about how he's left the old life behind him."

LJ nodded. "Have you been able to find out where Kane is residing?"

"Nothing concrete on Kane yet, but I have Vince running checks to find out where he has deposited the funds from all of the properties he's been selling over the last six months."

"Good - well keep at it Jake. We need to find out who Nash is buying highly sensitive military secrets from."

LJ turned slightly in his chair, so that he could direct his words at Inger.

"I've had your people at Interpol on the phone, Inger. They told me that Aleksey's girlfriend has been found murdered. They think she saw Aleksey's killer and had to be silenced. They're very keen to interview Kane. I'm going to speak to the French police tomorrow. They were the last people to see Kane. I'm interested to know what his movements were while he was in Paris. Your people have pledged their support in going through the hours of CCTV to patch together where he was and at what time."

The tiny hairs on the back of Dillon's neck stood up. "But you won't be talking to the police in the UK?"

"Not the police. But I'm afraid I'll have to inform the Home Secretary's office at the very least, they will insist on it, old son."

"Are you really certain about that? If you release this information then the police will be all over this like a rash. If they arrest Kane on a murder charge then we might as well all go home and play Backgammon. Nash is only staying in Dorset because Kane owes him a large sum of money and this operation they're involved in is Nash's payback."

"As usual Jake, you make a good case. Sometimes I think you should have been a barrister. I'll give you forty-eight hours, if you don't come up with anything on Nash in this time frame, then I'm afraid I will have no choice but to inform Dunstan

Havelock about the French murders. Keep me informed, old son." LJ terminated the conference and the screen turned to a constant powder blue colour.

"OK - the clock is running. Vince you continue to dig around Harvey's affairs."

"I'm already on it."

"Inger, you're with me. We are going to see an old friend of mine who lives just up the road."

Dillon parked the Porsche Panamera in the marina-side car park of Salterns Hotel. They passed through reception to the main bar area. Dillon spotted the man they had come to speak to immediately, he was sitting on a stool reading a newspaper with a pint of lager and a whisky chaser on the bar; every now and again he lifted the pint glass and drank from it. Dillon approached the bar and the man glanced round.

Frank Gardner immediately recognised Dillon and a broad smile appeared on his suntanned face. The former MI5 spy stood up and greeted Dillon warmly.

"Jake Dillon. Fancy seeing you here of all places, how are you?"

"I'm fine Frank. How are you? You old rogue?"

"Well, I'm wondering what has brought you back down to Dorset."

Frank Gardner was of slender build, somewhere in his late fifties early sixties with cropped fair hair, wearing a navy blue polo shirt and stonewashed denim jeans with a tatty old pair of deck shoes. He looked at Dillon through a pair of black plastic framed designer glasses.

Dillon bypassed Gardner's question and instead said, "Frank, let me introduce Miss Inger Lindberg. She's working with me for a while."

"It's a pleasure to meet you Miss Lindberg. What's your poison?" Gardner gestured to the optics behind the bar.

"A still mineral water will be fine, thank you."

Gardner ordered a mineral water and large single malt whiskey for Dillon. As he handed Inger her drink he said, "You know it's most likely tap water, don't you?"

Inger smiled at Gardner, "I think you're teasing me, Mr

Gardner."

"Please, call me Frank. Of course I'm teasing you, Inger."

They went and sat down at a quiet table by the window.

"You haven't answered my question Jake? Why are you here? Because, if my memory recalls correctly. The body count ran into double digits before you were done last time."

"I need some information about a certain Detective Constable."

"Is he local?"

"Yes and no. He is with the Met, but is currently seconded to Bournemouth CID."

"What's he done to warrant your venerable interest? Or is it a case of him having pissed you off?"

"I think he might be on the take and that's pissing me off."

"What's his name?"

"Steven Harvey."

"OK, leave it with me. If he is bent - then I'll find out."

"Thanks Frank, I appreciate your help."

"Oh, don't thank me until I have what you want. But it's going to cost you, mind."

"Yeah, it always does. Just find out for me, Frank. I don't care what it costs - just find out one way or another and as quick as you can." The older man nodded his understanding. Dillon added, "I'll call you in a day or two."

They left Gardner sipping his pint and drove straight back to the rented house. Vince was still running various searches for any bank accounts that Harvey might have hidden away overseas. The big Australian looked up briefly as they came through the door and Dillon knew the look from working with him for many years, and carried on walking through to the kitchen. Dillon picked up an iPad from one of the quartz worktops and tapped the command icon to roll back the outer doors and allow the panoramic view of Poole's natural harbour into the room. He tapped another icon and a panel opened in the ceiling to allow an ultra-slim flat screen television to drop down. He booted-up his laptop which immediately connected to the house secure wireless network and switched the television to receive mode. He looked up to check the screen and was pleased to see that the laptop home page was now appearing on it.

Dillon and Inger pored over the files for another three hours, cross-referencing information, trying to make sense of the facts. It was eight-thirty. They were thinking of taking a break and going to grab a bite to eat when an email arrived in Dillon's mailbox. It was from Vince in the next room with the instruction to open the attachment. It was a recording made by Nash when he had been talking on his mobile phone. They listened to it in amazement. It gave them Nash's agenda for the following day. Dillon made notes about times of meetings, locations, and most importantly of all - confirmation that the drugs operation had been brought forward due to a hitch at the dockyard and was now planned for the next day. The biggest prize for Dillon was a heavily coded message that Vince had picked up during Nash's conversation that he would also be contacted by his source the next day. The code had been sophisticated and had taken Vince's software over six hours to decipher.

"I don't believe our luck," said Dillon. "We've never had such a strong lead drop into our lap before. Looks like we got the bug in place just at the right time, so much for the signal blocker he's been using." Dillon said with satisfaction.

"Look at the print out, Nash was making a mobile to mobile call at the time of the recording. By the look of this report both phones are pay as you go unregistered sim cards." Vince commented.

Dillon called LJ on his home number. They would have to work through the night to organise the teams.

* * *

It was Thursday morning and Kane woke in the Canford Cliffs apartment that was owned by one of his offshore companies registered in Belize. This was the very first apartment he'd purchased sixteen years ago in the name of his first company and now he was living in it for the first time as a

199

tenant under an assumed named. It was a fourth floor apartment which he had always known would come in handy one rainy day. Over the ensuing years he had purchased the other seven apartments in the prestigious serviced building along with the freehold. Now he was back where he began, having sold all of his other properties. It was a curious feeling. It seemed as if the past years had been a dream. He felt cramped in such a confined space, which wasn't surprising since he'd rattled around in a ten bedroom mansion on the edge of the harbour until two months ago. Nevertheless, the apartment made a good pied-a-terre, especially since no one knew he was living there.

Going to ground somewhat limited his social life, but since he planned to leave England forever, he had little need for social camouflage. "Times are bad in this once fair land," he told those who thought they were his friends. "I've had to sell my home." Kane noticed how quickly they stopped inviting him to dinner, looking away awkwardly when they met him. He experienced a glow of self-satisfaction. He'd fucked their wives in discreet luxury hotels, drinking the finest most expensive Champagne while indulging in every conceivable pleasure of their feminine flesh. The wives loved the extravagance and the attention of the frivolous liaisons. He'd miss that part of it, although he might jet in from time to time and whisk one of them off to some remote country hotel.

He padded into the kitchen and switched on the Nuova Simonelli espresso machine which provided him with the endless cups of coffee he needed to sustain his existence throughout the daylight hours. He stared at the kitchen. It was a complete mystery to him. Perhaps he would teach himself to cook sometime. He ate at restaurants twice a day. His annual bill was over thirty-five thousand, but at the moment he saw no reason to economise.

He picked up his espresso and walked back to the bedroom. He looked in the wardrobe and surveyed his many hand-made Savile Row suits. He carefully picked out a dark blue wide pinstripe two piece and laid it carefully on the end of the bed. He picked out a pair of hand-made Italian leather brogues. He looked at his watch. There were three hours until his lunch meeting with Douglas Campbell-Fox. He took a shower, then padded back into the kitchen to grapple with the Nuova Simonelli coffee machine once again.

Kane had one more problem to solve. When the operation was under way he had to move around one hundred million pounds out of the UK. A million pounds wouldn't be a problem that would fit into a large suitcase, but a hundred million in hard currency would require some thought. In these days of security conscious border officials that amount of cash couldn't be transported by air and it would be equally as risky in the back of a truck. He would have to break it down into smaller amounts which could be concealed more easily in a number of different ways. He would find a way - a better way to transport such a large sum of money.

Razor and Cracker had offered to transport the money for a two percent fee, but in view of Razor's latest escapade at Heathrow it was clear they weren't as organised as they claimed. Anyway, it would put Razor into too powerful a position. Not only would he be investing in the consignment as well as importing it, he would also be dealing with the profits. When Razor grasped that fact he'd be after much larger percentages.

Kane had better people than Razor to handle the money. He had a genuine banker in the form of Douglas. He had first met him five years ago at an invitation only society ball in aid of cancer research. They were standing outside the marquee, Champagne in their glasses, smoking the finest Cuban cigars, looking down the lawn towards the English Channel. The dappled sunlight picked out the guests on the lush lawn. On the one hand Kane despised all of these wealthy people, but they were supporting a truly worthy cause. On the other, he craved admission to this exclusive club of the rich and famous.

"Only on days like this do I feel I'm still in the England of my childhood," said the man standing beside Kane. "I feel an overwhelming nostalgia. This scene suggests those bygone days of the 1940s."

"I know what you mean," said Kane. There was safety in such gatherings. Here one was beyond the law, securely ensconced in the bosom of the class system. On days like this, and in places like this, police cars didn't exist. Kane soon discovered that Douglas's family were old money and reached back over centuries.

"I'm afraid the old England's long gone. We shall have to accept that we are never going to see those halcyon days ever again." Kane said.

"What makes you say that?" Douglas asked, his eyes narrowing.

For the very first time Kane took stock of Douglas Campbell-Fox. He identified him immediately as coming from the peculiar arena of the upper class. He had been educated at only the best public schools so as to bring the best out of his abilities and talents. Physical prowess was clearly not his forte. He was of average stature with a bulging paunch. His teeth were his most striking feature and had been looked after by a very good, and no doubt, expensive dentist who had ensured that his smile was as near perfect as possible. He was aging fairly well and Kane hated him for it. He had a successful commodities trading company based on the Sandbanks peninsula. Kane had only been invited to the function because he had once fucked the attractive middle aged function coordinator when she had been stoned, and had gone out of his way to supply her with cocaine on a regular basis.

Kane decided it was worth taking a chance. "A few months ago I did a property deal with a Russian who had twenty million he wanted transferred to a numbered Swiss account. I told him, it wasn't that simple. That a sum of money that large would need special handling if he didn't want it seized by revenue and customs."

Douglas laughed. "That happens these days. It's only to make things difficult for the criminals. I'm surprised your client wanted to move his funds to Switzerland. If you're not English this is still the best country to keep your money. If you're English, then Switzerland or the Cayman Islands are best." Douglas turned to Kane, looked serious and added. "If you find yourself in the same situation again, give me a call. Over a billion pounds of foreign currency changes hands in the city every day. I know people who trade and who would be happy to accommodate your needs in such transactions."

Kane probed a little deeper. "Are these guys any good? I hear that this type of trading is not only illegal but getting harder by the year."

"Things are tougher now because of the tabloids constantly reporting; that this trader was insider-trading or that firm was fixing-share-prices. That won't stop a bit of irregular trading going on. It depends on whom you know. That's how it works and how many bankers have become very wealthy in days gone by. A word here and a word there - they never feel guilt or believe that they're doing wrong. As they say in the city, it's all in a day's work."

Happy days! Kane had hit the jackpot. Kane had been introduced. Over the next four years he contacted Douglas at various times and found him as good as his word. They had become good business friends. They lunched together once a month, and every now and again Kane went with Douglas on golfing weekends. Although Kane was a competent player, he could only stomach playing so many championship courses and talking nothing else but golf over dinner.

As Kane waited in the expensive restaurant he wondered if Douglas would balk at the sheer size of the deal which he was proposing this time. Douglas had never previously questioned the large sums of bank notes which Kane had delivered. He was either very trusting, or a gullible fool. Kane suspected the latter.

At last Douglas arrived and they were both shown to their table. They had ordered their lunch and were waiting for the waiter to bring the wine, the mineral water and the antipasto. In the meantime they watched the live shellfish in the large salt-water aquarium moving dangerously; powerful claws bound together. The two men shuddered.

"Can't say I give much for their chances of survival," said Douglas.

Kane didn't answer. His face expressed a look of distaste. He was wondering whether he really wanted to eat lobster after all.

It was only while they were sipping their coffee that Kane brought up his proposition. Douglas didn't bat an eyelid.

Kane wondered if Douglas understood the physical aspects of the proposition. "Sterling's so bloody bulky. You'd think the Bank of England would print a one hundred pound note at least. Even the American's have a hundred Dollar bill," he said lamely.

"Yes. I can see the problem Max," replied Douglas. "If I bump into the Chairman of the Bank of England I'll have a quiet word with him."

Kane looked at Douglas but couldn't tell if he was joking.

Out of the blue, Douglas said. "I heard somewhere that the drug cartels use women to count their cash. That they lock in them in large rooms with no windows and make them count the notes without any clothes on so they can't steal anything."

"That sounds really exciting Douglas," said Kane, who'd heard the same thing from one of Don Rafael's business associates.

"Is that the method you use Max?" Douglas leered.

Kane smiled. So Douglas had guessed the source of the money. "I'm afraid not."

"That's a pity," said Douglas, and laughed.

"If that's your thing Douglas, I know of a place where we could go and have as many girls counting money as you want." Kane said. A few choice images of Douglas in compromising positions might come in useful.

"Yes that could be amusing," said Douglas.

It had been bound to happen eventually, thought Kane. Douglas had to get greedy at some stage. It was human nature after all. So things were not cosy Douglas. Perhaps Kane would be putting Douglas's young wife to bed after all.

"By the way, I should remind you never to phone me on the office number. It's far too dangerous, especially as all calls are monitored and recorded for regulatory purposes. There used to be a time when a man's word was his bond. But now you have to prove it digitally. It would raise questions from above if they wanted to know what business I was conducting with you." Douglas said.

"That suits me, Douglas."

"It's a sobering thought, isn't it, big brother watching and listening!" Douglas threw in casually.

"Yes, sobering."

"You really needn't worry though, Max," continued Douglas blithely.

"All the same," said Kane thoughtfully, "It's not a pleasant thought. That's how they catch even the smartest criminals."

* * *

It was Thursday, 25th April, 1900 hours. The private Learjet appeared for the briefest second through the clouds over Surrey. The co-pilot made contact with Air Traffic Control, who started to issue flight instructions to the approaching aircraft.

England was always wet and windy in April, and cold anytime of the year. The Lear loomed out of the grey clouds suddenly, throttling back with a roar, hung over the tarmac and then dropped down. There was a shriek from the wheels as they spun into life, tyres smoking for a second.

Two men sitting in the Range Rover Vogue watched the private aircraft as it sped past, and out of sight. One of them glanced down at his watch, looked across at the other, and said, "He's bang on time."

Chapter 12

Jasper stood outside the Haven Hotel by the water's edge. He instinctively knew that somewhere in the darkness a member of Dillon's team or undercover police officers were watching him. He glanced at his watch. There were only a couple more minutes to wait. In London, Parliament was sitting and a lively debate to a packed house was in full-swing about the question of stemming the flow of illegal immigrants into the UK. During the many heated exchanges and much standing up to enforce the seriousness of what was being said - no one noticed the tall fair haired man standing by the entrance sending the email from his mobile phone to Jasper Nash.

Jason Villiers reclined the A4 Skyhawk pilot's ejection seat, which he had purchased and had converted into a stunning executive desk chair. The plush office of his most profitable restaurant offered him a place to keep an eye on his modest empire. Jason Villiers was waiting impatiently for a call which would tell him he could begin marketing. He had six vans ready and waiting, and had checked his dealers were all available to trade.

Jasper had rehearsed the red-herrings he was going to drop into the conversation for the benefit of those listening in. If things worked out, Dillon wouldn't follow him the next morning. He would still be extremely cautious when he rendezvoused with Jason's six drivers and their vans. He had decided to get Razor a Ford Transit Jumbo van. He was pleased with himself. That would cause problems for Dillon and his team. The adrenaline was running. He sat down on a wooden bench and made the call. He felt a pang of guilt. Jason would be horrified if he knew what was going on. The mobile phone bug would automatically start to download the number dialled, but Jasper knew that Jason would dispose of the sim-card immediately after he had finished the call. Jason never took unnecessary risks.

A few minutes later, and the conversation with Jason was over. The last pieces of the operation had been set in place. Jasper walked home to Martha. He'd taken care of everything, except for Martha. He could not keep lying to her. She must have guessed that he was more involved than he pretended. All he needed were a few more days, and then it would be over.

When he entered the luxury apartment he found Martha waiting for him. "Where have you been?" she asked bluntly.

"Walking, I needed to clear my head."

"Oh, I thought that was it," she said, pausing for a moment.

"I don't want you to insult my intelligence any more. I know you're doing far more than helping Max Kane. You promised me you would quit. I've decided that I can't go on like this. It's over, Jasper."

"Listen Martha..." Jasper began.

"No, Jasper. I don't want to listen to your bullshit anymore. Believe me. It hasn't been easy to make this decision. So don't make it harder. At least leave me some dignity, please."

Jasper said nothing. He poured himself a drink, picked up the glass and looking at it in his hand, swirled the whisky around a little. He looked at Martha. She was standing across the room by the window. He wanted to move to her and take her in his arms, but knew that she would simply push him away. It was his fault that things had come to this. Her patience had finally given out. He didn't believe that she meant it. The best thing would be to suggest having a trial separation, and once the job was done and the money had been transferred to his offshore numbered account he could see her again.

"I'm sorry, Martha. So sorry that it's come to this," he said. Tears started rolling down her cheeks. She made no attempt to brush them away. Jasper went over to her, and put his arms around her. She didn't push him away, but she didn't respond either. "I'm very sorry," Jasper repeated. "The last thing I ever wanted was to make you unhappy."

Martha shook her head. "It's over. You forced me to make this decision."

"I didn't mean to. Things have got out of control. I'll move out until this is over. Then we can see where we go."

"It's too late, Jasper. It's simply too late. This afternoon I called the solicitor and told her we wouldn't be proceeding with the purchase of the manor house." She pushed him away, suddenly.

Jasper looked at her, startled. "Whoa. Why are you so angry about this?"

"You really can be so bloody stupid, Jasper." She picked up her keys on the way to the front door, turned before leaving and said. "I'm going out for a while. Please go away Jasper. Because if you don't, I will, and you will definitely never see me ever again." The door slammed behind her.

Jasper went into the bedroom and packed some clothes into a suitcase and holdall. He only needed enough for the next few days. It would be all over then. He'd take Martha for a holiday.

Jasper looked around and sighed. It was time to go. He left his door keys on the dining table and after casting a glance around the apartment for one last time, pulled the door gently behind him as he left.

Outside on the pavement, Jasper felt the darkness cloak itself around him. He wondered if there were any surveillance crews working overtime. He couldn't take any chances, and it wasn't going to be easy to lose them carrying the suitcase and heavy holdall. He took a taxi to Bournemouth International Airport. The car hire firms were always open at the airports. Once he had a car it would be easy.

After picking up the car, he headed west towards Wareham. When he finally reached the boat, having made many detours to confuse or lose anyone following, he was confident that he'd shaken off any surveillance.

The heater on the power boat was still warm. He made sure that the diesel tanks were full, and generally checked around the once luxury power craft. Satisfied, he took out a sleeping bag from one of the lockers and prepared for bed, and set the alarm clock on his mobile-phone; he had an early start and a busy day ahead.

* * *

The dock supervisor had hand-picked the crew working with him. There was a complicated shift system at the port, designed to prevent conspiracy from occurring. However, on a couple of days a month he could almost guarantee that the four men with him would be working together. They had only a weeks' notice of when they would be on the same rota, but that was all the time they needed. As soon as they knew the dates they informed Razor. He then flew down to Casablanca and made the arrangements for the consignment to be loaded onto a ship bound for the UK. The dockyard team would be working the same rota scam as their UK counterparts. They are all being paid a considerable amount of money in return for no questions and reliability. All they had to do each time - was their jobs - nothing more and nothing less. But they all signed up knowing that their families would be harmed if they ever broke ranks.

Once the containers were safely on their way, Razor returned to England and contacted his lead in UK Customs who would put him in touch with an officer looking to make a year's salary in one night by looking the other way when the containers were unloaded from the ship and taken to a holding warehouse. Razor had never used Poole to bring a consignment as large as this one into the country, so he had to be extra careful about everything and every step of the way.

When the ship docked in Poole, and the containers were about to be craned off onto the quayside, the customs rummage crews went to work. They trawled through every inch of the vast ship with sniffer dogs in search of anything that shouldn't be there. They were also looking for hidden compartments behind the ship's interior structure that had been manufactured for the concealment of drugs or contraband by the crew. Once they'd finished their task the fright handlers removed the containers by crane, including the containers with Kane's consignment of cocaine in.

The container seals and manifests would be checked after they were unloaded onto the quayside; this caused a problem as the paperwork would show that they had been loaded aboard the container ship in Casablanca from a ship sailing out of a Colombian port. Such was the Colombian cartel's power and menace, they had their Moroccan contacts destroy the original documentation and erase the computer files. The shipment had now temporarily disappeared from the system, until the new manifest details had been re-entered. Now when they were inspected everything looked as it should do. When the time was right, it only left for them to be collected.

If, for any reason, the containers couldn't be removed from the ship or the collection didn't take place, instructions would be forwarded and they would be off-loaded at the vessel's next port of call, usually Rotterdam on the Dutch coast.

Now the container ship was securely against the quayside waiting for the customs officers to board and start their searching. The dock crew was waiting patiently inside their tea-room. They weren't in a hurry. It wasn't their problem if they weren't working because customs were taking their time. A couple of them were playing cards at a table in a corner. Now and then one of them went out to see whether customs had arrived.

Finally four officers with German shepherd dogs arrived and went straight up the main gang-plank. The wind whistled through the port and whipped at their clothes. There was the sound of a horn as the cross-channel ferry left port on her way to France. The lead dog laid its ears flat on his head as they neared the top of the gang-plank. The next moment all four officers with their dogs had disappeared into the maw of the vast ship. The dogs were let off their leads as two officers went down to the lower decks to search and sniff out any drugs from the bottom up. The other two customs men looked around the fright to be unloaded. It was cursory check. They had not had any tip-offs, but still had to be vigilant as the ship had sailed out of Morocco.

One of the dock crew stood at the entrance to the building. He was smoking a cigarette, watching the quayside with indifference, watching the ship with keen eyes. He was looking for any signs of unusual activity as the customs officers emerged. He'd been alerted by something as insignificant as the Alsatians looking perkier, ears pricked and tails wagging, indicating that they'd been rewarded for their find. He watched for any hint of urgency in the officer's return. Bloody dogs! Of all the ships waiting to be searched why choose to take four bloody dogs onto this one instead of the usual one or two.

If things looked wrong the dockers would have to be extra careful. They would have to find out if the officers had suspicions. They'd have to make a decision. It might be another cargo which was under suspicion. They always had the choice of letting the freight continue to Rotterdam. Rain started to lash down. The customs officers were taking a long time on board the ship. An hour was usually ample time.

Suddenly the customs officers appeared at the top of the gang plank. They descended to the quayside and ran through the rain, heads down, expressions hidden by the peaks of their caps. The freight handler started to pull on his yellow waterproofs. The officers burst through the door of the building and brushed off the rain. The Alsatians shook themselves. The freight handler stared at the dogs and wished someone had the guts to poison all four of them. Sniffer dogs didn't last long as there was a five thousand pound bounty on the head of each dog offered by the cartels. All of a sudden the largest dog turned its head and looked directly at him. Inadvertently he looked away.

"It's over to you guys," said one of the officers. The freight handler nodded. He alerted the rest of the team. Three of the officers went off to make themselves a cup of coffee; one remained just inside the main entrance ignoring the no smoking sign as he lit a cigarette.

Once aboard the ship, the team didn't waste any time in locating the containers holding Kane's consignment. The crane lifted each one off and onto the quayside. There were two more things to do. The original documentation in Morocco had been substituted with others. They were excellent forgeries and would pass any scrutiny.

Nice - thought the team supervisor. The fifty grand was as good as in his pocket. He didn't care that Razor had said they shouldn't spend the money straight away. He'd earned it and was going to buy himself a new car. Maybe a big Mercedes or even a Range Rover - yes a luxury four by four would look good on the drive of his ex-council house that he'd purchased many years before.

* * *

The alarm on his mobile phone rang at five o'clock in the morning. For a moment Jasper forgot where he was, and then stretched out a hand to silence it. He lay in the warm sleeping bag for a few moments contemplating the day ahead, wondering if he had overlooked any detail. He always planned for a consignment to be dock-side on a Friday because the dealers went to work at weekends. On weekdays, people had to work and had no money. On weekends, police resources were usually over-stretched, dealing with binge-drinking party-goers in the centre of cities and towns, and the constraints of overtime due to the Government cut-backs meant that they were less likely to be on normal duties. Dealers normally wanted two weekends of credit to put the cocaine out on to the streets. Jasper wondered if Max had even bothered to check what day it was. He doubted it. He struggled out of the bunk. There was no point in worrying about the day ahead; it was a luxury he couldn't afford. He barely felt the cold as he put on the kettle. He had other things on his mind.

By six he was on the towpath taking a shortcut to where he had left the hire car. Dawn had just broken and with it came a light mist swirling and fanning itself over the still water of the River Frome. Dew laden cobwebs floated in the morning air. A dog ran past him on a route it had obviously travelled many times before. There was the occasional caw of a crow in a nearby tree. He drove back to the outskirts of Poole and parked the car in the car-park of a large DIY store. He took out a sports bag and started walking towards the road. The town was waking up now and a cold sea breeze blew off the harbour.

He found the Ford Transit Jumbo van that Jason had come up with, as arranged, in a side road of a nearby trading estate a few hundred meters away. He put his hand up under the front nearside wheel arch and retrieved the magnetic key holder. He put his gloves on, unlocked the cab door and slid into the driver's seat. The vehicle documents lay under the seat. He opened the sports bag he had been carrying and pulled out a pair of blue overalls and struggled into them. He placed a clipboard on the dash. He was behaving like a van driver about to collect or deliver goods consignments; except his heart was pumping faster and the adrenalin surge was making him feel like he'd actually been snorting the old 'Billie Hoke' himself. He still had time to kill. There was always time to kill because he always made a point of being early for appointments in case something went wrong. If the van didn't start, then he would need extra time to start it. If he was late then Razor would be gone. If he had to make all of the arrangements a second time then the risk factor would be too high to be safe.

He drove the white van through the trading estate and along the dual carriage way towards Poole Quay, turning off and doubling back on himself a couple of time to see if he was being followed. He kept his speed low and a vigilant eye on the rear view mirror. There was no one there - sweet - he thought. He looked at his watch; it was time to make the rendezvous with Razor. When they had made the arrangement to meet at Baiter Park it was for the benefit of anyone eavesdropping in on their conversation at the pub. Jasper had then discreetly slipped Razor a piece of paper with the real meeting place written on it. Unbeknown to Kane and Cracker, one instruction was explicit - not to tell anyone else about the switch of location.

Jasper drove slowly down Turks Lane and parked the large van at the edge of the unmade parking area of the Parkstone Bay Marina. He picked up the clipboard off the dash and took a few moments to make a circuitous inspection of the surrounding area. He walked across the car park to the waterside café located right next to the water's edge. Razor and Cracker were sitting outside drinking coffee and smoking cigarettes. Razor sported a full-length black leather coat with black trousers and black shoes. They stuck out like a couple of sore thumbs, and Jasper groaned inwardly. Razor looked at his watch confirming that Jasper was on time. Cracker stretched out his hand. "Keys," he snapped, failing to observe even the most basic of usual niceties.

"Good morning gentlemen," said Jasper, shaking his hand before giving him the keys.

"Where's the truck parked?"

"White Ford Jumbo van around in the car park, you'll find the registration number on the key-fob."

Cracker stared at him. "Right - you really are a toffee-nosed git."

Jasper looked at Razor. A man driving a white van dressed in black from head to toe was certainly worth a second look. "Have you ever done this before?" Jasper asked Razor.

"What?" said Razor, taken aback.

"I'd put a pair of overalls on over your nice black clothes before driving that van."

"Fuck off." Razor said. "You mind your own business and keep your nose the fuck out of ours." Jasper shrugged. He doubted a policeman would believe anyone could be fool enough to drive a load of 'class A' drugs around in that outfit. It was probably safe after all.

Jasper decided he would be guarded about recovering the van when it was returned fully laden with the consignment. At least he had a couple of hours to have a coffee, make a couple of phone calls, and wander around to see if the terrain had been staked out.

He watched Cracker slide in to the driver's seat of his Subaru Impreza and put his mobile phone to his ear. Razor went and got in the van. Jasper went back to the café and ordered a breakfast and strong black coffee, and memorised the features at each of the other tables. He didn't want to see any of them in the vicinity an hour or so later.

In five hours it would all be over. In the meantime he would enjoy the relaxing setting of the café and forward the encrypted email that he had received twelve hours before from his source in Whitehall to his handler at the embassy of the Democratic People's Republic of Korea in London. All he had to do then was to wait for the confirmation that a payment had been sent to his numbered account in the Cayman Islands. He forced himself not to look at any of the other people sitting around him as he touched the screen of his smart phone to retrieve the contents of the message and to format it using the application provided by the embassy. He hadn't lain idle while he was incarcerated in the Hong Kong high security prison. Instead he had gone out of his way to pick up a sound working knowledge of Mandarin and Korean.

His stomach felt much better after the breakfast and two mugs of coffee. He left the café and wandered off along Turks Lane. His trained eye didn't pick up signs of any surveillance teams. At nine forty-five he activated the small pocket-size mobile signal and GPS blocker, and made a phone call, carefully reading the number from the paper napkin. The call was answered immediately with the tones indicating that the phone at the other end was also using a signal blocker. He recognized Jason's voice. He told him to be ready and waiting in an hour at the rendezvous point, to follow him back to the lock-up warehouse located in a side street of Winton just north of Bournemouth town centre. He hung up. Jason would recognise the van, and tail him at a safe distance to make sure he wasn't being followed.

Nobody had noticed the attractive young Scandinavian woman jogging or the man washing the Citroën DS3 in the driveway of a house he had just walked past or the young long-haired man sitting in the Ford Focus talking on his mobile phone. And he hadn't spotted the tall rugged looking man with unruly hair wearing blue overalls scrubbing off the deck of the sailing boat that was on a cradle in the boat yard...

Jasper surreptitiously screwed up the paper napkin with the phone number on and dropped it down the nearest roadside drain. He walked along Sandbanks Road, turned left into Elgin Road and continued a short distance until he came to the entrance of Parkstone cemetery. In due course he found that his hunch was right, and he waited five minutes to see if there were any signs of a tail.

Razor and Cracker were waiting impatiently in the car park of the café when he finally returned. Razor tapped his Breitling Super Avenger watch. "You want to get yourself a decent watch mate," he said. Cracker tossed him the keys to the van. Jasper walked across the car park to the van. He wondered what someone watching this little scene would have made of it. As he approached the van, he reached into his pocket for a handkerchief and pretended to sneeze. Still holding the handkerchief he opened the door and jumped into the driver's seat. He slammed the door behind him. He pulled on a pair of latex surgical gloves from his overall pocket and slipped them on. He wore them so as not to leave any fingerprints on or in the van. He couldn't help but notice that Razor and Cracker - had not worn gloves at any time. He watched Razor and Cracker drive away in the Subaru; their job was over. He started the engine and took possession of the consignment.

Jasper knew he had a ton on board from the sluggishness of the van's diesel engine in response to the throttle. He pulled slowly out of the car park and back out on to Turks Lane, at the junction he ground the gears as he pulled out onto Sandbanks Road and headed towards Lower Parkstone. He turned right into Britannia Road that led him to Ashley Cross, where he turned right again at the traffic lights on to Commercial Road and drove around the block a couple of times. He then spotted the black Ford Focus pull out behind him and then disappear, only to reappear a moment later at another junction. Jason was following in a Mercedes Vito van, tailed from a safe distance for a while, watching intently, and then peeled off and headed east towards Winton. Jasper spotted him and decided to cut through from Lower Parkstone avoiding the main roads and keeping to the side streets that would afford him a lesser chance of being stopped by the police who were operating a random stop and search operation on vehicles throughout the area. They were stopping drivers who were only too willing to have their vans gone over for road worthiness and searched in the interests of law and order.

If Jason had stayed back and turned on his side lights it would have been a different story. Then, Jasper would immediately know that he was being followed. He would drive to the large DIY store car park where he had left his car. The store had two entrances and the parking area covered at least two acres. The police wouldn't stop him because they would be hoping to catch the person or persons he was meeting as well. Jasper only had to leave the van in amongst all the other ones parked and walk away. The police would be welcome to the van and its contents.

Jasper turned on the radio and pumped up the volume. He was a good driver, and had driven all types of vehicle from sports cars to juggernauts. At last he arrived outside the lockup in the side road just off Winton high street. He pulled up and slid across into the passenger seat to let Jason climb aboard and drive.

"I'll take us around the block a couple of times just to make sure there's no one lurking and then drop you off around the corner," said Jason.

"No," said Jasper. Jason wasn't going to like this. "There's one box that I've got to take with me. Take me into town. There's a car that's been left at the Hinton Road garage."

"Hang on a minute, Jasper. You said I was taking the whole lot."

"I know. That's what I thought. This was landed on me at the last minute. Unfortunately I had no option but to agree to this condition."

"Well my old mate, this puts a completely new perspective on our deal." Jason pointed out.

"I don't like it any more than you do. The Colombian cartel wants this particular box delivered to a third party."

"Oh come on, Jasper. You know where that leads. It means that my dealers will come up against competition and that'll slow down the deals while they wait to see if there's a price fluctuation."

"I wouldn't worry about any competition. If my hunch is right that one box contains Methamphetamine and is heading for a private buyer somewhere in the Middle East."

"You promise me that box won't hit the streets."

"I promise." Jasper said looking his friend in the eye, as he said the words.

"OK," said Jason grimly. "Let's get going." Jason drove the van into Bournemouth centre and drove into the Hinton Road car park.

Jason had grumbled all the way into town, and as Jasper got out of the van he looked round and said, "Look on this little discrepancy as a giant favour to me."

"I've a good mind to tell you to fuck-off. Why should I expose myself to unnecessary danger?"

"How do I know that this consignment wasn't tagged with GPS trackers, which is why they haven't got anyone tailing us?"

"It's not tagged. I swept the interior of the van with a bug detector before I set off earlier this morning."

"How do we know that this car wasn't followed here or that someone isn't watching it right now?"

"Because it would have been left at least three days ago and moved to different levels of the garage car park at least four times. Not only would that precaution have been taken, but the car would also have been monitored via a wireless camera link by the person who had parked it. So you see - we're perfectly safe."

Jason swung the van around a corner and up to the next level.

"Over there, pull up as near as you can to that blue Kia estate car." Jasper pointed at the grubby looking car.

Jason drove into a free space next to the grubby looking and dented Kia. "I still don't like this," said Jason, shaking his head. Jasper ignored him. He looked at the boxes and immediately identified the one larger box he had to remove immediately. All of the others were smaller. He noticed the freight labels were still attached. He started peeling them off. Razor and Cracker had much to learn. If the boxes fell into the wrong hands the labels would lead an investigation back to the port.

"What are you doing?" Jason asked.

"I'll be finished in a minute or two." Jasper replied.

He reached the larger box and peeled off the label and found older ones underneath. This box had originated in Hong Kong, not Colombia. He quickly stuffed the incriminating evidence into his pocket and moved the box to the rear of the van. He jumped out of the van and joined Jason.

"What the hell are you doing Jasper? We shouldn't be doing this in broad daylight in a busy municipal car park in the centre of Bournemouth."

"No one is going to take any notice of two blokes in boiler suits driving a white van. And anyway all we're doing is unloading one large nondescript box and placing it in the back of an old estate car. No one gets suspicious if you do things out in the open. Stop looking around and chill-out, will you?"

Jason grunted, and shook his head again. He didn't help Jasper carry the heavy box to the rear of the car. He slammed the van doors closed.

"Hold on!" Jasper said, as Jason jumped behind the steering wheel. He picked up the clipboard and scribbled on a piece of paper, which he passed to Jason. "There's your delivery ticket for the benefit of anyone who might be watching."

Jason looked at the meaningless piece of paper, then folded it slowly and put it in his top pocket. He'd really had enough. "Call me Friday. We'll meet at five-thirty, at the usual place."

Jasper watched him drive away. It was almost two o'clock. He went to the lift, waited a moment for it to arrive. Pushed the top floor button, the doors closed, and he got out of the boiler suit. He threw it in the corner of the lift. On the top level he walked briskly to the stair well and descended all the way down to road level. Westover Road was busy with traffic and pedestrians. Within seconds he had vanished amongst the throngs of shoppers. Jasper weaved his way through the arcades, along a couple of side streets and eventually was sitting on a bench in the Central Gardens. He rang Kane's mobile phone and the voicemail cut in - he hung up.

When Kane phoned a moment later, he answered.

"Everything is now in place." He kept the conversation brief.

"Good," said Kane. "Just one problem, I'm afraid you're going to have to kick your heels for twenty-four hours before your next meeting."

Jasper hesitated before replying brusquely. "Why?"

"A payment was expected this morning, and it hasn't

been transferred," Kane said.

If Kane wanted advance payment for the single-box consignment it meant he didn't trust anyone. If Kane didn't trust these people then they were as dodgy as they can get. One thing was for sure now, he wouldn't be making the delivery when it was arranged. Kane would have to find someone else.

"Just put the stuff to sleep somewhere very safe," said Kane. "Do not unpack the box. I don't want any arguments with the owners about whether they've been short changed or anything. If we leave it alone with the seals intact they can't complain."

"Suits me," said Jasper. "I'll call you about this later."

"No. Call me tomorrow at this time."

"OK," said Jasper and disconnected the call. He looked at his watch, pleased that he'd kept the call under three minutes - two minutes and forty-five seconds - anyone monitoring the call would have been really frustrated because he had not given them enough time to do anything other than listen. Always assuming that they had been able to break the code for the GPS blocker that he carried with him at all times. He smiled smugly to himself. He'd go back to the Hinton Road car park and retrieve the large box from out of the old Kia estate car. He couldn't risk leaving it in the car. He'd rent a car and take it back to Wareham and stash it on board the boat. Kane had pulled another stroke on him.

* * *

Dillon felt despair as the surveillance teams each came back to him with negative reports on the day's watching and listening activities. He gave each of them the order to return to Ferran & Cardini in London.

Inger, Vince and Dillon would remain in Dorset.

This assignment was going nowhere fast and Dillon knew what he had to do. His optimism of three days ago was waning, but he still felt lucky. Everything was falling into place - but just not fast enough. He was now certain that Max Kane had overlooked something. He was now sure that Jasper Nash was the man who had been selling military secrets to the North

Koreans. But where and from whom was he obtaining the information? This assignment was a far cry from his previous one, perhaps that's why LJ had given it to him - a stroll in the park, he thought. From the very beginning they had been given the slip by Nash, who had a liking for sophisticated electronic gadgetry that no ordinary member of the public should ever possess, let alone be using. The information they had gathered from the intercepted mobile phone calls had proved worthless. The surveillance on Nash's luxury apartment had been a total waste of time.

"What do you think, Vince?" Dillon asked when they were sitting on the sun-deck overlooking the harbour.

"You want my honest opinion mate, or something that'll boost your confidence about this charade?"

"Why not try the honest route first?" Dillon said lighting a cigarette. Smoke drifted up into the warm air.

Vince lifted the overly large wine glass he had found in one of the kitchen cabinets, held it up to the sky and swirled the rich ruby red liquid around the glass. "If you ask me mate I reckon we've been sent down here on a fool's errand." He sipped from the glass and let out a noise that said this wine is so good, that words fail.

"Expand - and make it good."

"OK. But some of this is merely supposition mate! I think, as usual, Dunstan Havelock has been economic with the facts. We've been led to believe that Jasper Nash is a traitor. But I think there's more to it than Havelock's letting on."

"Like what?" Dillon interrupted.

"Well, about the only thing we know for sure is that Nash is in deep with Maximilian Kane and that together they've been smuggling large consignments of cocaine in to the UK for the Colombian cartels. We're told that he is a traitor - selling our country's military secrets to one of the most aggressive regimes on the planet, but have virtually no evidence of this." Vince paused, sipping his red wine.

"I agree, what I don't understand is how Nash got into the high treason game in the first place."

"Do you think we've been deliberately misinformed?"

221

Vince asked.

"No. That's not Dunstan Havelock's style. I think we've probably been trying too hard to catch Nash out and forgetting that a few criminals are smart and cunning. How do you think Kane and Nash have remained at liberty for so many years?"

"Look Jake, I know that you and Kane have some unfinished business, but you mustn't let it cloud your judgment mate."

"Bollocks!" snapped Dillon

"I'm sure he's got two, mate. But you know what I'm saying - the fact is that although it's no one's business except yours, you can't let it affect our success in catching Nash."

"Point taken, and thanks Vince. You know I always appreciate your blunt honesty. The last thing I want is to bring my personal dislike of Kane to fuck up the assignment."

Inger had been listening and was shocked by the lack of support for Dillon. She walked outside and sat down on one of the reclining chairs. "Do you English always have such a negative attitude?" She directed the question at Vince. "You should be positive and support Jake, not berate him. You sound like you're covering your backside."

"You're entitled to have your opinion. You should stay out of this. Your Interpol brief is to observe and assist where necessary - not to stick your nose into our business," said Vince.

"I'm afraid he's right, Inger," agreed Dillon.

"Look," said Vince, "you know that I'll give you all the support I can. I'll admit things looked good on paper. The phone bug appeared to be getting us somewhere. On the other hand when we were monitoring his calls from the mobile registered to him things soon became mundane very quickly. He's obviously using a minimum of two, if not three mobile handsets with unregistered throwaway sim cards."

"Nash must be getting details of the police operation and perhaps even ours from someone on the inside. The question is - who?" Dillon paused.

"The obvious source is the local police." Vince commented.

"Or perhaps he simply knew that he was being bugged.

I'll speak to LJ; maybe he can use his old cronies' network to find out." Dillon said lighting another cigarette.

Dillon went back inside; on the wall, the large plasma screen linked to Vince's laptop had a rotating cam-link icon drifting across it indicating an incoming video-call. It was Edward Levenson-Jones, sitting as large as life in his office in London, accompanied by Brodie Stevens, another one of the Partners who had offered LJ support at the highest level for over ten years. LJ wanted an update of the assignment so far.

It was six-thirty and it was usual for him to still be in the office. He didn't waste his words on niceties; instead he cut straight to the chase.

"Good evening LJ." Dillon said, knowing that the politeness would annoy his boss."Is it, Jake? I've just come off the phone to the Home Secretary who has been giving me a very hard time because Nash is still walking around a free man. He asked me if I thought you'd gone soft after the battering you took during the Chimera assignment."

Dillon ignored the comment saying. "Nash is slippery. He appears to be one step ahead of the surveillance teams at all times, which indicates to me that someone is tipping him off along the way. What we don't know - is who it is."

LJ stood up and started to pace up and down his vast office, lighting a cigar at the same time. "Do you think the intelligence was unsound?"

"It appeared to be good, but Vince and I have discussed the possibility that we weren't told everything by the Home Secretary's office, or MI5 are up to their old games of miss-direction and being selective with the intelligence they pass on to us."

"Oh not that old chestnut, Jake - one has to ask oneself this - what could they possibly gain from such deviancy. Needless to say, I've looked over the files and reports pertaining to this assignment, at length. The Partners wanted justification for the continuance of the assignment and for me to discover if there were any discrepancies. What I ascertained was that each and every file and report has been carefully doctored. Let's look at the matter of Kane and this Russian, Aleksey. The

French police authorities apparently wanted to interview Kane in connection with Aleksey's murder. I've been on the phone to the department dealing with the investigation. They told me they were still searching for the killer. The only lead they had was from Miss Lindberg, who told them that Kane may have been involved. They assumed that if Interpol were involved they would have evidence on which she based her suggestion. She has managed to compromise our entire investigation with one phone call. Worse than that - she has deliberately misled us all as to her real purpose for being here."

"I don't think Inger has misled anyone. I believe that Kane's involvement with Nash provides adequate premise to continue with the investigation into whether Jasper Nash is a traitor or not."

"Well I'm not convinced. The only thing that Nash is so far guilty of is conspiring to smuggle 'class A' drugs into the UK. I have an uneasy feeling about this assignment - that Dunstan Havelock has so eagerly sent our way. Inger Lindberg has been compromised by her involvement with you, and her reputation has been damaged for the future. I told you at the very outset of this assignment that your personal dislike of Maximilian Kane cannot and will not jeopardise this operation. Do you understand that old son?"

Dillon looked at the screen for a moment without saying a word, thinking what a patronising old git Edward Levenson-Jones was. "Oh absolutely - was there anything else?"

"Don't be facetious. You are supposed to be setting an example to the others and showing Miss Lindberg how professional Ferran & Cardini International is. I reiterate old son - Kane is of no importance to you or this assignment and you will leave him alone."

"I'm sorry you have such a low opinion of me, but it's not just Kane and Nash involved is it? They're playing with the organised criminal gangs. Not only that. I think that one or both of them has a contact in the police and possibly the customs service, and is paying them for information."

"I'm really not interested in your conspiracy theories old son. What I expect you to do Jake is catch Nash in the act of selling our military nuclear secrets to North Korea."

"Fair enough," said Dillon.

"Oh, and Jake - let's not fill up the local mortuary this time..."

LJ broke the secure comm-link and the screen became a passive light blue again.

Dillon stood for a few moments thinking about the assignment, and whether LJ was getting cold feet about having been persuaded to put him back on active service after the physical and mental beating he had taken during his last mission. Perhaps he should have taken the advice of the doctors and the shrinks, and retired for good. But he'd tried taking time away from the job before, and had soon become bored with the quiet life in the Scottish Highlands. The demon inside his head had lain dormant during this time, giving him peace. But, whenever the stress and the shooting started - it surfaced with a vengeance - once again enabling him to stay alive.

* * *

Jasper hauled the large wooden box into the day cabin of the power cruiser. He powered up the heating system, and then looked for a screwdriver and a pair of tin-snips in the boat's toolbox. The box was too unwieldy to transport and he wanted to re-pack the contents in to a military style rucksack, despite Kane's specific instructions that he shouldn't open it. This would make it easier to carry and less obtrusive.

Anyway, he was curious. He wanted to see the purity of the drugs inside. It would most likely be good quality Lebanese or Turkish hash. Too expensive to be commercially viable on the streets, and was probably destined for one high-end dealer who specialised in this type of exotic gear.

He manoeuvred the box to the far end of the day cabin cut off the high-tensile security bands and unscrewed the plywood lid to reveal the metal air-tight liner inside. It was very heavy, but he managed to pull the box out and place on the floor. Jasper picked up a long flat bladed screwdriver and pierced the top and then used the tin snips to start cutting it open. He could smell nothing, which meant that the packers had done their job well. At last the hole was big enough for him to put his hand inside and pull out the packages. They were covered in brown tape so he couldn't see the contents. The first thing he noticed was the unusual shape. Normally the hash came in rectangular or oval blocks, but these weren't even hard.

He pulled out every package and placed them all on the sofa next to him. When it was dark he would take the box and after weighting it, sink it in the river. He placed the packages in the rucksack he had purchased specially. Finally he took a knife and carefully cut the Tape off the last package.

For a moment it did not register. He thought he was looking at a new type of wrapping material. Then he realised he was seeing traces of a white powder. He pushed the knife into the package and sliced it open. He licked the blade, unnecessarily, for confirmation. He knew exactly what it was before the bitter taste hit him. The powder didn't sparkle. It was dull and lifeless, like chalk. It was heroin that had already been partially cut with other drugs of a similar colour and effect, as well as other adulterants such as; sugar, starch, powdered milk and quinine. But this street heroin still remained around forty percent pure and was packed ready for the wholesalers and distributors to cut many more times before it ended up in the end user's body.

He carefully sealed the package again, walked to the other end of the cabin and picked up a half bottle of Jack Daniel's and took a long swig.

He sat back down on the sofa and looked at the now full rucksack. He didn't know what heroin was worth on the street, but guessed the thirty or so kilos were worth a million at wholesale prices. They were certainly worth a life imprisonment term, and represented immeasurable long term misery to millions of addicts.

Kane knew that he would not get involved with handling heroin at any cost. They had an understanding about this. Kane would be as shocked as he was to discover that someone had done this. He immediately suspected Razor and Cracker. Kane had told him how they had demanded more of the action than had been agreed in return for the dockyard facility. Well, they were in for a little surprise. They were going to have to wait for their delivery, and they might be waiting a long time.

Something gnawed at the back of his mind. A few moments later it became clear. Kane had refused to postpone the operation even when he knew they were under some heavy surveillance. Jasper cursed; what a naïve idiot he had been, he should have guessed there was something different about this deal. Kane had been insistent that he should not open any of the boxes. That meant he knew what was inside them. Kane was involved after all, and that changed everything.

Jasper began packing the small bales of heroin into the forward bulkhead locker and covering them with an old tarpaulin. It was out of sight, but not out of mind.

Chapter 13

It was midnight, Dillon lay stretched out on one of the luxuriously comfortable sofas in the vast living room of the rented house that he was sharing with Vince Sharp and Inger Lindberg. There was a half full bottle of single malt whisky on the floor, positioned precisely where he could lower his arm and lift it to pour with the minimum effort. He had given up thinking about the assignment and was listening to a little light jazz on the state-of-the-art Bose sound system. From time to time he picked up the thread of a thought, had another swig of the smooth amber liquid, and skipped a couple of tracks to something more sympathetic to the melancholy he was feeling.

So long as he didn't move there was little sensation that he had drunk far too much. It was movement which made him feel unsteady. He fumbled with the screw top lid and finally managed to twist it back onto the whisky bottle. Of course, he wasn't going to give up on the assignment - it simply wasn't in his nature to do such a thing. He wasn't going to scamper back off to his home in the Scottish Highlands, either. No way. He would be back on the case first thing in the morning, and this time he would be doing things his way. The old way - without the rule book...

All this pretentious crap about not upsetting Nash and leaving Kane alone was just that - crap. Dillon laughed. He'd leave the pussy-footing around to the various law enforcement agencies involved and tell them nothing. You could never be too sure who you were talking to, or who they might be passing information on to.

His thoughts were interrupted by the front door opening and a moment later the light going on in the kitchen adjacent to the open plan living room. He looked at his watch. It was just past midnight. He listened to the fridge door being opened, a bottle being lifted out and liquid being poured into a glass.

Then bare footsteps padded towards where he was lounging on the sofa.

"Hello," Inger purred, she smiled and sat down in one of the easy chairs nearby. "I thought I might find you down here somewhere." Christ, she thought, he was half way through that bottle of whisky and must surely be wrecked.

"Sorry, I wasn't expecting to see you this evening," said Dillon defensively. He hauled himself into a sitting position and immediately regretted having moved. He ran fingers through his dishevelled hair and then scratched at the stubble on his chin.

Why couldn't she have just gone straight up to her bedroom, "I'll make you a double espresso, you look as if you could do with one."

"Thanks, do I look that bad?"

"Believe me; you look far worse than bad." Inger laughed at her own joke and wandered off to make the coffee.

Dillon heard the espresso maker working and then Inger padding back with a cup in each hand, setting them down on the low table in front of them. Dillon picked up the first espresso cup and downed the strong black liquid in one gulp.

"Damn that is good." Picked up the second cup and did the same again.

Inger looked at him in astonishment and said, "Good?"

"Very good, thank you. How's the Pinot Grigio?"

Inger glanced down and swirled the almost clear Italian wine around the glass she was holding. "Well, it's fresh, a little fruity with a smoothness that only the Italians can carry off well." She liked Dillon and she knew that her secondment would not have been anything like as entertaining, if she had been paired up with anyone else. She had overheard Dillon's dressing down by Edward Levenson-Jones on the comm-link earlier that evening, and felt he had been overly harsh with his comments and his assessment of her motive for contacting the French authorities about Kane. She knew what it was like to be a loner, working alone, having to make instantaneous decisions in the blink of an eye, or end up on a mortuary slab. Dillon hadn't worked it out yet, but they had more in common than he knew.

"Fresh and fruity, right - and smooth like an Italian - God, that must be good." Dillon smiled, his face softened and he thought what a lovely person Inger really was. What did LJ know; anyway, she must have had a good reason for contacting the French police about Kane. He would ask her when he was sober.

"Do you drink yourself into oblivion for a specific reason?" Inger asked. She meant it kindly, not so much a criticism as an outsider observation. He looked up sharply. She'd touched a nerve.

"What. No…" Dillon felt annoyed and probably looked embarrassed. "This isn't drinking - this is pure pleasure and a small reminder of the property I own in the Scottish Highlands. Falling into a state of utopian oblivion - now that's what I call drinking." Dillon smiled as he said these last words.

"Well, let's drink to that," said Inger, raising her wine glass to Dillon, who hesitated for a brief moment, then grinned.

"We should have got in Champagne and caviar."

"That would have been nice, but the wine is doing good, thank you."

The air was bursting with sexual tension between them. Inger was sitting opposite Dillon with her long legs crossed, making it impossible for Dillon to concentrate on their conversation. He stood up and walked over to the Bose system and changed the playlist, almost immediately soulful sounds started to emanate from the walls.

There was an awkward silence between them. Inger broke it. "Maybe you should look at this assignment from another angle?"

"Maybe I will," said Dillon after a long pause. He looked at Inger to see if she understood.

"Good," she said and smiled.

He sat back down on the sofa and poured out a small tumbler of single malt, asking Inger, "Would you like another drink?"

"No. I must get to my bed." She stood up. "Until tomorrow Jake," Dillon stood up and she kissed him on each cheek.

"Until tomorrow Inger, and thanks for the company."

She walked across the room and stopped at the doorway, turned and said, "We must do this again, but next time I will show you how we Scandinavians drink. Good night."

"Well, if that's a challenge, I accept and look forward to it." He felt as if he had an ally, and a new friend.

* * *

Kane expected to be marginally less bored at the dinner party than if he were dining alone at some restaurant. He was killing time. His host was a Conservative Member of Parliament and his hostess a biochemist for the Home Office; from time to time she donned an apron and spent a day relaxing in her kitchen cooking a veritable feast for friends and a few fellow charity patrons, Kane being one of the charity crowd who donated large sums of money for local good causes. There were ten guests; amongst them a Spanish diplomat and his wife; a couple from Hereford who owned a small holding, whom Kane carefully avoided; a frumpy woman who owned a local estate agency, who had been inappropriately invited for his benefit. The Right Honourable William Kelsey was the most interesting person present although his wife cast doubts on that epithet. He was the Junior Minister in charge of developing committees that would debate the fight against drug smugglers and organised criminals. The irony of it always made Kane smile when he met him.

Kelsey proved that he was a social liability over cocktails by arguing why banning smoking in UK prisons would do nothing more than cause unrest and possibly rioting in a room full of non-smokers. He rebuked those individuals who preached that passive smoking contributed to cancer. Kane found the gaffe in such earnest company almost memorable. Unfortunately Kelsey was not impervious to the hostility of his fellow guests. He gulped his drink and plied for conversation. He was met with indifference.

At the dining table Kane found himself seated between the frumpy estate agent and William Kelsey. He politely informed the estate agent that he had moved out of property in the UK in favour of more attractive overseas investment opportunities, and she wilted predictably in the direction of the farmer. Kelsey seized upon a moment's silence to recapture lost ground. "Do you know the funniest thing cropped up at the committee hearing I was chairing last night." One or two of the guests turned their heads, "The fight against the illegal drug smuggling trade is turning a corner." More heads turned and Kane inadvertently coughed with a mouthful of asparagus soup and brought the napkin to his mouth. He dreaded this subject.

"Our experts predict that there will be new legislation passed through Parliament and the House of Lords within the next decade enabling high-court judges to pass the death penalty to anyone caught, and found guilty of, smuggling 'class A' drugs into the UK. I say it's about time this country and others, grew a pair of big balls and eradicated the scum, who peddle this filth, from the face of the earth." Kelsey paused and smiled expectantly, "You see, we must face up to the global endemic of illegal drug abuse and be ready to wield the heavy weight of the law when this legislation is passed." Kelsey delivered another expectant smile.

There was a stunned silence around the table. "Do you mean to say that the Government is at last waking up to the fact that there is a drugs problem?" It was the frumpy estate agent who asked the question.

"We are merely at the debating stage, but yes, if we can push this through during this term in office then we have an extremely good chance of bringing back the death sentence to the UK," said Kelsey.

"Well, I think there's more likelihood of seeing a pink pig fly through the air," said the farmer.

"Oh I don't know. A number of high profile individuals have voiced their support for bringing back hanging and the House of Lords is unanimous on reinstating the death penalty as a warning to anyone thinking they can bring drugs into the UK." Kelsey said.

"It will never happen," said the Swiss diplomat sitting at the other end of the long oval table, "Unless the British can convince the rest of Europe that the death penalty is the last resort in the war against drugs. Well, you can forget ever getting your debate past that - a debate..." He sneered.

There was a murmur of agreement, followed by a silence. The ensuing conversation omitted Kelsey.

Kane bided his time. The opportunity was too good to miss. He turned to Kelsey and said. "You know, William. I'm inclined to agree with you. I think that with enough momentum your lot might just be able to pull it off. Make it the ultimate deterrent and make sure that there are examples made in the public eye."

Kelsey turned to Kane with eagerness. He hadn't expected support from any quarter. "There are many of us who believe that this is the only way to eradicate this scourge of our society. We have to take the initiative now, if future generations are to be safe. Because the fact is, the illegal drug trade doesn't stop there; organised gangs all over the planet trade not only in drugs but also in human trafficking, prostitution, and slavery. They are not interested in human rights or anything like - so why not treat them without consideration. The punishment must fit the crime."

"Quite," agreed Kane. He wondered how he was going to word his question. "Apart from debating the subject, has any further action been taken?"

"We've done a considerable amount of research. But that's as far as it's gone so far. Unfortunately our budget is fairly small, which means progress is slower than we'd like. But we'll get there in the end."

Kane could barely contain his enthusiasm. This was usual for anything that was deemed as a non-starter in politics. "Unfortunately times are tough financially for everyone, but I wish you success William." A sudden beeping noise silenced the table. For a second Kane thought it came from the other end of the room, then realised it was the mobile phone that Jasper Nash had given.

"Excuse me," he apologised. Shocked faces turned towards him. He switched the mobile phone to silent. "I'm expecting a very important call." Bloody hell Jasper! He looked at the number he had to dial in five minutes. How bloody embarrassing. "I'm frightfully sorry William, but I have to make this call." Kane stood up.

"Certainly," said his host, stonily. "You'll find the front of the house has the best reception signal."

Kane turned to Kelsey. "We'll finish that conversation when I return." He turned and left the room, gently closing the door behind him.

He wondered what Jasper wanted. They had an arrangement to talk the following day - and not before. Why had Jasper contacted him? He didn't like changes of plan. He hoped that nothing had gone wrong. He pressed the speed-dial on the mobile phone. It was a rare pleasure to make a business call from such a safe house. He listened to what Jasper had to say. It was not good news. The fool had done precisely what he had been instructed not to do! He had opened the box.

"Why don't we discuss it tomorrow? You pass it on as arranged, and then it won't be an issue any more," said Kane calmly.

"No Max. I'm having nothing to do with it," said Jasper brusquely.

"I wouldn't recommend you adopt that attitude. You could jeopardise the entire deal."

"Fuck your recommendations. Fuck your deal. You've crossed the line and you're well out of fucking order." There was menace in Jasper's voice.

"What do you mean? It's nothing to do with me. This is as much a shock to me as it is for you. I had no idea what was going on. The Russian Aleksey and Razor must have made a private arrangement."

"You're talking bollocks, Max."

"I'd rather you didn't use names," said Kane controlling his anger and his voice.

"You knew it was heroin."

"Do not use that word."

"You deliberately told me not to open that box."

"I think we should talk about this in the morning." He wondered if anyone was lurking in the shadows listening to his

234

conversation.

"You're joking. I'm not discussing it. Not now, and not in the morning. When I finish marketing the candy, my part of the deal will be over. Then I'll be in touch. I'll let you know where the other stuff is hidden and you can pick it up yourself."

"I really wouldn't recommend that. You don't mess around with these people. They don't listen to reason like normal people," Kane spat out the words in a whisper.

"Max - you can fuck off. You should have thought about that before you decided to take me for a fool, and that's final. You'll be hearing from me," said Jasper.

"I think we should meet. Things will turn nasty if you continue with that stance." There it was again - that hint of menace in Kane's voice.

"Trust me Max, things are already nasty. Goodbye." Jasper disconnected the call.

Kane stared at the mobile phone. Bad news - and tomorrow three million pounds was being paid to Jasper. It would be transferred electronically to a numbered bank account in Belize - which only Jasper knew the pin number to. Minus expenses already incurred, which included the one hundred and fifty grand for the port facility, and the same again as an advance for Razor and Cracker. The buyer would not be amused to hear that it would be a week before he could have his goods. It was going to be more than bloody embarrassing.

The trouble with the white dragon market was that the money had to be paid in advance. The fuckers couldn't be trusted once they'd got their noses or their needles into the gear. Really it was the buyer's fault. If the money had been ready when Jasper had got to the car then he would have made the drop and been none the wiser about the contents. It was the warehousing which was the problem. Warehousing was always the problem. Unfortunately the buyer was definitely not going to see it that way. Nevertheless, Jasper was overdoing the moral angle, and he ought not to have talked about it over the phone.

Kane pondered the problem as he returned inside to the dinner party. He realised there was an answer. He would let Razor and Cracker off the leash and they'd find Jasper soon enough.

Kane sat down at the dining table again, harbouring an apologetic smile. "I'm terribly sorry," he said. "It's to do with a very complicated deal in Australia. My lawyer needed to talk to me."

He finished his cold soup quickly. "Absolutely delicious," he said to the hostess. He turned his attention to William Kelsey again.

* * *

Dillon wouldn't have been surprised if Jasper Nash had come to Martha's door in answer to the intercom. He wouldn't put it past Nash to have returned home having accomplished what he set out to do when he had evaded the surveillance teams. However, it was Martha who looked at him through the CCTV intercom and released the electromagnetic lock of the outer door. Her face betrayed her fears as she stood facing him inside her apartment.

"Hello, Martha," Dillon smiled as he greeted her.

"What's happened?" she asked, alarmed.

"I need to speak to you," Dillon said.

For Martha, events seemed to be repeating themselves. Dillon's appearance made her aware that she not only had strong feeling for Jasper, but also what murky waters he was swimming in still. Was Dillon here to inform her that Jasper was dead or that he'd been caught and was back in prison?

Dillon remembered the lavish living room and the awesome uninterrupted view of the Solent over the blue flag beach. Things hadn't changed since he'd been there over two months before. There was a large painting easel standing in front of the wall of glass, a plain drape covering the work in progress below it; the u-shaped seating arrangement worked well in the bright room with a large Persian rug and rectangular glass topped coffee table in the middle. Everything in the room was the kind of expensive but tasteful items dirty money could buy. Most people worked for years so they could afford to decorate a room like this. He wondered if Nash gave her an allowance.

But Martha had changed. She was looking fresh and vibrant with a new hair style that gave her a sharp business look, and the lack of concern at his sudden appearance was undisguised. The sneaking admiration he once felt towards Nash had turned to disdain. A contempt, because he was proving to be so stereotypical of someone with a disregard for everything that was honest in life, and hatred, because he was proving to be as slippery as an eel and far harder to catch in the act of treason than Dillon had given him credit for. Dillon decided to not let Martha know this.

"So, Mr Dillon - what's this all about?" Martha asked. She had walked over and was standing by the window.

"It's about Jasper," began Dillon, somewhat unnecessarily. He was hardly there to discuss the state of the economy. He decided to wing-it, forget his scripted questions and see what information he could get out of her. "Do you know where he is?"

"No," said Martha, shaking her head. "We're no longer together. Things have not been so good since he returned from Hong Kong."

"I'm sorry to hear that," said Dillon. "You were so positive about your future together when we last spoke."

"Yes I was, wasn't I? It's funny how wrong you can be about someone you think you know so well?"

"Have you any idea where he might lay low for a while?" Dillon asked.

"No. I asked him where he was going as he walked out. I don't think he knew himself."

"Martha, it's in his interest to talk to me. He's up to his neck in something that will either get him killed or at least a life term prison sentence in a high security facility. The type of place they send terrorists and the like. I'm also told that he is up to his old tricks with Maximilian Kane."

Martha looked at him. "No," she said firmly. "No, I don't think he is. He wouldn't do anything like that, especially after what happened to him in Hong Kong," she said defending Jasper Nash. She didn't blink or look away. Her stare was almost a challenge.

Dillon admired her for the loyalty she was showing in defending Jasper. "Well, I'm afraid he is involved with Kane again. I've had him under surveillance, but he's now gone missing."

Martha reacted quickly to this news, looking suddenly away toward the sea view through the wall of glass. She realised he knew she was lying.

"Normally the disappearance of a suspect would give no cause for concern. We'd assume that he had got wise to the surveillance teams and was countering them by altering his routine, places he visited regularly, things like that. But this time things are different. One of Kane's partners in France, a Russian man named Aleksey, has been found murdered. Shortly afterwards his girlfriend was also killed because she could identify the killer. Max Kane is implicated."

"Jasper wouldn't be involved in anything like that," said Martha hastily.

"Oh no," said Dillon. "I don't think he knows anything about it." He hesitated, to add emphasis to this conclusion. "I'm concerned that the same demise might befall him as well."

Martha's eyes opened wide in horror. "No," she exclaimed. "Why should it?"

"Don't be too alarmed." Cautioned Dillon, pleased by her reaction to his goading. "There's no reason to think the worst. I have to consider all the possibilities. That's why I need to locate Jasper." He knew he wasn't playing fair with her, but there was no other way of finding out what he wanted to know.

"Are you expecting Jasper to call you?" Dillon asked.

"No," said Martha, and then corrected herself. "Well, yes. I sort of expected him to call to collect some of his things. I think he'll call anyway. He didn't believe the relationship was irrevocable. I did, at the time. We've still got a lot to sort out."

"That's good," said Dillon. "If he calls you, tell him I must talk to him. He won't want to talk to me - so tell him he's got nothing to lose. Tell him to call my mobile number, so he knows that I'll be able to answer from wherever I am." Dillon scribbled his mobile number on a piece of paper. "Here," he said, passing it to Martha. "Tell him not to try and run -

because if he does I will simply track him down and when I find him - I will kill him. If he doesn't want to talk to you on the phone, then try and arrange a meeting with him and I'll be there. Trust me Martha. I'm not a policeman or anything like. I work for firm that gets involved with investigations that are thought to be of a special nature. We don't report to anyone but the highest authority."

Martha nodded, though she looked dubious. "What are you then some sort of spy?"

Dillon looked at her for a brief moment before answering. "We only want to talk to Jasper, Martha."

"I want to know when you find out anything."

"Of course," said Dillon. He turned to leave. "By the way, I'm also interested in the whereabouts of Max Kane. You wouldn't happen to know, would you?"

"No. But if I did, I'd most definitely tell you. He is one person whom I hate with a vengeance." The vehemence in her voice told him she wasn't lying. "I'm sorry that you're caught up in the middle of all this." Dillon said gently.

"I'm not involved, Mr Dillon. I just had the misfortune of falling in love with Jasper Nash. Sometimes you don't get a choice."

"Well, it can't be easy for you at the moment."

"I'm coping."

"I'm sure you are." Dillon smiled. He opened the door to let himself out. "Don't forget, if you hear from Jasper you must call me."

Martha nodded. She looked worried. "Thank you," she said, as she closed the door, leaving Dillon feeling a little guilty for a moment.

The guilt didn't last long. It was replaced by elation that he had painted such a clever picture. When Martha told Jasper what had happened to Aleksey, it would be news to him; if it wasn't, then he was in the deep end with Kane.

And now, as always, it was a waiting game.

* * *

Jasper woke to the natural sounds of the riverbank and

the feeling of damp air inside the boat. He peered out through a porthole at the swirling fog cloaking the river. It was so thick it had turned the trees in to ethereal shapes. It emphasised his sense of isolation. He lay staring at the grey gloom outside and reminisced about his life. It had always been like this, waiting for something to happen. Waiting for someone to come into a room; and he was always alone, even with Martha there seemed to him to be a loneliness and all because of his inability to share his fears and worries with her. Not that there was anything worth sharing, except for what the money could buy. Then there was never a shortage of people with whom to share the cash. There were always good-time girls ready to go out with him, alive on a line of coke, who gave the brief illusion that they were part of society. There had been plenty of them before Martha; and they had left him empty and alone.

He would phone Martha. He'd made a dreadful mistake. She'd known what he couldn't see until now; that his trust had been misplaced and that he was being used by people around him. He needed Martha. He loved her. She was the only genuine thing in his life. She was his anchor on reality. It was not as if things had been easy for her, she fought for every success she had in her life. She never accepted refusal. Unlike his own life which was the antithesis of hers. Martha had a theme. Her life led somewhere. It led to a future.

Over the years he'd forgotten just how many illegal activities he'd been involved in. He'd forgotten what had gone down. He'd also forgotten the names and faces of people he'd worked alongside. He'd run from one thing to another. He'd been on an express train all his life, watching life flashing by, going from one drugs deal to the next. He never imagined the train would pull into a station and actually stop. This time it had and he was stepping off. After all, he had to be extra careful now. His North Korean paymasters expected him to keep a low profile and off the law enforcement agency's radar. He smiled at the thought of the large amount of pounds sterling deposited into one of his offshore company accounts each month, money always made him smile. In exchange for this generous gesture, he supplied information about the UK's nuclear weapons' development programme; which he obtained from a high ranking civil servant inside the Ministry of Defence with a penchant for cocaine and male prostitutes. Of course, the public was told through the media that this type of weapons programme was no longer politically correct and had been shelved many years before. But in reality, this was not the case. As long as the North Koreans were in possession of a nuclear capability - the west would continue to keep a deterrent in place.

He was wide awake now, got dressed quickly, skipped coffee and left the boat. He made his way down the towpath in the thick fog. He could feel the promise of the sunshine trying to burn through. Time seemed to be moving slowly and he wondered if he would catch Martha before she went out. When he found a public telephone box he couldn't make the call because it had been vandalised. Frustrated by this, he reached into his jacket pocket and pull out one of his mobile phones, but stopped, he realised that although the pay-as-you-go sim had not been registered he couldn't use it. The agencies investigating Max Kane would have acquired the numbers of all calls to his mobile and land phone lines and would be using tracking software that could trace every call being made or received. All they had to do was crunch the numbers until they were able to determine the locality, within a couple of meters, that fitted the intelligence and send out surveillance teams to cover the ground. He walked briskly back to his car and drove for forty minutes until he was in Blandford Forum.

"Martha," he said, grateful to hear her voice. "I need to see you."

"I'm glad you phoned, Jasper. I've got something to tell you. Are you coming over to the flat?"

He wished he could, but he couldn't take that risk. "No. It's a bit tricky, but I really do want to see you."

"Are you alright? You sound a little preoccupied."

"Yes. Could we meet somewhere?"

"Where do you suggest?"

Jasper thought for a moment. It had to be somewhere he could see if she was being followed. Then he wondered why he was being paranoid. He had nothing to fear from customs or the police. They had nothing on him, so long as they didn't know about the boat. "How about that place we had tea on your birthday?" Surveillance would stick out like a sore thumb there.

"OK."

"When can you be there?"

"Well, depending on the traffic - about an hour."

"That'll be fine. Oh, and Martha, I'm looking forward to seeing you." He said.

"Be careful, Jasper." She said, and put down the phone.

Jasper was surprised that Martha was expressing concern for his welfare. It was the first time he could remember her having done so. She had studiously ignored his activities in the past. He was disappointed she hadn't said she was looking forward to seeing him too. Suddenly he was curious to know what it was she had to tell him.

He opened the web browser on his mobile phone and looked for the address of the car hire car company. He found one of their depots on the route. It was time to dump the car; he would be safer without it, as the authorities would be able to trace it and him if they checked his credit card transactions.

Martha was already waiting for him at the Royal Bath Hotel when he arrived. She was sitting in a corner at the rear of the room. It was the most private area of the luxuriously appointed lounge and he wondered if she chose it on purpose.

Martha didn't waste much time with niceties, "I'm glad you called me, Jasper," she said. "I had a visit from that special investigator, Jake Dillon, this morning." Jasper looked at her, surprised. He hadn't expected that. "He says he wants to speak to you. He thinks you're in danger. He says that a man called Aleksey was murdered in Paris along with his girlfriend. Do you know this man?"

"I've met him a few times over the years."

"Dillon says that Max Kane was involved." Jasper sighed. "Do you know anything about it?" When Jasper didn't answer, she asked. "You're not involved, are you?"

This time Jasper answered. "No. But I think I know

more than I want. And I wish I didn't. I think you were right about Max all along. I wish I'd listened to you. But, he did get me out of Hong Kong. I was blinded by that."

"Why do you think he might have had something to do with this Aleksey?"

"I can't tell you. I don't want you to get involved. If you know, then you're involved."

"So why not speak to Dillon?" Jasper shook his head.

"He'll help you. I know he will. He's not working with the police or customs, or anything like that; at least that's what he said."

"There are unwritten rules in this game."

"Even if Max Kane breaks them?" asked Martha astutely. Jasper remained silent.

"It's not my business. You don't go asking questions about other people's scams," he said reservedly after a moment.

"It makes me very sad to think it's come down to this. Max always wanted to be wealthy. It was something to do with his father. When I first met him he wanted to be a millionaire by the time he was twenty-five. He worked out the quickest way of getting there. He was cunning, inventive, diplomatic and of course charming. He could have gone into the diplomatic corps. He could have done anything he wanted. The fact that he went into a career of crime didn't change anything. He was determined to succeed at the expense of anyone who stood in his way. I thought I was an exception because I was his friend."

"I can honestly say, Jasper. I never had any such illusions," said Martha.

"I know you didn't. I used to think we were on some kind of crusade. It was such fun. Twenty-two years ago it seemed inevitable that drugs would be eventually legalised. Sure we were breaking the law, but we didn't harm anyone. When we were ripped off a couple of times we let it go. We made sure the word got around and the guys never worked again. We didn't break legs or anything heavy like that. I always thought we'd retire one day. We'd open a bar in the Caribbean or something. Max never committed himself in those conversations. He's never acknowledged any responsibility to me or as far as I know, anyone else. If he had anything to do with Aleksey's death then he's not a criminal. He's a psychopath. I hope to God he wasn't involved with Aleksey's death. I find it truly hard to believe though."

"Look Jasper, I don't want anything to happen to you," said Martha. She put her hand on his.

"It won't. I promise. You know, when I came back from Hong Kong I was so happy. I thought that for once everything was going to work out. I was going to retire from the business. I was looking forward to settling down in the country, away from it all. I even had a strange notion that we could maybe make a couple of babies. It wasn't always like this - was it? There was a time when we had fun wasn't there?"

"Yes, of course we had fun."

"Do you remember the time when I drove to Geneva with a million pounds in the boot of that Aston Martin I hired for the weekend?"

"Yes. I only found out when you drove into the underground garage of that Swiss bank and two security guards came to greet us. That was memorable; I'll grant you that, Jasper."

"Did you ever believe it could end?" Jasper asked.

"Yes. I could always see that it would end. Something had to give at the end of the day."

"I suppose you're right."

"I wouldn't go that far. But I have always been right about Max Kane. When you feel betrayed and neglected, you feel bad, but you shouldn't feel that it's entirely your fault. You'd be a fool to have let it get that far." They sat in silence for a moment. "I am sad though. I feel frightened that I am losing a friend. My best friend - we've shared a lot together. And you - how do you feel?"

"I agree. I am still reeling from what's happened." Jasper shook his head. "Something always happens. That's the only thing I've found out in life."

"So - what are you going to do now?"

"Well first off, I'm going to speak to Max. I want to know what happened to Aleksey. I have to know the truth. It will affect what I do next."

Martha looked in her bag and pulled out a piece of paper and gave it to him. "This is Jake Dillon's personal mobile number. I think you should call him."

"Maybe," said Jasper. He looked at the number, memorised it and passed it back.

"When will it be over Jasper?"

"Two days, and it will be over. We'll go away, if you want. Before we do that we'll clinch the deal on the manor house."

"Maybe," said Martha. "We'll see," she added and smiled for the first time since sitting down.

They lapsed into silence. A group of American tourists arrived in the lounge. They were all talking loudly as they made straight for the bar and swamped the bartender with their drink orders. One of the men broke free and went over to the dining room and studied the evening's menu greedily. The head waiter glanced at the group of ten and snapped his fingers for a table to be laid immediately. A moment later and the big American man and his entourage were being escorted to their table.

"Thank God for that," said Jasper.

"Are you becoming an old snob?" Martha asked with a wry smile.

"Not at all - it's just that Americans are so loud all of the time."

"I have to go," said Martha. "I have an appointment. Will you call me tonight?"

"Yes."

Martha stood up. "Kiss?" she asked.

Jasper looked up at her, and then stood up. She kissed him.

"Be careful."

Jasper smiled, and watched her leave. He lifted his hand for the bill.

* * *

Razor was furious. He'd tried calling Kane four times in the past twenty-four hours, leaving his three mobile numbers

245

that he could be contacted on. He'd done nothing but kill time in bars waiting for one of the phones to ring. Next time they worked together Kane was going to carry a mobile phone that he had given him or there wouldn't be any deal. He wondered if Kane was ripping him off. Something was definitely wrong. He had a quarter of a million in hard cash tied up in this deal, and no collateral security. He paced backwards and forwards in the lounge bar of his local pub. He looked at his watch repeatedly.

The initial payment of fifty thousand had been paid on time prior to the deal going through. But the first two hundred thousand pounds had not been paid, and now Razor was being aggressively asked by the dock workers for their whack. He had told them they would be paid within forty-eight hours of the consignment coming ashore...

Cracker had problems. He wasn't concentrating on the business any more. They'd been talking about Kane, when Cracker suddenly said, "You know what my mum used to tell me?"

"No," said Razor, baffled.

"Always remember son that you're unique. Just like everyone else."

"What's that got to do with Kane?" Razor asked.

"That we're all individuals," said Cracker. Then he stopped talking. Razor wondered if he was back on the drugs. He'd never mentioned his mum before, and was definitely not intelligent enough to be philosophical.

Razor glanced down at his watch and then checked each of the three mobile phones placed on the circular table in front of him.

A moment later and one of the phones started to ring.

"Hello. Hello," he said in a raised voice.

"Ah. There you are, Razor. I've been trying to get hold of you." Razor listened to Kane's irritatingly refined voice. It cut no ice with him.

"Well, you haven't been trying hard enough. Where's the fucking money you owe us?"

"That's what I wanted to talk to you about." There was a pause. The line hummed.

"I'm listening." Razor looked grim.

"There's been a slight hold-up."

"What kind of hold-up?" Razor shouted down the line, imagining northern European men with guns making off with his money. His worst nightmare was coming true. He should never have got involved with this fucking con man.

"Relax Razor. I'm sorting it out."

"Listen you asshole. Don't you tell me to relax! I want that fucking money you owe me - all two hundred thousand. I did my bit. You think I do this for my health? I'm not running a fucking charity. I want my dosh, and I want it in twenty-four hours or I'll come looking for you. You know what I mean, don't you? You'll need more than a private fucking hospital!"

"We've got a problem."

"What do you mean 'we'? You have the problem!"

"The friend I introduced you to, well he doesn't want to handle our special consignment."

"What?" Razor was perplexed. "What do you mean handle? What's the fucking problem?"

"He's developed a case of moral scruples. I must admit it caught me by surprise. I think he'll return the goods when he's finished marketing the main consignment of candy."

"You think?" said Razor. "You fucking think?" he repeated in amazement. Kane was out of his mind. Five million quid's worth of pure un-cut heroin and he was only thinking.

"It's not a matter of thinking. The fucker isn't paid to think. You give me that tosser's address. I'll sort it out"

"It's not that easy. He's disappeared. His girlfriend says he's moved out."

"Give me the address all the same. I'll find him."

"I don't think he'd take too kindly to that."

"I don't give a fuck if he takes kindly to it or not."

"Are you sure you want to deal with it? You could always leave it to me." Kane felt his conscience was clear. He would always be able to say he had tried to persuade Razor to be patient.

"I did leave it to you, and look what fucking happened," snarled Razor. "Now give me his address." Razor groped in his pocket for a pen. "Wait a moment," he snapped.

Kane could hear Razor shouting for Cracker to get him a pen and a paper napkin from inside the pub. He scribbled Jasper's address on a paper napkin.

"What's the creep's girlfriend called?" he asked.

"Martha."

"And what's her surname?"

"Hamilton."

"Right," said Razor. "Now dump that phone in the sea and buy yourself a new one. Call me so I've got the number. I want to stay in touch with you from now on. Maybe I'll have some news for you by tomorrow - got that?"

"Yes," said Kane.

"Good." Razor ended the call.

"You better prey I get only good news, Maxi baby," he menaced under his breath. He walked out to the BMW six series coupe where Cracker was sitting in the passenger seat. He hoped that Cracker would come down off of whatever drugs he'd been taking soon and didn't have the usual mood swings. All he was doing was staring as if he was disturbed about something from his past. No matter - right now they had a drive down to Sandbanks to locate, and sort out Jasper Nash.

Chapter 14

Martha heard the intercom impatiently buzz twice. She did not recognise the man on the screen. He was wearing an expensive looking black suit, but he was definitely not from the same ilk.

"I'm looking for Martha Hamilton?" He asked, abruptly in an east London accent.

"And you are?"

"Never mind who I am. Have you spoken to Jasper Nash recently?"

"No," said Martha, about to add she had seen him earlier, but then thought better of it. "Who are you?" She asked.

"My associate and I are friends of Jasper. He said he would be calling you," the rough looking man's voice sounded edgy and irritable. "He wants to see you. It's urgent, like. Said I was to pick you up and take you to him."

Martha wondered what had happened. Jasper had never asked her to do anything before. She guessed he needed her help; that was obvious. "OK, I'll just be a minute and then come down," she said, and went into the bedroom for her handbag.

She wondered if she should call Dillon, but then the intercom buzzer started again so she quickly picked up her bag and left. As she went down the stairs she started to write the text to Dillon. At the front door she was met by the man in the black suit and his associate, as he called him. He would win no prizes for being handsome.

"Excuse me, I just want to send a text message to a friend before we leave," she said.

"No texts and no phone calls," said the man, bluntly.

Martha looked at him, querulously. It sounded as if he was giving orders.

"I want to tell someone where I am going."

"No," said the man. "We don't want any phone calls."

"Where are we going?" Martha asked.

"You'll find out," said the man. "Now, let's go. We don't have time to waste."

"Why the rush - what's happened? Why does Jasper want to see me, we're not together anymore." Martha said, her voice now showing uncertainty as to the legitimacy of these two men. Something was not quite right. She didn't like being rushed. Jasper would have provided some explanation.

The man in the black suit took a step towards her; pulled a Smith & Wesson snub nose .38 calibre from the holster tucked into his waistband in the small of his back, and grabbed hold of her wrist. "We could have done this the easy way. But I really don't have the time to mess about with being polite."

He led her down the steps of the luxury apartment block, "Now I don't want any trouble from you out on the street. Just do as I say and you'll not get hurt" He still held her wrist firmly.

Martha was confused. She wondered why Jasper was involved with someone like this. She suddenly felt nauseous.

"No," said Martha, finding her inner strength. "I'm not going anywhere with you."

The man just stared at her. "No?" he asked in a voice that was barely a whisper.

They stood staring intently at each other for a brief moment. The man pulled back the hammer on the Smith & Wesson and prodded Martha in the stomach menacingly. "You come with us or I'll put a bullet in that pretty little head of yours without a second thought - you got that missy?"

Martha stopped struggling. She was stunned at what was happening to her. She realised that resistance was futile. She shook off the grip that the man held her with and followed him out through the front gate and on to the road. She hoped that there might be other residents around. She glanced up and down Banks Road. There were a few pedestrians in the distance, too far away to call out to, and the cars, although only travelling at thirty miles per hour, wouldn't be taking any notice of anything happening on the pavement. She wanted to put up a struggle and make a commotion, but it was pointless; people would only think it was a domestic argument. "Don't even think about it," said the man, stopping suddenly, and jerking her wrist. They had crossed the road and were now standing by a BMW 6 Series coupe. He opened the passenger door, dropped the front seat forward and pushed her into the rear seat. "Sit there and don't make a sound or any sudden movements - or I will kill you."

She looked up at the man. Studying his facial features, she might have to give the police or Dillon a detailed description of him later. The other man got into the driver's seat and started the powerful engine. She stared at him for a second. The BMW pulled smoothly away from the curb, drove to the end of the road turned right and joined the flow of traffic on Panorama Road. Martha glanced forward and spotted the driver looking at her in the rear view mirror.

As the car drifted across the road, the man in the black suit shouted, "For God's sake, Cracker. Keep your eyes on the fucking road or we'll end up in the drink."

Cracker glanced briefly at the other man, before returning his full attention to the driving. They were heading away from the peninsula along Banks Road. On the left, the harbour looked resplendent under a blue cloudless sky. Martha glanced at the driver again, she could see the upper half of his face in the rear view mirror, and she thought he had a squint. He looked at her. She looked away. She felt his eyes staring at her. She wished the man in the black suit had not mentioned Cracker's name...

* * *

Kane switched off his mobile phone for the night. He wasn't interested in negotiating with Jasper. He was waiting to find out if Razor had any success with Martha.

He phoned Razor's mobile phone the next morning from the Royal Bath Hotel where he enjoyed a full English breakfast overlooking the Poole Bay. He wasn't in any hurry; he never liked to rush his meals. Despite Razor's demands about getting another mobile phone in favour of the one he already had to ensure he stayed in contact. Well, he could go and screw himself; his phone had the numbers all recorded, and that was good enough to prove conspiracy. All he had to do was mail it to the police and that would help have those two East End ruffians, with airs of grandeur above their station, locked up for a very long time.

Kane was disappointed to hear that Martha hadn't told Razor where Jasper was hiding; but managed to calm him with some difficulty. Those two guys really had to learn the virtue of patience.

He wondered with morbid curiosity, how Jasper would respond to the news that Razor was holding Martha. He switched on the mobile phone and waited for Jasper to call.

Kane began to have serious doubts about Razor and Cracker. They might become too much of a liability, in which case he would have to consider dumping both of them. That would mean calling in the professional services of Mr Kipper, again. Forty thousand pounds, and Razor and Cracker would be history. The man would like the fact that the job was on British soil, he would fly down from Manchester to London on a shuttle and then fly back the same day. Those two would not know what had hit them. It was definitely worth considering. It might become necessary if he were to put Don Rafael in touch with Harvey Trent and his property development company Montserrat Holdings and they subsequently decided to collaborate. Kane didn't want people like Razor lurking in the background.

He should have never have got involved with Razor and as a result he had placed himself in more danger than he felt comfortable with.

The mobile phone started to ring in his pocket. He looked at the screen. It was Jasper. Kane answered, and was surprised to find him on the offensive. "I've heard that Aleksey has been murdered in Paris."

"What?" said Kane? He wondered how Jasper had found out. He quickly feigned surprise. "When did this happen? Who told you?"

"I'm surprised you don't know. You told me that Aleksey

and Razor were working together with the heroin switch. But they couldn't have been. Could they? Because Aleksey was dead before the plan could be hatched."

"When was Aleksey killed? Are you sure he was murdered and it wasn't some dreadful accident?" Kane tried to buy time.

"Oh, come on, Max. You must have known. I phoned a few friends in Paris. They told me that Aleksey's luck was running out. They say he backed out of a big deal just before he was killed. You told me he was still bankrolling you to cover yourself. You're a barefaced liar. You knew he was dead."

"It's more complicated than that. Look, we can't talk over the phone. Razor's pulling strokes on me."

"Were you involved with Aleksey's death?"

"No! I didn't know anything about it. You know that's not my style Jasper."

"How can I trust you?"

"You have to trust me. We're in this together now. Razor's fucked me up and now he's fucking you up. I warned you he was ruthless. I said you couldn't play games with these guys."

"What do you mean?" Jasper asked.

"He's got Martha, Jasper."

Kane was gratified by the stunned silence over the line.

"Jesus, Max! What's going on?" Jasper spat. "What the fuck are you playing at?" His legs were shaking. His heart was pounding. He felt nauseous.

"Not me, Jasper. It's Razor! He was like a pit bull terrier. I couldn't control him. He went round to your place and couldn't find you - so he took Martha as security."

"What do you mean?"

"He's kidnapped her. That's what I mean. He's holding her to ransom until you give back the consignment."

"You gave him my address?" Jasper asked incredulously.

"Of course not," Kane thought of an answer quickly.

"He got it off that copper, Harvey. Look, he's accusing you of ripping off the heroin. He's an animal. We should have expected him to do something irrational like this." There was silence down the line. "Are you still there Jasper? We should get together - soon."

"I don't want to see you, Maximilian. I want to see Razor. Give me his number."

"Sorry, don't have it. You see I have to wait for him to contact me."

"Bullshit. You know his number. You told me he uses at least four mobile phones?"

"Yes he does. But I don't know the numbers. I'll wait for him to call and tell him you want a meet. That way I can give him your mobile number and he can call you."

"Leave a message on Martha's answer phone. I can pick it up remotely from my mobile phone."

"No. I don't think that's wise. It's more than likely bugged."

"Of course you're right. So here's what I'll do - call you on that mobile I gave you every hour on the hour until you've got hold of that fucker. All right, Max?"

"Well, I hope he calls me sooner rather than later then."

"For your sake, let's hope he does, Max."

"Couldn't you simply deliver the consignment as planned?"

"I want a guarantee that Martha will be released unharmed."

"If you'd taken my advice and not opened that crate none of this would ever have happened."

"That's not how it was. You can't twist it like that. You knew there was heroin in that crate. You've tried pulling a fast one on me, Max." Jasper retorted.

"Think what you like. It's far too late for squabbling now. Your actions have made things very awkward." Kane complained bitterly.

"As if I give a fuck Max, you'll be getting my first call in exactly one hour. Make sure you've got that phone switched on." Jasper disconnected the line. Kane held the phone away from his ear. He shrugged. He was in the driving seat.

* * *

Jasper paced up and down until he'd calmed down a little, and then called Martha's home number. There was always the slim chance that Max was bluffing. He let the phone ring a long time before disconnecting the line. He wished he knew where Kane was hiding himself away. He had been moving around all over the place since this deal started and never stayed anywhere longer than one or two nights. If he could find him, he'd pay him a visit and slice off his balls with a very sharp filleting knife. He wondered if he should arrange to meet Max after all.

Jasper knew it was over. This was the end. Martha would never forgive him. All his efforts to protect her from his nefarious activities had failed. He had no excuses to offer her. His only hope was that time would heal some of the betrayal. Every time he thought of the future his stomach turned and he felt sick. A yawning chasm of empty hours and days spread out in front of him. He'd come so close to piecing together his life with her, and now it had been destroyed. He didn't want to imagine what she was going through.

But first he had to get her out of wherever they were holding her. He pondered over the conversation with Max. There was the slim possibility that Max had been double-crossed by Razor. After all, Max had sounded plausible; but there was only one way to find out if he was involved in Aleksey's murder. He scanned through his contact list for Jake Dillon's personal mobile phone number. He quickly typed in a text message asking him for a meet and then pressed - send. If Max Kane had lied to him then he was going to pay for it.

* * *

Martha cursed herself for being such a naive fool and opening the main door. She hadn't expected anything like being kidnapped, especially not in broad daylight. The journey in the back of the BMW had been a grim experience. After a short while she had felt feverishly nauseous and used every ounce of self-control not to let her captors know that she suffered from travel sickness.

Razor glanced around at Martha, noticed she wasn't

looking well and told Cracker to pull over and stop. He jumped out of the car and pulled the passenger seat forward, shouting at her to get out of the car if she was going to be sick. She shook her head, trying to force down the bile which formed in her throat. It was too difficult. She leaned forward and before she could get out, was sick. She watched the vomit spray the back of the front passenger seat. It dribbled down the luxury leather hide, dripping in globules on to the deep pile carpet. She stared at it for a moment and focused on a piece of pasta. She remembered what she ate for lunch. It seemed a long time ago. She was violently sick again. Razor was screaming in anger at her for ruining his brand new car. He slammed the seat back in place, knocking Martha's knees as it locked in place and he got back in.

Martha spent the remainder of the journey in a nauseous trance. Between the retches, her head lolled as the car twisted and turned through the country lanes of Dorset. She couldn't muster the energy or interest to sneak a glance out of the side window to try and identify some landmark which might suggest their whereabouts. She knew they had reached their destination because, with a squeal of tyres, the car came to a sudden halt and the two men jumped out and the next moment she was being hauled out of the rear seat.

"Get out of the car you stupid bitch," ordered Razor as he violently pulled her out through the doorway.

Martha caught her shoe under the squab of the front passenger seat, stumbled forward out of the car and landed on her elbows and knees on wet grass. Rough hands grabbed her under the arms and lifted her onto her feet. She gulped at the fresh air. Razor pushed her from behind and followed her in to a courtyard. The buildings which surrounded it were almost derelict. Creeping ivy covered every visible part of the brickwork. The guttering was shot. The site was ripe for re-development. She was pushed towards a door bolted with a large padlock. Cracker unlocked it. She followed him inside the building where the air was cold and musty and the gloom was everywhere. The windows were boarded with plywood shuttering. It looked like it had once been a country hotel. She could see the reception desk and dining chairs scattered askew in an adjacent room, before she was ushered up a flight of stairs to the first floor.

A thick layer of dust covered the surfaces. Their footsteps echoed along the corridor. Here and there floorboards had been prised up, as if a surveyor had been at work, and then abandoned the project as hopeless. She was pushed roughly into a room; a single low wattage light bulb was switched on. There was a rickety looking bed positioned against the back wall, some crumpled grey blankets which looked filthy and stained. On the lino-covered floor; old newspapers lay scattered around, an ashtray overflowing with cigarette butts and a dirty mug were on the top of the bedside cabinet. She assumed this would be her cell. The windows were nailed shut and were boarded over from the outside.

"I need to go to the bathroom," she said weakly. The man wearing the suit opened the door and she went in. She started to close the door behind her, but a shoe was wedged against it.

"No you don't." Razor said.

"Don't be ridiculous," said Martha, irritated. She wasn't going to have them watch her. "Do you really think I'm going to remove the nails holding the window frames, and then kick off the boards covering the windows with my bare feet? Oh, and I would then have to jump the twenty or so feet to the ground - without breaking either my ankles or my neck."

"What do you reckon, Cracker?" Razor asked.

"I think she should have a bit of privacy, Razor."

She now knew both their names.

She closed the door. She looked with utter disgust at the grimy toilet bowl. The seat was missing, she used it quickly. She splashed water over her face and started to feel marginally better, looking up she looked at herself in the mottled cracked mirror. She looked pale and haggard.

The door was rudely opened. "All right luv, we want to ask you some questions," said Razor. She returned to the bedroom, looking much more intently at Razor and realised the he dyed his hair. He had much lighter coloured eyebrows. It was a particularly unpleasant combination, and she wondered why he wanted to look like a ginger tom cat with the tinged hair colour...

Bloody hell! If she'd known Jasper was working with people like this she'd have dumped him a long time ago. He'd been astute to keep all the details in the background, dropping hints now and again, suggesting a nether-world romance to his activities. Well, he'd exploded that myth with the appearance of these two hobgoblins.

"We want to know where Jasper Nash is hiding."

"I've already told you. I don't know where he is," said Martha.

"I don't know because we are no longer living together. He moved out. If you happen to see him I would be grateful if you would tell him that any thoughts he might have about us getting back to together, evaporated when you introduced yourselves as friends of his."

Razor stepped forward, looked at her, and then struck her across the side of her face with the back of his hand. "You have no idea who you're talking to, you stuck-up bitch."

Martha didn't react. He grabbed a fistful of her hair in a tight grip. "You're making a terrible mistake," said Martha. "I really don't know where he is, and if I did know I'd tell you."

"We'll see," said Razor, releasing her hair. Martha's failure to react left him feeling awkward. He stepped back, looked her up and down, and then cupped his hand over her right breast and squeezed.

"Nice pair of tits," he commented. "If your boyfriend doesn't turn up soon luv, you and I will be getting to know each other a lot better."

Martha slapped him hard across his face.

Razor looked ugly. "You don't want play rough with me, luv," he said. "Not when you've got no one to come to your rescue." He grabbed the top of her arm, his fingers dug into the soft flesh, she screamed and he tightened his grip. "Not so tough now are you missy?" He dragged her across the room and flung her on to the bed. "Now you think long and hard about where your boyfriend might be hiding. Otherwise you'll get what's coming to you - if you get my drift?" He looked at her lecherously, "you never know - if you tell us what we want, you might just come out of this alive!"

"Don't get heavy now, Razor," Cracker said. "After all, there could be a happy ending to all this. We got to talk. I think Kane could have pulled a fast one on us."

They left the room, leaving Martha sitting alone on the bed with filth and dilapidation all around her. She was cold and she was miserable. She wondered how long this was going to last. She looked around, there was no way she was wrapping herself in those foul-smelling blankets. They could at least get her some clean sheets and blankets and a good book if she was going to stay for any length of time. Who was she kidding? She stood up and began to walk around the large room, floorboards creaked under her footsteps. She stopped and listened, there was no sound except for the wind howling and the rain beating on the window outside. Martha went and sat on the bed again. She heard footsteps outside in the corridor.

* * *

The taxi dropped Jasper outside a magnificent New England style luxury residence on the Sandbanks peninsula. He looked at the piece of paper with the local address Martha had given him; just to make sure he'd arrived at the right place. He stopped himself from approaching the high solid looking oak gates and pushing the intercom. He didn't know what Dillon knew. He couldn't afford to be arrested on suspicion of conspiracy. It wouldn't help Martha if he were locked up in a police holding cell. He backed off and walked along the road to the Haven Hotel, went in to the lounge and took a seat near one of the windows and dialed Dillon's mobile number.

"Dillon."

"Mr Dillon, this is Jasper Nash. I would like to talk to you."

"I'm glad you called, Jasper. When and where would like to meet?"

"How about now, if you're free, that is?"

"Yeah, I'm free now. Where do want to meet?"

"I'm in the lounge of the Haven Hotel."

"I'll be there in two minutes."

"Great," said Jasper, and disconnected the line.

Jasper glanced down at his watch, checked the time, and kept an eye on the main entrance. He wanted to see how long it took Dillon to get there. If he took too long it probably meant that he was organising his team into position around the hotel. In the event it only took Dillon two minutes before he came through the main hotel entrance and Jasper stood up as he approached him.

"Good of you come at such short notice." Jasper said, his eyes darting around the room nervously.

Dillon grinned. "You needn't worry. This is off the record for now."

"Good," said Jasper. He wondered whether Dillon was naïve or very clever. It was absurd to think that he was going to trust Dillon on the basis that this meeting was - off the record. Jasper wondered if he was talking to the wrong man.

"You told me the last time we met, that you would throw me a lifeline if I needed it. I need it." Jasper said.

Dillon didn't respond at first. He waited until the waiter had placed their coffee on the low table between them and had left. "I remember saying that I'd give you one chance to talk to me. But, you must realise that I can't do a deal. Not with the police anyway. But I can try and get some of the drug related charges dropped."

"Some of the charges, what do you mean?"

"Well, let's see. There's large scale cocaine smuggling in to the UK. Then there is the charge of bribing a police officer. Oh, and we mustn't forget the charge of conspiracy to murder. I think that covers the main ones."

"Bullshit! You can't pin any of that on me."

"That might be so at this precise moment - but I still can have you thrown into a high security prison, and the key thrown away for the rest of your natural life?"

"Sorry, I don't follow?"

Dillon was sure that Nash had suddenly developed a nervous twitch in his left eye, and his face had taken on the pallor of a ghost. "Forgive me, Jasper. When we had our little chat at Heathrow airport a few weeks ago, I had just been assigned the job of investigating you. The charge is treason - selling military secrets to the North Koreans is definitely frowned upon in Whitehall, you might like to know."

Jasper looked at Dillon and gave a wan smile that conceded he'd been outwitted without admitting anything.

"Look, the thing is I can give you a folder containing all of the names involved, as well as warehouse locations and distribution routes. All I ask in return is that you give me a twenty-four hour head-start to get away."

"I'm not interested in the smuggling operation." Dillon said with a tone of condescension. "I want everything and anything relating to the espionage that you've been involved in. That includes; who is supplying you with the classified information at this end, methods of communication and routes of delivery for mail, electronic and physical. I want every last fine detail about the cell you are involved with; and that means the names of everyone from the highest ranking to the lowest level in the chain of command. Now if you want to change your mind..."

"And if I do change my mind?"

"Well, your position is not looking good, Jasper. But why would you change your mind? It would definitely not be the logical option. Particularly as you're asking for my help - so it only leaves one question. Why do you really want to speak to me?"

"You spoke to Martha yesterday?" Jasper said. Dillon nodded. "She's been kidnapped to apply pressure on me."

"Let me guess, Maximilian Kane?" Dillon asked.

"No. A couple of his business associates called Razor and Cracker. I don't know their real names. All I do know is that they appear to be running the current operation with Kane."

Dillon picked up his smart phone, logged onto the Ferran & Cardini mainframe and seconds later slipped the phone into his jacket pocket and looked at Jasper. "Razor's real name is Ryan Edwards, he obtained the nickname 'Razor' for putting a blade across the face of a Latvian drug dealer who trespassed and touted for business on his territory in London. The other one known as Cracker is Conner Hawkins. He made his name by opening some of the toughest safes in the city. Of course, they're both well known to the Met. But, they also seem to be fairly well connected and so far neither of them has ever served a prison sentence."

Jasper looked stunned at the amount of information Dillon had gleaned on these two thugs.

"So tell me Jasper, what do they want from you?"

"I've got something they want."

"What is it?"

"I can't tell you at the moment."

"Why have you fallen foul of your friends?"

"Let's just say it's a question of morality and conscience."

"Morality you say?" Dillon questioned. "You're a drug smuggler and spy for an aggressive communist regime. Please, don't talk to me about morality."

Jasper stared at Dillon. He was definitely talking to the right person. However, whether he would help get Martha back was an entirely different question. "I take your point."

"Why don't you go to the local police?"

"I don't trust them and they wouldn't act quickly enough."

"Why?"

Jasper hesitated. He had to make every revelation count. "I'm giving you the first piece of information and I want something in return."

Dillon shrugged his shoulders. "That depends."

"There's a Detective Constable called Steve Harvey who is on Kane's payroll. I heard this morning that he's also tipping off Razor as well."

Jasper watched Dillon's reaction with interest. It was obvious the allegation had hit a raw nerve somewhere, but Dillon controlled his demeanour well. Dillon's face did stiffen a little and a muscle in his neck flexed, he ran a hand through his unruly hair. "I presume you can back this up with proof?"

"I set up the first meeting between Harvey and Kane

while I was being held inside a police cell."

"What else?" Dillon asked suspiciously.

"That comes later," Jasper replied.

"No. That comes now, chummy," said Dillon aggressively.

"Later," said Jasper calmly. "You'll have to trust me. First you've got to help me get Martha back safely." Dillon looked at Nash, and thought what a cocksure little shit he was.

"After all, you did invite me to come and talk to you," continued Jasper. "Or have you changed your mind, Mr Dillon?"

"No," said Dillon. "I'm not known for changing my mind. But if you want my help I'm going to need much more information than you've given me so far."

"Like what?"

"Firstly, I need to know where Kane lives."

Jasper frowned. "I'd have thought you would already know that."

"I'm not going to tell you what I know, am I? You're going to have to learn to trust me too. Remember this. Without me you don't have a hope in hell of finding Martha. So, let's start talking."

Jasper thought for a moment. Dillon was right. He did need him. "I don't know where Max is living. He moves around a lot."

"How do you communicate with him?"

"I gave him a mobile phone. I assigned times for both his and my phones to be switched on for ten minutes and then switched off again."

"What's the mobile number?"

Jasper wrote the number on a scrap piece of paper and passed it to Dillon. "Martha told me Max was involved with Aleksey's murder. Is that true?"

"The French authorities have a lead which makes him the prime suspect," Dillon lied. It would do no harm to let Jasper think the worse. He was going to be a lot more open if he was kept in that frame of mind. "The French are preparing the papers requesting that he be handed over to them for further questioning."

"What?" Jasper asked, baffled.

"The French authorities want Kane back in Paris to be interrogated when we locate him."

"They really think he's involved?" Jasper queried.

"They're certain," emphasised Dillon. "Now, when do you next speak to Kane."

"Not until later this evening. But I have tried calling him a number of times and he's not got the phone switched on. I want to contact Razor to make a deal for Martha's release. I left a message on his voicemail to arrange a meeting for us."

"When did you find out that Martha had been kidnapped?"

"Four hours ago."

"What have you said to Kane?"

"I told him I'd co-operate."

"Good," said Dillon. "I have to make a phone call now. I need one of my team to run a thorough check on Razor and Cracker. I want the information quickly." Jasper looked wary.

"I'll put my phone on loudspeaker if you want to listen in. I assure you I'm not turning you in."

"That's not the problem. Max has intimated that he has another contact, apart from Razor, who is high ranking and very well placed to protect him. I don't think it would be a good idea to let anyone know you're in touch with me."

"Are you saying that this person could be a serving officer in the police or possibly one of the other law enforcement agencies?" Dillon asked suspiciously.

"I don't know, but I don't want to run the chance."

Dillon pondered this revelation for a moment. "No. I don't buy that. It's not feasible. Razor yes, I see where that's coming from."

"You have no idea what's at stake here. We're talking around five to seven million pounds a month. With that kind of money Max can buy anyone he chooses. For half a million I could buy you."

"Let's not be presumptuous now." Dillon said with a steely coldness.

"Think about it," said Jasper. "At least sleep on it. Five hundred thousand pounds paid into a numbered Swiss bank account every month. Are you so principled, Dillon?

Dillon remained silent. He punched in the Ferran & Cardini secure line that would automatically scramble the conversation he was about to have with Vince sitting at his laptop in the rented house on the peninsula. This was standard Ferran & Cardini company policy, and acted as protection against the electronic eavesdroppers listening in. He only had to wait a brief moment before Vince answered. Dillon gave him the details of Razor and Cracker, but left out Jasper.

Dillon hung up and immediately caught the attention of a passing waiter and ordered more coffee.

"That was a strange conversation you've just had with your assistant."

"Why's that?"

"You didn't once tell him that you were meeting with me."

"Oh that. Yeah, if I had told him you would now be in the very real danger of being arrested by a member of an MI5 tactical squad. Taken to an interrogation facility and questioned for twenty-four hours - without an interval. That's why I left you out of the conversation. But while we're doing questions and answers, tell me how you managed to give my surveillance teams the slip."

Jasper couldn't resist a smile. "We knew through Harvey that there was an independent surveillance team working alongside the police and possibly customs teams. The only thing we didn't know was who you were. It was easy to feed wrong information along to you all via the telephone taps, and no doubt you also tried listening in to mobile conversations as well. With no luck, I'd guess?" Jasper looked smugly satisfied with himself.

Dillon winced at the mention of Harvey. He would settle Detective Constable Harvey's hash soon enough.

"Of course, the GPS mobile signal blocker you use is very effective. But you might not have been aware that it can be countered. You haven't met my colleague Vince Sharp yet.

It took him about three minutes to locate and hack into the encryption of your box of tricks, and de-activate it!" Dillon said with satisfaction.

Jasper looked uncomfortable at this revelation.

"So tell me something about Razor and Cracker that's not in their file?"

Jasper paused for a moment, as if he was considering his reply. "Razor and Cracker have a team of freight handlers on Poole docks and another team of eight at Heathrow airport. The Poole docks team lifted the consignment of cocaine for Kane a couple of nights ago. The Heathrow team lift special freight off of the private jet fleets about twice a month."

"Do you have the details of these people and which ships and planes are involved?"

"Sorry, but you know how this sort of thing works, I'm hanging on to that information a little longer."

Dillon decided not to comment. He looked at his Omega Seamaster. Five minutes to the hour. "Isn't it time to make the call to Kane?"

Jasper made the call. They waited patiently for Kane to answer his phone, but the voicemail cut in to leave a message. Jasper hung up immediately. As the minutes ticked by, Dillon noticed Jasper growing increasingly nervous. He continually fiddled with and systematically destroyed the coasters on the table. Dillon caught the waiter's disapproving glance. He came over to them and swept the debris onto the tray he was holding.

"I think Harvey is the quickest way to find out where Kane is living at the moment," suggested Dillon. "If Harvey has done his job properly he should be able to tell us about Razor. He might even know where Martha is being held."

"Harvey's not going to volunteer the information just like that. He doesn't know where Max is, because I had to arrange the meeting between the two of them. If you approach him, then Razor and Max are going to know. I don't think that's a good idea."

"Then again, it might force them to make a move," said Dillon. "But I don't want to take chances with Martha's life. I think I'll arrange for Harvey to be taken out of circulation."

"What do you mean?"

"I'll have him lifted off the street and detained for a while. Preferably, in one of the isolation and interrogation facilities that are used for terrorist suspects." Jasper felt reassured for the first time during their conversation. Dillon was proposing action, and not simply propelling words at him.

"Do you mind if we move on from here? I don't like hanging around after using this mobile phone. Harvey might be able to figure out where I am using their triangulation software. I really don't want Max Kane to come looking for me."

"I understand," commented Dillon. They stood up. "Why don't you come to the house we're renting here on the peninsula? We can talk there. There are more questions I want to ask you."

"All right," said Jasper after a moment's hesitation. "But I want to make something absolutely clear to you. If you attempt to arrest me I will give you no cooperation at all. Your investigation will come to an abrupt halt. A brief will have me back out on the street within minutes, because you haven't actually got a shred of hard evidence against me at the moment."

"Point taken," said Dillon amiably.

For the next hour back at the house, they smoked cigarettes and drank coffee outside on the south facing deck. Jasper walked down the landscaped garden to the water's edge to call Kane. Dillon did not bother to follow him, and each time he returned, despondent that Kane was not returning his calls. Kane was making him sweat. They barely spoke because Jasper had made it clear he was not answering any more of his questions.

Jasper stood up quickly when he heard movement inside the house. He looked at Dillon nervously. Dillon shook his head calmly, and looked at his watch. It was Inger and Vince returning from their visit to London with the information he had asked Vince to obtain on Harvey. Inger had brought her suitcase with her, as Dillon had suggested earlier. He was pleased to notice how well she had hid her surprise at seeing Jasper Nash. He made the introductions and brought them both up to speed with recent developments.

"So, the plan of attack," said Dillon. "From this point on, Jasper, you will be able to contact Inger, Vince or myself at all times by dialling this four digit code into your mobile phone," Dillon gave him the number on a piece of paper. "If I'm not available, you will automatically be transferred to one of the others. Nobody else will know that we are in contact with you. Vince and Inger are the only people I am prepared to trust until we find out if Kane has a paid informer other than Harvey. Do you find that acceptable?" Dillon looked at Jasper. He nodded in reply. "I'm going in a moment to have a video conference with my boss in London and bring him up to date with what we're doing down here. Inger will show you up to one of the guest suites. I am going to need his support and the firm's considerable resources when it comes to it."

"What about Martha?" Jasper asked. "Securing her release is the most important priority."

"Of course it is," answered Dillon. "That's why I'm going to have Harvey lifted off the street, and then I'm going to interrogate him myself."

Jasper nodded.

"Just one last thing, Jasper - you're not here as a prisoner and you can leave at any time. But if you do decide to leave, then remember this; I will come after you and I will find you..."

Jasper nodded again.

* * *

As Dillon wandered off towards the lift that would take him up to the top of the house and the crow's-nest. He wondered if Nash was setting him up.

The crow's-nest study, a lavishly furnished circular room located at the west corner of the waterfront house. Floor to ceiling glass open the room to uninterrupted one hundred and eighty degree views of the harbour and across to the Purbecks in the distance.

He wouldn't put it past Kane to have organised this. After all, they'd set him up previously. This might be Kane's parting shot. He'd feel a lot better if Nash had produced information pertaining to the person or person's feeding him the classified information.

For a moment Dillon wondered if he was going soft, allowing his hatred of Kane to affect his judgement; but he was too far down the line to back off now.

* * *

Vince had opened a secure video-link between Poole and London with the live imaging now appearing on the fifty inch plasma monitor in the crow's-nest. Dillon stood with his arms crossed in front of the large screen waiting for his boss, Edward Levenson-Jones to appear.

"This had better be good, Jake," said LJ. "And damned important to pull me out of a meeting with the Home Secretary?" He looked at his watch, emphasising that it was inconvenient having to talk to him.

Dillon waited for LJ to sit down behind his desk. All the time thinking; the man belonged in some antique shop in Brighton.

"So what is so important, Jake?"

"There have been developments down here in Dorset," he said.

"Which are?"

"I have been approached by Jasper Nash. He requires my help in finding his partner Martha Hamilton who has been kidnapped by two of Max Kane's associates."

"He wants to trade for this service, I assume?"

"He says he is willing to blow the whistle on Kane's entire operation. Everything, details of the distribution routes, Laboratory and warehouse facilities, and the names of those involved along the route of distribution."

"But we're not interested in Kane." LJ looked up sharply at Dillon.

"This is true. But it's not quite as straightforward as that." Dillon kept his voice calm.

LJ stared at Dillon. "Is this some sort of joke, Jake? You've got Jasper Nash in the house, saying that he'll sing like a canary and you are saying it's not straightforward."

"I see nothing funny in any of this. We still don't know where Kane is hiding. We don't know where Razor is holding Martha Hamilton. And we don't know where the consignment of cocaine is being warehoused." Dillon said patiently.

"The deal is that Nash will give us Kane and then himself in exchange for us finding Martha Hamilton." If LJ went on with his constant negativity he would get a good kick in the bollocks the next time Dillon met him. "However, Jasper Nash has given the name of a bent Detective Constable who is on Kane's payroll and who gives him forward warning of any operations concerning surveillance." Dillon paused for a moment and then decided it was time to give LJ a heart stopping fright. "He has also told me that the information he passes onto the North Korean Embassy comes from a high ranking officer at the Ministry of Defence."

Dillon watched LJ jump up out of his leather recliner chair and walk around his desk so that he was closer to the screen. "That's a very serious allegation."

Dillon didn't say anything. The implications of what he had just said were beginning to dawn on him. Something made him uneasy. He was thinking of LJ's negativity about his involvement with the assignment from the outset. But the nagging question was - why?

"Do you have any suspicions?" asked LJ.

"Not at the moment. But, like I said before - after we locate the woman for Nash he'll loosen his tongue. I have no doubt about that. Of course, if Kane has a bent copper on his pay role and he most likely has a customs officer or two as well. That could make things tricky for us to keep our involvement quiet." Dillon decided that if LJ didn't support him then he would automatically become a suspect; and even if he did, he still wasn't to get away with whatever it was he was up to.

"What course of action do you suggest?" asked LJ.

"I'd like to put together a small team that I can trust and I already know who these will be, and I know they will keep to absolute secrecy with no fear of leaks. I've got a few leads on Kane which need investigating. Hopefully, with Nash's help, we can catch Razor with the consignment and the woman."

"What about Nash?"

"Everything depends on his co-operation. Without him running scared and wanting to cut a deal - we have nothing."

"When do you want me notify the Home Secretary's office that you have Nash?"

"Not at the moment. Ultimately it will depend on what sort of case we can build against him. At the moment it's all circumstantial. It might remain that way."

"I hear what you're saying, old son. I don't want anything that suggests a deal. In the UK, you know as well as I, we do not condone plea bargains."

"Of course, and I hear what you are saying."

"OK, Jake. Get on with it, but keep me in the loop at all times."

"Thank you." Dillon said.

"By the way Jake - have you told anyone else that the leak is coming from the Ministry of Defence?" LJ asked casually.

"Only you," said Dillon.

"I think we should keep it that way for the time being. We don't want to scare him off."

Dillon agreed with his boss and was about to terminate the video-link when LJ said. "Oh Jake - it's good to see that you haven't lost your tenacity, old son."

The screen went blank, leaving Dillon standing in the middle of the crow's-nest looking out over the harbour, and wondering how the hell he was going to find Martha Hamilton...

Chapter 15

Dillon had driven the Porsche Panamera back to London and made a phone call to the police station where Harvey worked from, discovering that the Detective Constable was working with another force for the next two weeks; then he told Vince to set up the comm-link between the HD infrared video glasses that he was wearing and the house on the Sandbanks peninsula.

Vince had watched Dillon's back on many assignments and was the only person Dillon trusted unconditionally.

Dillon was keen to break into the first floor flat. Any delay put him in danger of being discovered, as there was always the possibility that Harvey would return unexpectedly. He looked at his watch, and heard Vince's Australian accent in the earpiece confirming the link had been successfully made.

He crossed the road and walked a short distance to get a better view of Harvey's first floor flat before calling his home number. He looked casually up at the windows while holding his smart phone to his ear. No lights were turned on. There was no answer. He looked at the phone for a moment, and then tried calling Inger. He wanted to know how she was getting on with Nash. There was no answer.

Dillon spoke quietly to Vince, but the link had been broken. He tried again, but all he got was silence. He looked at the windows of the flats. Only a few were lit. He was committed now, and would go in, with or without Vince monitoring his movements and sound remotely.

Dillon crossed the road and rang the bell of Harvey's flat as a precaution. There was no answer. He rang the bell again, and waited a few moments.

Coming from inside the communal entrance hall a couple opened the main door and breezed out, passing Dillon. He leaned forward and lowered his head ever so slightly, pretending to look more closely at the name plates of the flats, which partially obscured his face from them. As they passed, he stood up quickly and moved inside before the door swung closed.

The door to Harvey's flat was made of solid hardwood, he knocked three times. There was no reply and everything seemed quiet inside the flat. He tested the door with his shoulder unobtrusively. He put his hand into his pocket and pulled out a slender leather pouch containing a set of lock-picks. He unzipped the pouch and carefully chose one of the jigglers and one of the twisters. He ran the tip of his forefinger over the face of the lock before sliding the jiggler and then the twister into the cylinder barrel. Ten seconds later the door opened and he stepped into the darkened hall. He shut the door quietly behind him. He stood just inside the room listening to the sounds of the building while his eyes adjusted to the gloom.

The flat smelt dirty and neglected. Plastic bags of rubbish lined one wall. A television blared from one of the adjacent flats. No worries about being heard, that tenant was obviously hard of hearing. He smiled to himself in the darkness, and shone the small LED torch around the hall. It was grim, tatty wallpaper and worn out carpets. The furniture had seen better days, miss-matched and secondhand. The block of flats had looked reasonably modern and well-kept from the outside and throughout the communal areas. But Harvey's place was a hovel and he obviously lived alone. The living room had a view of the road, so he decided to leave that until last. It wouldn't take him long to search the rooms. He started in the bathroom. It was a health hazard. He inadvertently held his breath as he levered away the bath panel. He looked inside the cistern, and scrutinised the floor tiles to check if any of the grout was missing or cracked. He drew a total blank. He went through to the kitchen and started with the obvious. The fridge contained an assortment of decomposing foodstuffs. The ice in the freezer compartment had been recently hacked away. He removed a packet of frozen hash-browns and found a plastic bag. He pulled it out and peered inside. There were five neat bundles of fifty pound notes, each containing five thousand pounds. He took them all back into the bathroom and hid them behind the bath panel. He was now looking for an address book. There was nothing else of interest in the kitchen. He tried the bedroom. Harvey had run to form so far. He hoped to find something in his sock drawer, but there was nothing, except for three pornographic DVDs. He tipped up the mattress, but there was nothing underneath.

Dillon suddenly froze. He heard a key in the front door lock. He switched off his torch and opened the bedroom door a fraction. There was a moment's hesitation. That would be Harvey wondering why the second deadlock was open. His subconscious would be throwing out alarm signals and his conscious would be allaying the fears. He'd open the door, turn on the light, and look around. Then what? Search the flat maybe.

The front door opened and the light turned on. There was another moment's pause. Then another door, this time in the living room; the loud click of a switch being turned on - most likely the electric wall heater that Dillon had spotted while he was searching there. The door to the kitchen was closed. It had been open. He probably never closed it. It was exasperating how slowly Harvey's thought process worked. What was the worst thing that could happen? The money - he was thinking about the money. He'd open the door cautiously. Turn on the light. He'd open the fridge.

The doorbell started to ring insistently - urgently. It stopped for a moment before starting to ring again. It must be something urgent. Harvey probably half turned and then his subconscious threw up the questions. If someone was in the flat, that might be the warning signal from an accomplice downstairs on the road. The bell stopped ringing. Harvey opened the kitchen door. He turned on the light. Dillon moved behind the bedroom door. Harvey looked in the bathroom. He approached the bedroom cautiously. There was only one place someone could be hiding now.

Dillon flattened himself against the wall and braced himself. The door opened slowly. He could see Harvey's shadow on the opposite wall. He was turning on the light.

Dillon propelled the door away from him with as much force as he could muster. He heard Harvey grunt as the wind was knocked out of him as it slammed into his shoulder. A moment earlier and it might have smashed his hand into the door jamb. Dillon grabbed hold of the door once again, brought it back and slammed it close again on Harvey's advancing figure. There was the sound of wood slamming into flesh and bone as Harvey took the full force again. A grunt, then a short sharp kick, and the wood splintered as the hinges gave way and the door was projected into the room and down onto the floor with an enormous crash.

He was tougher than Dillon had expected and most likely trained in Karate or kick-boxing. Dillon felt the adrenalin surging through his body, his heart pumping at full throttle and then a deep stirring in his subconscious. He closed his eyes for a fraction of a second, and when he opened them - everything was black and white and he knew what he had to do. Dillon stood back and reminded himself that he was dealing with a corrupt police officer. This one would not be pulling his punches. He didn't waste time; dropped down low on one foot, half turned and snapped his left leg forward as he came back up. A classic Karate kick that should have made heavy contact with Harvey's stomach, but he managed to react quickly and absorbed some of the blow with blocks using his forearms. Dillon broke the grip on his ankle and stepped back as Harvey's momentum brought him fully into the darkened room. He stood in the gloom for a brief second, backlit by the hallway light, perhaps wondering if there were two intruders. He stood for a fraction of a second too long. Dillon took the initiative. He drove his boot hard down the front of Harvey's shin and as the policeman's head dropped Dillon delivered an uppercut with all the strength he had. Harvey doubled up. Dillon shouldered him backwards out of the bedroom on to the floor. Harvey covered his face with his hands. There was a trickle of blood between his fingers.

Dillon's wrist was numb. He wondered if he had broken a bone in his hand when he'd punched Harvey's jaw. He nudged Harvey warily with the toe of his leather dealer's boot. There might still be some fight left in him. "Come along DC Harvey.

Let's be having you in the living room"

Harvey groaned. He moved his hands painfully from his face and tried to focus on Dillon for the first time. He was surprised to be called by his name and rank. "Who the fuck, are you?" He asked, in a nasal voice.

"Get up, and make it snappy asshole." Dillon ordered, kicking him in the back.

Harvey tried getting to his feet. He made it to his knees before saying. "You're making a massive mistake."

"Really?" Dillon spoke coldly, kicking him again, so he was not in any doubt about the intention towards him.

Harvey let out a gasp, and made a concerted effort to stand, finally balanced unsteadily on his feet, and shuffled along the hall to the living room. Dillon pushed him into a chair. At the same time there was a knock at the door.

"Who is it?" asked Dillon.

"Is that you, JD?"

Dillon recognised the voice of Jack Buchanan from the Special Projects department at Ferran & Cardini International, and opened the door. He'd forgotten about the tracking device inside his smart phone.

"What are you doing here?" Harvey asked.

"Oh, let me think now. Yes, I'm illegally searching your skanky abode for anything incriminating."

"Well you have made one big fucking mistake breaking in here," snuffled Harvey undaunted.

"I don't think so you nasty little scuzzbucket," said Dillon. "I come with impunity issued at the highest echelon of Government."

"Fuck off," said Harvey. "You won't find anything to incriminate me around this dump. I only use this place as somewhere to crash."

"Well, I'm afraid your life is about to take a turn for the worst. It's not looking good, DC Harvey. You're taking bribes from Maximilian Kane; you've aided and abetted a kidnap, and that's just for starters. So I'm sure we can tie you into the drug smuggling rap as well."

"What?" Harvey said. He was holding a dirty

handkerchief to his bloodied nose. His eyes were beginning to swell from Dillon's punch. "You've got nothing on me."

"Cuff him, Jack," said Dillon. He walked into the bathroom and retrieved the twenty-five thousand he'd previously removed from the freezer compartment. "I found this little bundle of pocket-change earlier." He stared at Harvey, now holding the bloodied handkerchief in both hands.

"Yeah - so you found my life's savings."

"I don't think so. You're a bent copper and this is dirty money from Max Kane."

"You must be joking, Dillon. You're so fucking wrong, it's wrong. Yeah, I did speak with Kane and Nash. They both made me propositions. It was part of my brief to keep them on the hook because he's a known associate of two very dangerous suspects."

"I'm not interested in you or the complexity of your predicament. I want to know where Razor might be holding someone he's kidnapped."

"I wouldn't know."

"How about Kane - how do you contact him?"

"I met him once in a pub."

"Where does he live?"

"I don't know."

"Let's see if your memory comes back later. Jack, take DC Harvey to the lockup. I'll take the money to LJ for safe keeping. When you've got DC Harvey settled in, ensure that he is introduced to the drug and then top-up the dose every hour."

Harvey's eyes widened in horror, "What do mean drugs, and what the fuck are you going to do with me?"

Dillon had started to walk away. Stopped - and then turned to face Harvey. "We're going to pump you full of heroin and then make sure you're given a top-up every hour for, say, twenty-four hours. Oh, don't worry. We don't want you dead - just on the way to being addicted. Our doctors have calculated the exact dosage that we should be administering to you based on your height, weight and age. After which you will be well and truly on your way to becoming reliant on it. Then my colleague will stop giving you the drug. After six to twelve hours your body will start withdrawing. This will make you crave for more heroin hits. But, unfortunately for you; there will be no hit until you've answered the questions I want answers to. And believe me, at this stage in the proceeding you will sing like a canary. If you decide not to, then within a few more hours you'll be shaking uncontrollably, vomiting and experiencing stomach cramps and diarrhoea. You will literally be begging for more of the evil shit to be pumped into your veins, just to stop the pain racking through your head and body."

"You crazy bastard - you wouldn't dare."

"You don't know him, then, do you?" Jack said casually from where he was standing near to the window. "Because, if you did, you'd realise that he will not have any problem doing exactly what he's just described to you." He smiled.

Harvey looked at Dillon, who said. "When you're done with him Jack, hand him back to his own people at the Met. They might like to investigate his drug habit that will lead them to the root cause of his lack of integrity. Now, I'm going back to the office to get one or two things, and then I'll be going back to Dorset."

Jack grabbed the chain of the handcuffs and pulled Harvey to his feet. Harvey shook his head. "I wouldn't want to be in your shoes," he said.

* * *

Jasper Nash glanced down at his watch, stood up and walked out of the living room. He stopped at the door and said, "I'm going for a walk and to make a phone call to Kane." He was not hanging around to wait for Dillon to return from London and have him arrested by his pals at MI5.

"I'll come with you," said Inger.

Jasper shrugged.

She followed him around the block to the Haven Hotel. He went across to the seafront alone and sat on one of the benches. Jasper made the phone call to Kane, got the voicemail and left a message for him to ring back. After ten minutes he gave up waiting and walked back to the hotel entrance and joined Inger. They went inside and ordered two Jack Daniel's on ice. "Kane will call me. He can't afford to lose what I'm holding."

"What is it?" Inger asked.

She looked at him, but he didn't look at her. He was preoccupied, and she knew better than to interrogate him. She sensed his dilemma. He would talk when he was ready. In the meantime her job was to make him talk about anything to gain his trust. The art of interrogation was to create a bond between interviewer and suspect. Dialogue had to be maintained. It didn't matter who asked questions or who gave answers because the process created the illusion of a relationship.

Inger floundered for subjects to talk about. She tried to remember what she had read in Nash's file. Nothing came to mind; only that he had been in prison.

"What was it like in the Chinese prison?" She asked.

He didn't reply immediately. She listened to other people around them talking and laughing, thinking that he had ignored the question, and then he began speaking. "If you want the honest truth - it was bloody horrific. Everyone tells you that prison is bad. But a Chinese prison is hell on earth. You don't believe it at first; you think that because you're a foreign national they will treat you with at least a small degree of leniency. Not likely. That thought was beaten out of me every day for the first two weeks by the guards, who have nothing but contempt, who dealt out the beatings with an unhealthy fervour. You're cut off from everything. Worse than that, you're cut off from civilisation and reduced to the state of an animal." He hesitated. "I won't ever do time again, I'd sooner be dead."

Inger wondered if he realised that he would receive a custodial sentence, whatever the outcome of this assignment.

"I think you're doing the right thing talking to Dillon. And, for what it's worth, I think you've been betrayed by your friends," she tried to reassure him.

He ignored her. "The best way to protect yourself in prison is to let people think you're going mad. That way, they leave you in peace. That way, you gain some privacy. I spent a week walking up and down an imaginary line without speaking a word. Killing time - thinking - contemplating! Then

I spent the next week slapping the ground with the palm of my right hand, pretending to hear voices under the soft earth. The other prisoners treated insanity like a contagious disease. After you've been in a Chinese prison like that, you don't believe in humanity or morality any more. Some people deal in arms to make money. Those people aren't in prison. Compared to them the prisoners were fairly decent really." He paused for a moment. "In this country what percentage of the population has a criminal record?" Nash asked out of the blue.

"I don't know."

"Then take a guess," he said, irritably. "Driving offences don't count," he added.

"This is purely a guess, say fifteen percent?"

"No. Thirty-three percent of men and nine percent of women are convicted criminals in the UK. That equates to one-in-three men and one-in-eleven women. These people are; physically and mentally abusing their spouse or partner, burgling homes, robbing banks, and much worse. They're all candidates for corporal punishment. They're all polluting the planet and our societies and some of them are making vast sums of money. The laugh is that forty-two percent of the great British public is a convicted criminal. And another thirty percent is getting away with it but should be convicted."

Inger didn't get the point of what he was saying. "You shouldn't be so bitter." She said.

"Oh, I'm not bitter. I'm not even pretending I'm a saint. I wheel and deal a highly addictive drug that's been around for centuries. When it's abused - it does kill people. These people all know the risks, and if it wasn't cocaine they were sticking their snouts in, it would be something else."

This was the moment thought Inger. This was the moment when the suspect unburdened himself and started to let things out. At moments like this people blurted things they hadn't intended, or remembered things they thought they had forgotten. The key was to keep them talking.

"Whilst I cannot and do not condone the peddling of cocaine, there is also a side of me that has no sympathy for the idiots who use it either. And, at the end of the day, if there is demand, then someone has to supply." Inger said, cajoling him into trusting her. He looked at her for a second, surprised. She had evidently got his attention and now his curiosity was getting hold as well. "I am Scandinavian, we think much differently to you British, more liberal and lateral thinking towards many areas of life."

"I was never involved in anything where people were hurt. We didn't go around breaking legs," he replied defensively.

"Yes, I understand. But now the Russian, Aleksey is dead, and his girlfriend Natalya. She was an innocent." Nash didn't respond. Inger continued. "Somewhere, sometimes there is always some person who is being hurt in this business. Maybe it is the small farmer in Peru or Colombia, where life is cheap. This is the problem. You are part of this system. You are intrinsically responsible."

"OK! I know I'm guilty," retorted Nash angrily. "But we are all guilty of something by association."

"We can make a choice," said Inger. She wondered if she was pressing him too hard in her search for the information she sought.

"You're missing the point," said Nash. "It's the intention which is important. You buy cheap clothing from well-known high street brand names, but you don't want the little children in India, Pakistan and China being exploited and paid virtually nothing to produce them."

"So you think you have a morality because you do not deal in heroin?" Inger said. Nash didn't reply. She had a flash of insight. "Is it this which is causing the problem? Kane is dealing in heroin?"

"Yes," said Jasper Nash, bitterly.

"And now you've hidden it?"

"Yes."

Inger remained silent for a moment, sipping her drink and thinking; there was something strangely attractive about him. Stupid but attractive, it was his criminal naivety, and like so many he had no idea of the consequences of his actions. He believed that fundamentally he was a good person, and never saw the contradiction in his life. But, she knew what he needed

- encouragement and reassurance. "So you've told me what it is. But you haven't mentioned where it is. You know that by helping Dillon with this drug thing, that you'll be free."

"If I help him then I will be killed."

"Why? He will protect you. Dillon has access to all manner of resources. Safe-houses being just one of them!"

"You know that's not true. If I give evidence against Kane and the others, someone will put a bullet in my head. Or, if they don't I'll go to prison too and with certainty be murdered on the inside. Whatever you think Dillon can do - he can't. The British establishment does not do deals with the likes of me."

"I think you should trust Dillon," said Inger.

"Listen luv, I don't trust anyone."

"What about your girlfriend, Martha? You do not trust her either?"

"Love is not trust. Love makes you vulnerable. Love is a state of fear."

Inger looked at him sharply. He actually believed what he was saying. She was shocked. She hoped never to enter a world like that. She wondered what had happened to him in the past to make him feel like that. "So what will you do about Martha?" She saw his face harden.

"I can't turn the clock back. I know that. But I'm going to salvage what I can. Make amends for her sake. Max has betrayed me. So I'm going to betray him. That's what I'm going to do for Martha. I'm going to tell you all about Maximilian Kane. Let's not have dinner for the moment. Let's have another drink here in the bar." He turned in his seat and caught the attention of a waiter and ordered two double shots of Jack Daniel's. "I'm going to tell you a story. And you can switch on that voice recorder you always carry around with you, and record what I'm about to say."

For the next three hours over dinner, Inger listened to stories about smuggling. She learned how vast sums of money were moved from country to country in order to launder it. She was told of where the money was banked over the years. He included the account numbers in Switzerland, Belize and the Cayman Islands. Nash, she soon discovered, had a photographic memory for dates and numbers. People who committed nothing to paper remembered the finest details. Jasper concentrated on the banking. He told her about the people involved with Kane. He was hitting him where it would really hurt. Without the money Kane would be nothing. Money always left a trail; and in the end people had to explain where it had come from. Jasper had just opened the prison-cell door for Kane.

When Jasper Nash had finished unburdening himself, he stood up from the table and without excusing himself left, leaving Inger no opportunity to stop him.

"Please telephone me tomorrow," she said turning off the voice recorder.

He stopped, turned and looked at her, and said. "Of course, your part of the deal is to find Martha."

* * *

It was nearly one in the morning before Dillon returned to the house on the Sandbanks peninsula He went through to the kitchen and poured himself a single malt whisky over ice. Went into the living room and discovered Inger asleep on one of the huge sofas. He placed the whisky tumbler on the low glass table and went off to find a blanket to drape over her. By the time he had returned, she had woken and looked round as he came through from the hall.

"Sorry if I woke you, I went to find a blanket," Dillon said, sitting down in the chair opposite her. "Is Nash in bed?"

"He's gone. He went after dinner." Inger said apologetically.

Dillon was irritated by this revelation of incompetence. He had hoped that a highly qualified and experienced Interpol case officer would have been able to keep him at the house for thirty-six hours. However, his irritation vaporised when he heard that Nash had given her details, and allowed Inger to record their conversation, regarding to Kane's banking operations and the name of his banker. He told her to keep her mobile phone close at all times and to have one ear open to its ringtone, even when she was asleep. Feeling exhausted, he needed to rest, sitting down in the reclining chair by the window. He leaned back and immediately felt more relaxed, and slept in the chair for five hours.

When he finally woke, it was barely light outside; a small group of large herring gulls were making mayhem near to the rear windows. He got up and padded barefoot across the heated travertine tiled floor. Fixed an espresso coffee from the machine and went back to the sofa, Inger had gone to bed, and slumping down on it booted up his tablet computer. It was six-thirty in the morning. The early hours were always the best, quiet, no one around to make any noise. Dillon always found that this time of the day was the most productive. In the early hours the broadband response time was quickest because no one else was blocking up the Internet. He'd have done a day's work by eight o'clock. After that time his phone would start to ring and people wanted his attention, they wanted his experience, they wanted him to sort out their problems. He began by accessing the main servers at Ferran & Cardini International, that would re-route him through to the Police National Computer and allow him to familiarise himself with Harvey's investigation into Kane, Razor and Cracker. It didn't look like it would be too difficult to pick up the thread of the trail; but what he wanted to know was what Harvey had failed to log on to the computer.

He would send a couple of experienced field officers to search Razor and Cracker's homes in London. If the properties were empty, access would be gained and they would be gone through with a fine-tooth comb. They would be in and out in less than eight minutes, without anyone seeing them or any suspicions being aroused by any of the neighbours.

He had asked Vince to run a check on Kane's mobile phone; this had revealed it had been registered by a man called, Milton Haramhat, and the pay-as-you-go tariff topped-up by the same person using a credit card. Vince had then hacked into the phone company's main server with relative ease, and accessed all of Kane's phone records for the last five days, including; SMS messages, data, images, and voicemail messages. Dillon now wanted the address of Mr Milton Haramhat, and for that; the big Australian would have to hack into the bank's computer system. This would be an insanely and highly fortified citadel; designed to keep out the world's most dangerous hackers and cyber terrorists.

Vince arrived back at the house shortly after nine that morning. As he walked through in to the kitchen, he spotted the note that Dillon had left for him on the granite worktop.

Dillon was standing with his back to him looking at the fifty inch plasma screen in front of him. "How did it go with Harvey?"

"He's a stubborn little fucker, that one." Vince said with exasperation.

"Did they manage to get anything out of him?" Dillon asked.

"No. They've been injecting him with a combination of barbiturates and amphetamines for the last twenty-four hours. He should've sung like a songbird on the downward spiral. But, no matter how long he was left in a state of depression, he stayed schtum. Which was very frustrating for the Doc, who by the way did a great job? He made the guy actually think that we were injecting him with heroin. What a jerk."

"What are they doing with him now?" Dillon typed a command into his tablet keyboard and text appeared on the large screen.

"LJ has arranged for him to be brought back to Bournemouth. When the police find him he'll be stoned out of his brains, carrying a semi-automatic sidearm, and in an area frequented by prostitutes and druggies. The report of an armed man will be put through to the local nick anonymously." Vince said.

"That's good, and very creative. I want him well out of the way, locked up so he can't foul up this assignment any more than he has already."

"Well, he won't get in the way or be able to tip off Kane where he's going. That's if he doesn't get himself shot by the SO19 guys first." Vince said with satisfaction.

"Right - disappointing that he didn't tell us anything, though." Dillon guessed that Vince was wondering what was going to happen now with finding Nash's girlfriend.

"So, what do we do about finding the girl?"

"Well, Nash is one hundred present sure that she is being held somewhere by Razor and Cracker, and enquiries have shown this to be correct. A couple of rough looking men answering their descriptions were seen helping Martha Hamilton into a car. That coupled with Nash disappearing, leads me to believe things are not as they should be in Kane's camp."

"Vince nodded. "Sounds like a lot of hearsay and supposition, if you ask me, mate."

"What do you mean?"

"Well, it's not as if there's much in the way of hard facts to base our actions on."

"Have you never heard of deduction," commented Dillon nonchalantly.

Vince grunted, "Where is Inger now?" He asked.

"She's running errands for me," Dillon lied.

"Oh. So what's the plan?"

"We are going to need two of the surveillance teams back down here as soon as we locate Razor. You organise them and put them on stand-by. After you've done that, have a look through the Kane file again and see if you can come up with anything we might have overlooked before. After all, Kane is not infallible, he must slip-up sometimes."

"OK." Vince sounded sceptical. He knew that Dillon was the best person to catch Kane and Nash. But there was more to this assignment than had been divulged by Dunstan Havelock. "What are your plans now?" Vince asked, as Dillon grabbed his jacket from the back of the chair.

"I've got a couple of meetings," replied Dillon enigmatically, leaving the room. He had an unofficial meeting with Dunstan Havelock at the Chewton Glen hotel, to report on the progress of the Nash investigation.

* * *

Dillon finally returned home at three o'clock that afternoon. He was exhausted. When he opened the door to the luxury house he couldn't tell if any of the others were there or not. Inger was sitting on one of the sofas working at her laptop. Her long legs suddenly reminded him how long it had been since he'd been close to a beautiful woman. How inappropriate to think about that now, he thought. He looked around and realised that she was alone. "Is Vince around?"

Inger closed the laptop "No. Mr Levenson-Jones recalled him back to London. Some sort of crisis with the main server at Docklands."

"Has Nash called?" He asked.

"Yes. He's called two times and on both occasions has asked if you have found Martha yet."

"What did you tell him?"

"I told him you were making progress. He told me to tell you that time is running out and he will call again."

"How did he sound?"

"He sounded angry and sort of nervous at the same time, if that makes sense."

"The next time he calls tell him I want to see him. Tell him I have something to say to him."

Dillon went upstairs to his bedroom, showered and shaved. He put on a crisp white shirt to compliment his dark navy blue slim-fit suit and left to meet a case officer from MI5 who might be able to supply crucial information about Jasper Nash.

Spooks weren't Dillon's favourite people; he'd had his fair share of run-ins with MI5 over the years, and they had very rarely done him any favours. He arrived early at the main gate of the Special Boat Service barracks. An armed guard thoroughly searched the Porsche and then him before checking him in. Dillon was then given directions to the officer's mess. Dillon was kept waiting for twenty minutes before he was shown into a vacant conference room.

With unconcealed dislike, Clive Powell continued writing and looked up at Dillon and pointed at a vacant chair with his pen. Dillon pulled it close to the desk and sat down.

"I must make it clear to you, Mr Dillon, before we begin this brief interview, that it is not the policy of MI5 to divulge any information concerning an on-going investigation.

The only reason that I'm down here in Dorset and talking to you is because of an instruction from the Home Secretary."

"Interesting - firstly, I do not like to be kept waiting, especially when the British tax-payer is footing the very large bill, Clive." said Dillon irritably looking at his watch. He didn't have the time or the inclination to waste, bandying around with this idiot. "I will make one thing clear from the start. I am a senior field officer with Ferran & Cardini International. We take our instructions from, and answer to, one office and one person only. The Prime Minister... I am investigating a matter of national security and I expect full co-operation. I believe you have a file on Jasper Nash and his recent criminal activities. Furthermore, I want to know every detail about those individuals he corresponds with. Do I make myself clear, Clive?" He deliberately used the spooks Christian name for the second time; the over-familiarity was making him very uncomfortable.

There was a ponderous silence. Dillon glared. The spook absorbed the threats with horror. He struggled to control his agitation at Dillon's assertiveness and obvious ability to out rank him on all levels.

Dillon continued. "I would also remind you that refusing to assist me in this investigation will result in you being suspended from active duty."

The spook's greasy complexion had turned decidedly sweaty. He took out a handkerchief and mopped his forehead.

"I'm sorry," he said finally. "I didn't realise how much clout you guys have. Let me assure you I checked Nash's file as soon as I was told to meet with you. I can only say that all of the information you require is in the file."

This last sentence made Dillon immediately suspicious. Something about this file made Clive Powell nervous.

"Have you met Jasper Nash?"

"No. I've only ever seen interview footage of him."

"What about Maximilian Kane?"

"No. I'd remember if I'd met anyone with such a flamboyant name."

The intelligence officer shuffled through the file in front of him and was about to place it inside his briefcase, but Dillon interrupted him by stretching out for the papers. The file was grudgingly passed across the table without question. Dillon looked through the papers quickly.

"I want all of this information sent in digital file format to the Ferran & Cardini secure server in Docklands." His tone was clipped. He pushed the file back to Clive Powell, holding his gaze as he did so.

"I'll see that it is carried out as soon as possible."

"Make the call. Have it sent by the time I leave this room." Dillon recommended. The spook hurried out of the room to make the call. He couldn't be too helpful.

One of the papers made reference to Max Kane and a bank account that had been opened twelve years previously in the name of Mark Cane. A credit card had been issued seven years ago. Two years ago Mark Cane had apparently moved out of the UK and requested that no mail be forwarded until he provided a permanent address of residence.

Dillon flicked through more of the pages and came across twenty-four bank statements relating to the Mark Cane account, which he took a close look at. He assumed that they should have been forwarded had the bank had a forwarding address. Highly irregular practice and the bank manager would have known this. But the interesting thing was that whoever it was who had set the account up, knew the weakness of the system and how to play it to their advantage.

"Correct me if I'm wrong or being particularly stupid. But why is there information relating to Max Kane in the Jasper Nash file?"

Dillon allowed this to sink in before he continued.

"What is Max Kane to MI5?"

"I'm afraid, Mr Dillon. That is classified."

"Oh, classified. Well that's disappointing. Now Clive, I'm not a gambling man, but I'll wager that my security clearance out-ranks yours by at least ten-fold. You'd better call your superior officer and ask him to check for you. Because Clive, I want to know, what you know, about Max Kane."

Begrudgingly Powell pushed back his chair and stood up. "Please wait here, I'll go and make the call to London."

Dillon leaned back on his chair and waited for the spook to return. All he wanted was an address for Kane. Of course, Kane was too smart for that.

Soon Powell would return with a sheepish look on his face and the digital key that would give authorisation to access the information on Kane. Dillon made a mental note to contact an acquaintance in the Human Resource department at MI5. He was sure that Powell would benefit greatly from two weeks training with the SAS.

* * *

The rain was relentless. Kane spent a tiresome day making phone calls, attending to the complexities of his business affairs. He had a little blue book half filled with mobile and land line telephone numbers and the locations of all of the contacts and street dealers he had built up over many years. They were spread across the south coast, throughout the Home Counties, all over London and throughout Europe. Kane flicked through the pages until he'd found the number he wanted. Made the call and after confirming the first, last and third letter of a password. He was told that the down payment for the consignment Jasper held was safe in a Swiss bank account.

There were clouds on the horizon though. Harvey's usefulness had been short-lived. Kane heard he had been arrested, and wondered how Dillon had made the connection so quickly. Harvey would be alright, so long as he didn't talk. Harvey would be more aware than most of the dangers of incriminating himself. The voice on the phone assured Kane that the trail ended there. Razor would become the next problem, but he still had a job to do.

Kane looked at his watch. It was ten minutes to seven. At any moment a call would come through to his mobile phone. He was becoming accustomed to the reminders every three hours, though he'd finally turned off the sound. He scrolled through the last few text messages. He relished the thought of Jasper making those pathetic calls in the hope of having Martha returned unharmed. To hell with Jasper - he deserved to suffer for the problems he was causing. Although he was being careful to remain concealed, and cleverly ensuring that his contacts didn't spot him and immediately report back of his whereabouts. Unfortunately Jasper was too cunning for that; but not cunning enough. Now, Jasper would be getting desperate to make a deal for Martha's release.

The phone vibrated and Kane read the incoming number on the screen. It was Jasper. He remained seated enjoying the luxury and warmth of the hotel. He was dressed for dinner wearing handmade Italian brown leather shoes that had cost a thousand pounds, and a suit made for him by his tailor in Hong Kong. He looked through the window at the foul weather outside. The England he had been born to and loved, had long since gone along with everything sane. If things went well he would be leaving this dustbin of a land for ever, within the week.

"Good evening Jasper," Max Kane said, when he answered the phone.

"Hello Max." He heard Kane's unusually resigned voice at the other end of the line.

"I'm sorry to have been so long coming back to you. They've only just contacted me."

"Is Martha OK?"

"Oh yes," said Kane. He was going to keep this conversation short. He wasn't going to run the risk of the call being triangulated and traced. Maybe Jasper had recruited someone to his camp. "I've arranged for you to meet with Razor tomorrow, at one o'clock at the Castleman Hotel and restaurant."

"Where's that?"

"A place called Chettle village, which is a small hamlet in North Dorset. You'll find it a bit off the beaten track, but worth the drive out because the food is most agreeable. Have you got that? Don't forget that Razor holds the cards. You speak with him. You do exactly what he says then you can go back to playing happy families with Martha."

"I want guarantees. You release Martha - before I meet him."

"Oh come now, Jasper. You know as well as I, there are

no guarantees in this game." He had an afterthought.

"Well, there is one thing for certain, but I hardly need mention it. Razor was resolute that you turn up alone. Martha's good health depends on it." Kane terminated the call, got up and walked out of the hotel smartly.

The duration of the call was only 30 seconds, but it still made him nervous with all the smart software around these days. He reassured himself with the thought that Jasper would be a fool to make a deal with the police. He'd be lucky to escape a conviction even if he tried turning Queen's evidence. Anyway, he'd be risking Martha's life.

Jasper didn't seem to realise he already had a guarantee, because there was still the money from the sale of the cocaine consignment to hand over. He had become such a suspicious unappreciative bastard. Their business partnership was definitely over. Maybe he could find out who was marketing for Jasper. There weren't that many dealers, four or five at most, who could handle the distribution of a large consignment in such a short time period. There was O'Rourke in Dublin, but he had supposedly retired. Maybe it was Jack Stone in Brighton. Then again it could be the Stanislav the Russian in London or Kamal in Manchester. That left Jason Villiers - yes, Jason. He was the most likely. It wouldn't be too hard to check them out. He'd make a few calls in the morning. Then Jasper's guarantee would expire. Now that was an interesting proposition.

When Kane made it back to his own apartment, he poured himself a stiff drink, took off his damp clothes and stepped into a steaming hot shower, before changing into something casual. He slumped down into one of the easy chairs and sipped the brandy. The effect was instantly warming. He had one more phone call to make. He rang the agency in Bournemouth. He'd used them before. He gave them the credit card number. After he put down the phone he waited impatiently for the doorbell to ring.

He felt aggrieved. It had been like this throughout his life. Just when he thought he was about to realise his ambitions they were ripped away from him. Now Jasper had betrayed him. After all, they'd been friends since their university days.

He'd given Jasper every chance. He'd shared the good times with him, not to mention the bad times. Jasper would have been nothing without him. There was no reason why he should suddenly become so unreasonable. Even if he had a moral stance he had a duty to be loyal. It wasn't a question of money. That was always negotiable. No. Jasper had harboured resentment all these years, and was proving he wasn't trustworthy. It probably had something to do with the prison sentence in Hong Kong as well. Some people just couldn't hack doing time. Something cracked inside them. Well, Jasper would still be rotting in that Chinese prison if wasn't for him. He deserved some thanks for getting him released, at the very least. It would probably have been different if Jasper had gone to a public school. He might have learned loyalty and self-reliance. Now Jasper was going to learn the hard way. Jasper had fucked up big time, a deal which would have been worth around fifty million a year.

Kane walked into the bedroom and tidied it. It didn't need much attention. He was punctiliously finicky anyway. He went back into the kitchen. It was a matter of time now. Things were now under control. Razor and Cracker would ensure that Jasper did exactly what he was told. Abducting Martha was an extreme measure but it had produced the desired effect and result. Jasper was now co-operating.

Life had always been struggle - a battle. He hadn't seen his parents for twenty-seven years. This was his father's fault. He had always bullied him and made him feel worthless and insignificant. Then there was his mother's ultimate betrayal. She had found him in his bedroom, his trousers and pants around his ankles sitting on the edge of the single bed with his erect penis in his hand, masturbating. He was eighteen years old with hormones running riot through his body. She just stood in the doorway, a look of disdain across her hard bony face. She didn't say a word; she simply bent down and seized the pornographic magazine lying on the bed beside him. Her appearance in the doorway and quick intake of breath had startled him. It was her actions after leaving his room. She betrayed him. She went and told his father who immediately started to humiliate and ridicule him. Laughed at him and called him all manner of things. What ignorant individuals they both were. He had left home shortly after for university. From that point on, Kane had been alone. If he hadn't won the scholarship to university he would never have met Jasper, and they would never have embarked on their smuggling venture. He would never have been able to afford his ocean going yacht that enabled them to bring dope over from Amsterdam to various points around the UK. His father had been willing to give evidence against him when the young girl drowned herself after she had been on his boat drinking cocktails. It was only fortunate that he had friends who were well connected that the whole affair had been swept under the carpet. He was glad he had fucked Dillon's girlfriend before she had drowned.

The doorbell rang. He hoped they'd sent someone good.

Kane opened the door. The girl was no more than twenty, attractive and had a look of innocence about her. They seemed to come young these days. Uncannily, this one looked a little like the girl who had drowned. He closed the door and took her coat. He glanced down at the black stocking covering her slender legs. At least she knew how to dress. Well, she had no idea what he was going to do to her. She was going to do something for him she had never dreamed about. She was going to learn something about herself, and the power of money. Kane felt himself getting hard with the thought.

"We'll have the Champagne in the bedroom," he said.

The young call-girl smiled. He didn't care for her teeth, but then he wouldn't be looking at them.

"How do you feel about unconventional sex?" he said, with a sly look.

The girl sipped her Champagne, eyeing him carefully.

"Do you like water-sports, for instance?" he added.

The girl looked at him. "I'll take a leak on you if you want, but it'll cost you extra. And I definitely don't like pain of any sort." She said brashly.

"Of course," replied Kane. He picked up his wallet and opened it in front of her. He caught the look on her face as she gawped at the large wad of fifty pound notes inside. He was going to enjoy the negotiations.

There were plenty of ways to kill time, but this was definitely one of the best. He switched off his mobile phone. He didn't want any interruptions.

* * *

Jason Villiers gently raised his wife's slumped arm from his chest and eased himself out of bed at three-thirty in the morning. She stirred, turned over and continued dreaming. Jason pulled the duvet up over her shoulders. He slipped on his dressing gown and padded down the landing to the family bathroom. He locked the heavy oak door behind him. He didn't want to be disturbed, even at this ungodly hour. He went to the far side of the spacious room and stood facing the large floor to ceiling ornate gilded antique mirror. He leaned forward and after ensuring that he was in the right position, pressed one of the mouldings on the frame. There was a faint click; he pulled on the mirror and that entire section of the panelled wall glided forward silently to reveal a secret room. He had designed this eight by six foot niche when he restored the manor house. No one, not even his wife, knew about it. He entered the small room and lifted a canvas bag off the floor on to a work bench. He wasted no time in opening the bag, pulling out large bundles of money in denominations of twenty and fifty pound notes. He lifted a metal tambour roller shutter door to expose a state-of-the-art electronic money counting machine, and went straight to work.

Things were going well. Good cocaine always sold. He'd have the lot gone by the end of the weekend. It had been cut with a few other dubious substances and the weight doubled before hitting the streets. His instruction to the dealers had been simple - only sell at premium prices. There hadn't been a murmur, nor of any competitive gear in circulation and he had made an absolute killing. Jasper had been truthful about that aspect of the deal.

There should be six hundred thousand pounds in the bag. Give or take a few quid. The Manchester boys certainly knew how to shift the gear quickly; they'd sold out within eight hours of hitting the streets, clubs and pubs. A motorcycle courier had arrived at one of his restaurants in Dorset four hours after, with the canvas bag. Now he awaited the arrival of the London bag, and those from Glasgow, Newcastle, Birmingham, Bristol and Cardiff. Each bag would contain a similar amount of cash. He fed the notes into the machine. It whirred away. By six-fifteen he had counted all the money. It was fifty pounds short. A single fake note had been passed over to one of the distributors. He carefully put rubber bands around the now organised bundles and placed them in one of the empty wooden wine cases stacked at one end of the room. He had everything organised and ready for when the remaining bags arrived later that day. He had ensured that each of the bags was delivered to a different restaurant that he owned. He enjoyed making, and counting, money...

He left the tiny room and went back out in to the family bathroom, pushed the moulding again and the wall panel moved silently back into place, only a click could be heard as the lock engaged.

He went downstairs to the kitchen. It was still early and everyone was still asleep. He washed his hands, dirty stuff, money. He congratulated himself on how well he did business. He operated through some of the best dealers and that was proved when the money came back so efficiently and precisely. These days he wouldn't take on new clients. The streets were more dangerous than ever before with stories of distributors being robbed of their gear, and even murdered if they wouldn't give up the drugs or the proceeds. It was a tough dog-eat-dog world out there and far too many people were willing to kill to get ahead. The thought of the eastern European gangs sent a shudder through him.

He made a pot of tea, and returned to the bedroom. He woke his wife with a kiss on the cheek, then slipped into bed beside her and snuggled against her warm body. He liked his routines.

At eight forty-five Jason backed his ten year old Mercedes estate out of the double garage. He looked at his wife's brand new BMW 6 series convertible, and smiled. He liked her to have the best in life. It made him feel good. He watched the garage door close automatically. He did a three-point turn in the driveway and left for work.

He scowled when he saw the over-coated figure standing in front of his high wrought iron gates. His heart quickened when he recognised who it was. He pressed the remote and the gates started to swing open. By the time he reached the entrance he was in a fury. He lowered the Mercedes side-window. "What the fuck do you want?" He spat at Kane.

"I need to have a quick chat with you," said Kane.

"Get in," ordered Jason. Kane obeyed. Jason turned out of his driveway and slipped into the rush hour traffic. He took a careful note of the cars in front of and behind him. He looked at Kane. "I don't want to see you anywhere near my property ever again, no matter how urgent or important you feel it might be. Do you understand?"

"What I have to say is very important," insisted Kane.

"I don't give a shit. My family is very important to me. You are a danger. Do you understand? You're a fucking liability, Kane."

"Of course I understand Jason. I was particularly vigilant, you know."

"I should damned well hope so. What do you want anyway?"

"Jasper has left the country. He's got something else he's working on. He told me to give you instructions for handing over the paperwork."

"Why didn't you meet me at the prearranged rendezvous?"

So, thought Kane smugly, Jason was handling the job.

"Because you wouldn't be meeting me, it would be the police or customs, or worse."

Jason looked grimly at the road ahead. He didn't like the sound of this. It was definitely the last time he worked with this lot.

Kane took out his wallet and passed Jason a business card. Jason glanced down at it and stuffed it in his shirt pocket. "You should ring Herr Leitner; he will tell you what arrangements have been put in place for the handover. He is a

Swiss banker and very old-school. Everything is above board. He will ask you for your name. This is Klaus Wolff. He'll know what it's about. He will arrange to have the paperwork collected from you."

Jason thought for a moment. His gut-feeling was telling him to point blank refuse. Something wasn't right. He didn't like changes to the plan. He liked meeting new people even less; but refusal would result in a more complicated arrangement, and meeting Kane again.

"No problem," he said.

"Has everything gone well?" asked Kane. He wanted to know how much Jason was retailing the gear for.

"Everything was fine," replied Jason curtly. He pulled the Mercedes over to the kerb, outside Bournemouth's main train station.

"I'm going to a meeting now," he lied. "You can catch he train back to Poole."

"OK," said Kane. "I'll see you later."

I don't think so, thought Jason. A few minutes later he pulled over. He didn't trust Kane. He dialled Jasper's mobile number. There was no reply - just the voicemail.

Chapter 16

It was Razor who should have been meeting Jasper Nash at the Castleman Arms hotel at one o'clock that day but he was proving to be unreliable. Cracker didn't know what was wrong with him. He was in a world of his own half the time. Whenever Cracker asked him what was wrong, he said he was rationalising; that was if he answered at all. He'd always been a weird one, and when this business was over he needed to sort himself out.

Razor got edgy and paranoid if he wasn't in control or wasn't being kept in the picture. He needed constant reassurance. He didn't want to meet Nash at some country hotel. But he didn't want to guard the woman either. Cracker had told him to let her go to the toilet whenever she wanted to, and to make sure she had food and water. But don't make any phone calls and keep well away from the windows. Do not answer the door.

"Yeah, yeah, yeah," said Razor. His eyes slowly shifted towards Cracker. For one brief moment they looked coherent; and then they glazed over and he lost all interest in the conversation.

"How long am I going to be stuck in this derelict dump, then?" Razor asked.

"For as long as it takes. That's how long." Cracker thought that Razor might be depressed. Cracker had been like that when his Grandmother had died; he'd been exactly the same until his doctor gave him some little white pills to perk him up.

"I'll call you later," said Cracker, cheerfully. "You look after her, and everything will be fine," Razor nodded.

Cracker took one last look at Razor. Razor smiled back at him wanly.

Cracker convinced himself that everything would be

alright. That was four hours ago.

Cracker picked up his mobile and called Razor to check everything was fine. The phone rang for a long time. Cracker prayed Razor hadn't fucked up. If Razor stayed calm and did absolutely nothing it would be just perfect.

The phone stopped ringing. There was no voice at the other end.

"Razor?" asked Cracker.

There was an inordinately long pause. "Yeah, what do you want?"

"You sure you're all right?"

"Yeah, I'm good."

"Good. I thought I'd just let you know we'll be finished this afternoon. Is the woman OK?"

"Yeah, she's fine," said Razor, and hung up.

Cracker had parked up in a country lay-by so he could check on his emails. There was one from his London solicitor. It looked like the private investor was coming across with the half a million pounds venture capital for the nightclub. That had been a nice little investment. He saved the message and smiled smugly to himself.

* * *

The mobile phone woke Dillon at six forty-five. He looked at the clock on the bedside table as he answered it. He had overslept, and he still felt exhausted.

"Jake Dillon?"

"Yeah, this is Dillon."

"This is Jasper Nash. Have you got any news for me?"

"We had no luck with Harvey. We're concentrating our efforts on looking for Martha."

"Well how about Razor and Cracker?"

"Sorry, but so far we've come up with nothing. They appear to have disappeared off the face of the planet."

"I'm afraid, Mr Dillon. Time has run out." He disconnected the call.

Dillon struggled out of bed; his torso ached from years of rough treatment, and pulled on his clothes. He guessed Nash was going to deal with Kane, and give him the consignment of Heroin in return for Martha. There was nothing he could do to stop it. If he knew where Razor was hiding, he would be able to crack open this element of the assignment and then have a clear run at Nash for his dirty dealings with the North Koreans. But if he moved to quickly, he could blow the whole assignment and then Nash and the others would get away free of prosecution on trumped-up technicalities.

He went down to the kitchen and made a pot of tea for Vince and Inger, and a double espresso from the machine for himself. He placed everything on a large tray and carried it into the living room. He then sent both of them a text to get up and meet him downstairs. Five minutes later they both padded barefoot into the living room and slumped down in the chairs opposite Dillon.

"Good morning. Forgive me for disturbing your dream time. Nash has contacted me." Dillon said, pouring the tea for them. "Inger, I'd like you to hang around the house today, just in case Nash turns up in person or calls the house land line."

Inger nodded, and curled up in the luxurious easy chair. He knew she was frustrated with the lack of activity, waiting for something to happen, waiting for that single lead that would evoke some sort of action.

"I'm sorry," he said. "It won't be for much longer." Dillon finished his espresso.

"What do you want me to do mate?"

"I want you to do what you do best. Watch and listen. You never know, Razor might be stupid or arrogant enough to make a call from his mobile and, if he should, I want you to locate his position."

"Oh, is that all. You don't want much, do you?" The big Australian smiled.

* * *

Dillon went up to the crow's-nest and sifted through some of the paper trail that Kane and Nash had left behind them so far, hoping to find something they might have overlooked before. So far nothing worthwhile had been found. He came across some of Kane's old credit card bills. The credit card had barely been used during the past six months, and most transactions had been carried out throughout Europe, probably because he had no Euros in his pocket. He had used the card in the odd restaurant, but never the same one twice; and the chances of a waiter remembering a customer were long - so another dead-end.

Vince appeared in the room. Dillon turned and immediately asked how the surveillance team watching Cracker was doing and would he go and join them for the rest of the day. "It's wasting my time, Jake, sending me out there," he complained.

"I want someone I can trust, you're the only one I truly trust," said Dillon. "I want someone who thinks logically and remains calm when the shooting starts, and who won't lose Cracker when he hits the road. I have a gut feeling that something is going to happen today."

"Yeah?" said Vince. "From the time he checked into his hotel yesterday afternoon, until he reappeared four hours later at seven o'clock the only thing he did was order a cheeseburger and fries from room-service, made a couple of calls from his mobile and watched television. Our software is having problems deciphering his mobile signal because he hardly ever uses it. Why don't you let me hack the MI5 main server and take a look at their brief for Jasper Nash?"

"I really want you out there today Vince," said Dillon firmly. "Trust me on this, Cracker is going to make a move today, and when he does I want you right on his tail."

"How do you know this for sure?"

"Mate, I just know, alright."

Vince's eyes narrowed. "I'll do it, but you've really got to open up a bit more. And another thing, are you banging the girl?"

"How long have we known each other and worked together?"

"Too long - that's how long, mate." Vince said laughing.

"Well, Inger and I are most definitely not doing any banging, as you put it. Not that it would be any of your business if we were."

"Yeah but it's what other people think that matters, mate."

"Vince - you should know me better than anyone else. I don't give a fuck what people think."

"Well, perhaps you should." Vince said peevishly. He turned on his heel. "I really hope I'm not wasting my time," he mumbled.

Dillon watched him leave the room. He wondered if he should let Vince know that he was still in contact with Nash. It might make him a little more positive and enthusiastic about the assignment.

He looked at his watch. LJ would be in his office now. He went downstairs to the main living room plasma screen and prepared himself to deliver his daily report to his boss. He needed to persuade LJ that progress was being made and the light at the end of the tunnel could be seen. He wondered how long it would be before the police authority would start demanding proof that Harvey had been accepting bribes. They'd be busy with their own internal investigations at the moment, but by then he'd have Kane and ultimately Nash. He hoped.

Dillon's iPad notified him the there was an email waiting. He quickly opened it and discovered that Kane had used the Mark Cane credit card the previous evening. A payment of two hundred pounds had been made to The Orchid International Escort Agency. Dillon immediately Googled the company, this was a high class call-girl service aimed at wealthy business men staying in top hotels throughout the area.

He looked at his watch. It was ten-fifteen and time to video-link LJ in London.

"Good morning Jake."

"Good morning LJ."

"What progress to report?"

"We've got Cracker Conner under twenty-four hour surveillance. It's only a matter of time before he leads us to Martha Hamilton. Nash has gone to ground, which doesn't bother me as he phones in about four times a day to find out what's going on."

"Well that sounds promising. What of Kane?"

"Kane - well he made his first big mistake last night. He used his alias Mark Cane credit card to book a tart for the evening. Once I've contacted the agency, I'll get the address of the hotel and room number where he is staying, and then have him monitored as well."

"That sounds very promising - keep at it, old son. Has Nash met anyone whilst in Dorset?"

"Not that we're aware of. Vince has him bugged, there's been no phone contact either."

"OK. I'll report back to the Home Secretary and let you know if there are any changes to your brief."

The massive screen turned blue as LJ discontinued the secure link.

Dillon dialled The Orchid International Escort Agency. Their line was answered promptly. "Orchid International Limited. Carmen speaking, how can I help you?"

Dillon realised he had not thought through what he was going to say. If he said the wrong thing it could blow his chances of getting the information he wanted.

"Hello," said Carmen again.

"Oh hello," replied Dillon. "Your agency has been recommended to me."

"I'm pleased to hear that," said Carmen.

"I wondered if was possible to arrange an appointment with you."

"By all means, we always recommend that new clients visit us personally. When would be convenient for you?"

"Well, I'm not far away from you at the moment." He glanced down at his iPad. Are you still located in Lower Parkstone?"

"Yes."

"In twenty minutes?" asked Dillon, his heart rate rising.

"Certainly," said Carmen. "And what name is it, sir?"

Dillon hesitated, as he quickly thought up a plausible name. "Asher," he said fluidly. "Mathew Asher."

"Thank you, Mr Asher. I look forward to seeing you in

twenty minutes."

Dillon hung up. He grabbed his jacket, looked at the iPad screen once again and slipped it into its protective sleeve. Despite a trendy address in Lower Parkstone, the Orchid International Escort Agency was probably not as international as its name suggested, if Carmen was both answering the telephone and meeting the clients. He'd soon find out. He picked up the iPad and raced out of the luxury house.

* * *

The taxi dropped Dillon in Church Road. He walked down through Ashley Cross Green, passed the water fountain on his way to Station Road. He found the address that was a door next door to a gent's hairdressing salon. He rang the bell alongside The Orchid International Escort Agency's polished stainless steel name plate. The door was opened remotely and Dillon pushed his way inside. He entered a dingy narrow hallway with a sign telling the visitor to go up the stairs to the first floor reception. As he opened the door at the top of the stairs, he was pleasantly surprised by the contrast of décor and lighting of the entrance hall below. He was greeted by a woman whom he immediately identified as Carmen, who came and led him into her office.

Dillon looked round the small room. He tried to ascertain what this agency was really about. The office was very white and stark, with a desk, a white leather sofa, a white woollen rug and a glass coffee table. There were a few high-end glossy magazines laid out on the low table.

Carmen offered him a seat, and she closed the office door. He could tell she owned the business from the way she sat behind the desk. Her clothes were expensive, but lacked taste. She wore too much make-up that failed to soften her hard features. She looked fifty, but was more likely to be in her early forties. He'd met far too many women like Carmen, to recall, who had all had tough lives.

"As I said over the phone, Mr Asher, we do like our clients to peruse our portfolio of escorts in absolute comfort. You will soon see why we have the word international in our company name. Our escorts come from all over Europe, Africa, Asia, Indonesia, and the Americas." So that really was her game, thought Dillon. "If you make a note of the those that interest you then we can ensure that all your requirements are catered for when you call us in the future." Carmen hesitated briefly, and licked her lips. "Now, are you interested in men or women, or perhaps both?"

"Women," said Dillon. The trail to Kane was getting warm. Carmen typed in the command and almost immediately the image of an attractive black girl appeared on the monitor screen facing him. Carmen pushed a wireless mouse across the desk to him. "Could you tell me your terms?" Dillon asked.

"We accept bookings over the telephone using all major credit and debit cards. We will not however, accept calls from withheld numbers, or any bookings made by text. Our escorts are available twenty-four hours a day, seven days a week, three hundred and sixty-fives days of the year. Some of them only work evenings and others only during the daytime. Our booking fee is one hundred pounds. The escorts make their own arrangements with the client when they meet them, but generally their rates start around eighty pounds for thirty minutes and one hundred and fifty pounds for an hour of their company. If a client requires the company of the escort for the entire night, then I believe that is around one thousand pounds - all fees are payable in cash up front, when the escort arrives."

"I see," said Dillon. He used the mouse to scroll through the images as he spoke. The pages were full of escorts of all nationalities and there was no accounting for taste. Dillon noted that some of the girls seemed very young; perhaps it was because he was getting older. "Do you keep records of your clients?"

Carmen misunderstood his question. "We do, but they're kept on an encrypted database. I'm told by my IT man that it's impossible to break into. We take client confidentiality very seriously. After all, we don't want client information falling into the wrong hands."

"Does that include their addresses?"

"We make a note of the client's address at the time of

booking. The escort meets the client at that address. When the escort leaves she telephones to say that she's finished the job, and then we destroy the address he or she has just visited. Of course, all private addresses are kept on the secure database. We have to do that for the security of our escorts and ourselves." Carmen added, "Confidentially, there are some very strange people out there; we can't afford to take any chances."

"I quite understand," said Dillon." "So you record the addresses on that computer?" Dillon said pointing at the computer CPU on a low shelf behind her.

"No, we stopped doing that, just in case of the unlikely that there was a breach of security and their names and addresses were stolen. Can you imagine the scandal?"

"So how do you keep the addresses totally safe?" Dillon persisted.

Carmen looked at him suspiciously. The clients who asked the most questions were always the most difficult. "You're not the first client to be worried about that, Mr Asher." She pointed a deep red fingernail at a floor standing machine by her desk. "As I've just said, after we store the information on the database we destroy every piece of paper on this commercial shredder. Anything that is written down goes through the slot, which includes all credit card details, and there are no exceptions to this rule. Some of my clients are very important people and some are very high profile celebrities; but all of them are very satisfied with the escorts I send to them."

Dillon was undeterred. There had to be some way of finding out Kane's address. If he kept asking questions though he would either find out or be booted out of this tough lady's office. Although, Carmen had become suspicious and looked like she was definitely not willing to answer any more questions.

"Anyway," said Carmen, losing her patience. "If we kept all of our client's addresses we'd end up looking like the database of the Metropolitan Police."

Dillon smiled. Carmen made a mistake at last. She'd given him an idea. "You have a lot of clients?" he asked.

"Over one hundred a week," she replied, proudly.

"So when did you start the agency?"

"Just over three years ago."

"And I bet you could recall each and every one of your clients?"

Carmen shifted in her seat. "You ask a lot of questions, Mr Asher. That is, for someone who is looking for a tart for the night?"

Dillon nodded. "Yes, I am. I'm very sorry about that. No offence meant."

Carmen looked at him, "None taken Mr Asher."

Dillon closed down the monitor screen and pushed the mouse back to Carmen. He leaned forward, reached into his jacket pocket and produced his fake MI5 identity card, placed it on the desk in front of Carmen, and said. "You have something that I need."

"Oh, all the men say that luv. Of course I have something you need - girls that will fuck your brains out."

"You're mistaken," said Dillon stonily. "What I want from you is located on your computer. I want the address of one of your clients - a man called Mark Cane."

"On your bike, Mister Asher, or whatever your name is. I don't give out client's confidential information to anyone, not even MI bloody 5. Now get out before I call the police." Carmen reached across the desk and picked up the telephone.

"Please do. Call the police, I mean. When they arrive, I will quickly tell them that I had come here to find an escort to accompany me to a business charity function, and was offered a number of high class call-girls. With my connections in Whitehall, you will be locked up for running a business that profits from the activities of prostitutes. So please, call the police now." Dillon said affably. He took out his mobile phone and laid it on the desk top.

"You can't be serious," said Carmen. She scrabbled in a drawer and produced a packet of cigarettes. She lit one.

"I couldn't be more serious," said Dillon. "I want that address and I will leave with it - one way or another." Dillon kept his voice low and calm.

"But I could be ruined if it got out that I'd divulged a client's personal details." Said Carmen desperately, and took a long draw of the cigarette.

"No one will ever know, and you can carry on your business as usual. I have no interest in seeing your business go down the pan." Dillon said.

Carmen stared at him. "OK, I believe you. What do you want?" She was used to paying off bent coppers who ensured that she could operate unhindered.

"Like I said before, I want some information."

Carmen's eyes narrowed and even with Botox, lines appeared across her brow. "What sort?"

"First, I'm going to give you a word of warning," said Dillon. Carmen's face hardened. "By agreeing to give me information, you will from this point forward be bound by the Official Secrets Act. If you should speak about this meeting or impart any information about what has been said here today. Then you will be arrested and charges will be brought against you, followed by a lengthy prison sentence. Do you understand?" Dillon said sombrely.

Carmen nodded, relieved that this whole strange affair was going to stop with this conversation.

"I need the address of Mark Cane a client who saw one of your girls last night."

"Mark Cane you say." She adjusted her designer glasses on the tip of her nose. Opened up a new window on her monitor and a list of information appeared. She had no qualms about indiscretion any more.

"Yes, Mark Cane." Dillon spelt out the surname for her.

Carmen scrolled down the page and then clicked on one of the entries. "If I tell you, will that genuinely be the end of it?" She asked.

"Yes." Dillon said. "But I not only need Cane's home address. I also want the address where the girl went last night."

"You need to talk to young Lexi," said Carmen.

"What's her real name?"

"Lucy Brookes."

"Call her up and tell her she has a client now."

"She has another job during the day. I don't know what

she does, but she's never free much before three o'clock. I have to leave a message on her mobile voicemail, and then she calls me to get the details."

"I want her mobile phone number and address."

"I only have her mobile phone number," said Carmen. She scribbled the number on a piece of paper.

"I want to meet Lucy Brookes at three-thirty, sharp. And make sure she is here. If she doesn't show for whatever reason I will make sure you are very, very sorry," warned Dillon. "Is that understood?"

Carmen nodded. Lucy would be there. She'd make sure of that. She picked up the telephone and dialled the number. The answer phone cut in and she left a short message. "Lucy, this is Carmen. Pop in to see me at three-thirty; don't be late as I've got something perfect for you." She replaced the handset on its base unit.

Dillon stood up. "I'll show myself out. Three-thirty sharp remember." He closed the office door gently as he left Carmen sitting behind her desk, still stunned by what had just been said to her.

He walked through the outer office, placed a tiny pin-hole surveillance camera in amongst the foliage of a pot plant standing on the reception desk, and left the building.

* * *

An hour after Cracker called, Razor became conscious of a repeated knocking coming from upstairs. He got up out of the chair and climbed the stairs. He stood outside the bedroom door. "What do you want?" He asked.

"I want to go to the bathroom," said Martha.

"You'll have to hang on." This kidnapping lark wasn't for him, and this woman was driving him mad with her whining. It irritated him and interrupted his thoughts.

"Listen, you..." Martha held her tongue, thinking better of antagonising him, "I can't hang on, I'm afraid."

Razor unlocked the door and Martha walked past him into the toilet. She shut the door. Razor thought for a few moments. She didn't speak to him. She didn't look at him. He knew the reason. It was his eyes. He listened, but couldn't hear anything behind the door. Maybe she was attempting to escape out through the window. He opened the door.

"Get out!" Martha screamed.

Razor stepped back and shut the door. It was a scene from a voyeur's fantasy. The woman was squatting above the toilet. Her legs were apart, and he couldn't quite see if she was shaven or not. His heart rate was racing and he felt hot and sweaty. He waited patiently in the corridor, and thought about his other fantasies.

Razor had been daydreaming for what seemed like a long time, when the woman came out. Something was gnawing away at the back of his mind. He couldn't put his finger on it. If only he could remember what it was?

"Where is your friend?" Martha asked.

"He's had to go out."

Martha walked back into the bedroom and shut the door. He stared at the door. He imagined her naked and tied to a bed. "Look after her and everything will be fine." Razor walked down the corridor to his room and booted up his laptop. He watched the catch-up channels on the iPlayer.

He remembered what it was he had forgotten. It came with crystal clarity. They couldn't let the woman go. She knew too much and she'd seen their faces and knew their names. It didn't matter what he did now then.

He hadn't been with a beautiful woman before; he usually went with hookers in the back of his car or in a seedy room somewhere.

* * *

Jasper waited for Razor in the foyer of the Harbour Heights Hotel on Haven Road in Canford Cliffs. He was early for the meeting. This second meeting had been hastily arranged when Cracker had turned up for the meeting at the Castleman Hotel instead of Razor. Jasper had thrown a wobbly and told him that he would only deal with Razor.

Soon Martha would be free. He would try and persuade her to take a holiday with him to ease away the nightmare. He now regretted every decision he'd taken over the past week. If only he had played along with Max. If only he'd listened to Martha in the beginning. Contacting Dillon had been a waste of time. Even with the resources at his disposal, he had been unable to find out where she was being held. Dillon had been jerking him around, playing for time so he could locate Max.

Jasper reviewed his options. He was still in a strong position. He would hand the heroin to Razor. They'd have to honour any deal while he still had the couple of million pounds to collect from Jason. He looked at his watch. There were still fifteen minutes until the meeting with Razor. He looked around the foyer for any signs of surveillance. There were none. The pace and atmosphere remained the same. He made a phone call to Inger Lindberg. He was giving Dillon one last chance. If Martha was free there was no need to meet with Razor, but he was disappointed to find out that there had been no developments on that front. He declined the offer of a meeting with Dillon, but told Inger he would phone again. He didn't want Dillon to know that he had an appointment with Razor.

Jasper saw Razor's BMW pull up in the hotel's car park. He reached it before Razor was out. He opened the passenger door and got in.

"Where's the gear?" Razor asked.

"Somewhere safe for now, we'll go and collect it soon."

"You wouldn't be trying to pull a fast one, would you?"

"Steady Razor, no fast ones are being pulled."

"OK then, which way?" Razor barked.

"You need to head towards Poole centre and then follow the signs for Upton." Jasper looked out of the window. Razor was still failing to take the most basic precautions, the least of which would have been to hire a car for this transaction. It was only ten minutes before he spotted the car tailing them.

"You're being followed," Jasper pointed out. "There are at least two vehicles, four cars back is a white Mercedes Vito van and one car in front of the van, is what looks like a Ducati Streetfighter S." He should have guessed that Dillon would be tailing Razor.

"You must have been tailed to the hotel," said Razor.

"You were told to come alone." Razor said, his tone mocking.

Jasper ignored the remark. He wanted to be sure no one witnessed the transfer of the heroin. It was most likely the only concern that he had in common with Razor.

Razor pulled into a petrol station and filled up the tank of the BMW. Then he set off in the opposite direction. After a few miles Razor confirmed they were still being followed.

"I've always followed one simple rule in life," he said finally. "If you've got unwanted company the best thing is to let them know - you know, that they're there. Then they back off and leave you alone." He circled the roundabout two times and took off down a road leading to Lytchett Minster village at high speed. He came to a sudden halt in the middle of the carriageway causing chaos as the sound of screeching rubber on tarmac from the vehicles behind followed a split second later. Some vehicles were forced to weave their way past. The BMW remained motionless in the middle of the road, its hazard warning lights blinking in the gloom until it was clear of cars following them. In the end the surveillance teams abandoned the operation. "That's taught them the lesson," Razor said, pleased with his success. "Now let's get down to business."

"What about Martha?" Jasper asked.

"I get the gear, and then I make a call to Cracker. He then lets her go someplace, and you go and pick her up. That arrangement is not open to negotiation."

"Pull over and stop the car." Jasper said suddenly.

Razor stopped the car.

"Listen pal - before you get anywhere near to picking up the gear, you will make a call and I will talk to Martha. Otherwise, you can fuck-off - and let me tell you. That is not open to negotiation, either."

Razor stared at Jasper for a long moment. He was appraising the demand. Finally he nodded. He reached inside the jacket he was wearing and pulled out his mobile phone and made the call.

"Put the girl on the line," he snapped. He listened a moment.

"I don't care," he said. "Put her on."

Jasper watched Razor intently. He waited impatiently. Razor stared out of the windscreen, avoiding any eye contact with Jasper.

Finally Razor awkwardly held the mobile phone to Jasper's ear.

Jasper heard muffled sobs.

"Martha," he said. "It's Jasper..."

"Jasper..." he heard her gasp, "Please... I can't bear it any longer. Get me out of this. You..."

"Martha, it won't be long!"

Razor snatched the phone away and disconnected the call. He started the car. "So, let's get moving."

Jasper was frantic. He had never heard Martha so upset before. "Instruct Cracker to let her go," he said coldly.

"When we're done and I have the gear safely stowed in the boot of this car - then she'll be released."

"If anything happens to Martha I will kill you," he said with menace.

"Yeah?" replied Razor. He nodded as if assimilating the information. "Let's drive."

* * *

The first doubts entered Jasper's mind as he led Razor along the tow path to the boat. They were the only people walking in the drizzle. "Can't stand the bleedin' countryside," complained Razor.

Jasper said nothing. Wareham riverbank was hardly deep rural Dorset.

"Makes you stand out like a sore thumb," Razor added.

His sudden affability aroused a sixth sense. Jasper looked over his shoulder. Razor's Italian shoes suffered as they slithered on the muddy path beside the riverbank. Away from the familiar camouflage of the concrete walls he looked curiously vulnerable, staggering around in the open with not a building to be found.

"Here we are," said Jasper, stepping on to the boat. Razor looked at the boat with wariness. He looked at the gangplank which rested precariously on the edge of the deck. He looked at the black water between the side of the hull and the sheer wooden sleepers retaining the river-bank. He gripped his mobile phone firmly, stepped cautiously on to the gangplank, grabbed the side rail, and finally stepped on to the deck.

Jasper had unlocked the hatch in the cockpit and was already down in the cabin. He fumbled in the darkness by the chart table for the light switch. A distress flare rolled across the table. Razor clambered down.

"So where's the gear then?" Razor asked, taking in his surroundings.

"It's stowed forward," said Jasper, leading the way into the bows of the once luxury craft. He opened up the forward bulkhead cover, pulled aside the tarpaulin cover and started to retrieve the small brown bales of heroin. Razor carried them back to the main cabin and placed them neatly on the chart table. When all of the bales had been retrieved, Razor counted them. They were all there. He put the small packages in to a large holdall that he had brought with him, and then went to the cockpit, placing the holdall carefully on the wooden deck.

"Now my part of the deal," said Jasper. He had come up from below and was now standing in front of Jasper in the cockpit. He casually leant against the control panel, the distress flare gun held firmly in his right hand behind his back. "Where is Martha?"

"We've got a problem," said Razor. He reached into his coat and pulled out a three-five-seven calibre Smith & Wesson snub-nose magnum. He smiled.

"No way," said Jasper. "Aren't you forgetting I am the only one who can collect the money from the sale of the cocaine?"

"Oh yeah, I forgot to mention. Your mate Maxie has arranged to collect it himself, that is, once he'd found out who it was handling the deal."

"What about Martha?" Jasper asked. When the gun had first appeared he'd frozen, but now he could feel his heart pumping. He was being forced to do what he had anticipated, but dreaded.

"Who gives a fuck about some stuck up tart when there's ten million at stake?" Razor said, unpleasantly.

"What strikes me about you Razor is that you're not a cold-blooded killer. You're probably quite a pleasant person deep down. I mean, you're not a hit man. You've got to have something personal against your victim, so I'll tell you something. I'll make it easy for you." Razor looked baffled by this train of thought. Jasper leaned forward. He was staring at Razor intently, willing him to hold the stare. The hand gripping the flare gun came round and remained silently by his side; he lifted the muzzle a fraction of an inch. "There's an old nautical saying," he paused for moment. "He that is embarked with the devil must sail with him. I think you're sailing with the wrong team - arsehole!"

For the briefest second Razor's expression registered incomprehension. Jasper squeezed the trigger of the flare gun. There was a deafening bang and then the whoosh of the flare leaving the barrel. Jasper stepped out of the cockpit.

Razor's eyes widened and the look of incomprehension turned to one of shock and horror.

The flare hit Razor in the stomach with such force it knocked the wind out of him and doubled him over - he dropped to the floor. Blazing its fourteen thousand candles of light the flare erupted into an uncontrollable fury of sparks that flayed around the cockpit. Razor screamed as the acrid smoke seared his lungs. He was temporarily blinded, had dropped the Smith & Wesson as he fell, and was now incapable of seeing anything.

Jasper waited until the flare had almost extinguished itself before moving back into the cockpit. Through the acrid smoke he could see Razor's body crouched in a corner. Jasper now had the upper hand; he could see the gun lying on the floor. He picked it up and stuffed it in his pocket. He turned, found the remnants of the flare casing and using an old cloth he'd found in a locker, picked it up and dropped it into the water. It boiled on the surface for a moment before floating off downstream.

He looked back into the boat. Razor was curled up,

his jacket smouldering. Flames licked at the cushions. Jasper pulled the fire extinguisher from the bulkhead and sprayed dry powder over the flames.

Finally there was silence. Except for Razor's rasping breath. At least he wasn't dead.

"Razor!" he shouted. "I want the address." Razor didn't react. Jasper stood behind him, gun ready in hand. He grabbed Razor's jacket collar, and pulled him. Razor twisted uncontrollably. Jasper looked away instinctively. Razor's hands had been burnt to the bone, and were splayed like talons. His hair was all but gone. His face was no longer identifiable. His features had become morphed. Jasper forced himself to look back.

Razor might have been looking at him, but it was hard to tell. The eyelids had taken much of the force of the flames. Slowly his head shook from side to side.

"Listen carefully, Razor. I'll ask you again, give me the address. I don't care how long it takes, I will get it." He walked out onto the small rear deck area and breathed in the fresh air. When he went back inside he had the gun in his hand. He knelt down beside Razor, "I have your gun pointed at you." He cocked the hammer back. "I will blow your kneecap off if you don't tell me where Martha is."

Jasper listened. Razor's rasps seemed to be coming quicker. He was speaking, but his lips weren't moving.

"I can't hear you," he said.

"Look in my pocket. Letter," said Razor, with difficulty.

Jasper pressed the gun to Razor's right kneecap and felt in the jacket pockets. He withdrew the mobile phone and car keys from one pocket. In the other he found one letter.

"...help me," Razor muttered.

Jasper ignored him and unfolded the letter. It turned out to be an estate agent's property auction notice for a derelict former hotel just outside of Dorchester.

"Is Martha being held in this property?" Jasper asked holding up the piece of paper.

Razor nodded.

"I hope you're not lying to me?"

Razor shook his head.

"OK, well this is how it's going to play out. I'm going to this old hotel and I'm going to release Martha. If I find her unharmed, then I'll call the paramedics to come and sort you out. If not - if Martha is not there or she has been harmed in any way. Then I'll come back and sort you out myself." Jasper hesitated a moment. He passed his hand in front of Razor's face. There was no reaction. Blinded! Well tough shit. "You sure you're telling me the truth?"

Razor slowly lowered himself on to his elbows. He rocked backwards and forth like a small child. Jasper leaned over Razor and picked up the holdall containing the heroin; he might still need a bargaining tool. He left the boat's heater on low and closed the rear hatch door. He stepped out in to the daylight. It was good to breathe the fresh air.

He ran back along the tow path to the car and before driving off, he dialled the number Dillon had given him. Inger answered. Dillon was not there. He gave Inger the address of the derelict hotel just outside Dorchester where Martha was being held, and told her to find Dillon.

He felt pangs of anxiety run through him at the thought of what might happen to Martha, if Cracker didn't hear from Razor.

He needed to speak to Dillon. It was time to make a deal. Maybe he was already at the place where Martha was being held. He dialled the other mobile number that Dillon had given him.

* * *

Kane took more precautions than usual when he returned to his flat after the call from his source inside Ferran & Cardini International. He felt uneasy. Although the source said there was no need to worry, something warned him that it was time to leave. Of course this person didn't want to prematurely sound the alarm bells; he had received three hundred and fifty thousand pounds up front, for digitally oiling the official wheels in Morocco, and would receive another one hundred and fifty thousand pounds on completion of the deal.

The man was keeping Kane in the picture. Only, Kane didn't like the picture.

Dillon had found out too much and was closing in. Razor was too hot to contact. It appeared that most of the law enforcement agencies were after him as well, even though he'd given them the slip. He probably had the heroin and well on his way to getting it onto the streets by now. Kane would keep the advance. One day they might meet and settle accounts. If Razor was smart he'd put the heroin to sleep somewhere safe and wait for the heat to blow over. Dillon would pull him and Cracker in for questioning soon; but they'd had plenty of practice at being interrogated over the years. They'd say nothing. They valued their lives.

Kane felt the briefest pang of regret for Jasper. They'd been so close in the old days, but they wouldn't be chatting over coffee anymore because Jasper had made the cardinal mistake. He had spoken to Dillon. Kane had worked it out; it explained how Dillon knew Martha had disappeared.

It had been Razor's idea to murder Jasper once he had possession of the heroin. Now Martha would join him in the foundations of a luxury home in Canford Cliffs. Jasper was a stupid son-of-a-bitch. It could all have been resolved so amicably.

Tomorrow Kane would slip over to southern Ireland, and then fly from Dublin to Stockholm in Sweden; from there he would fly business class to Singapore. He had an appointment to call his Ferran & Cardini man in a month for a debriefing. Things should have cooled down by then. There would be sufficient change to pay him off from the eight million which Jason Villiers was delivering to him as part of the new arrangement. He came expensive at two million, but worth every penny to ensure he received the money. If everything went to plan, he and Villiers would plan a new venture together. After all, it would be such a pity not to use all of those connections to the full.

Kane pottered around the flat with a large black bin bag, cleaning up. He didn't want anything nasty lurking in the kitchen when he came back in a few months. He changed the sheets on the bed and put the soiled linen in the bag. He reflected on the sex he had experienced with the tart the night before. Sex was a messy business. He hated losing control of himself.

Chapter 17

Vince paced around the spacious living room of the Sandbanks house. He was nervous. He didn't like it when Dillon disappeared, following some lead of his own. It was hard to know what course of action to take when he was kept in the dark.

His phone rang. He pulled it out of his pocket and answered the call. It was Dillon.

"How's it going?"

"We lost them," said Vince. He didn't have time to explain how Razor had made surveillance impossible, before Dillon was snapping down the line.

"That's inconvenient, Vince. How the fuck did Razor and Nash give you the slip with two teams on the road following them?"

"They knew we were there, and not because they spotted us. Jake, they'd been informed that we were going to being tailing them. From the minute we turned up we didn't have a hope in hell of succeeding."

"So who do you think it was that told them?"

"I'd make a guess and say - it's got to be an insider who has access to our daily schedule files."

"A member of the surveillance crew, do you think?"

"Could be - but whom, is anyone's guess."

"Well, dig up everything on all of them. If you find anything call me immediately." Dillon terminated the line, annoyed that the big Australian had not been that concerned about the possibility that someone was leaking information to Nash and possibly even Kane.

Vince slipped the phone back into his pocket again, and grinned. He was managing to keep things together. He was taking risks, and paving the way, but that was what he was paid to do.

The surveillance operation on Razor and Nash almost brought the whole scam to a crashing end. Vince congratulated himself on his cunning. It hadn't been easy to ensure Nash spotted the white Mercedes van and Ducati rider. Razor wouldn't have noticed at all. He grinned at Razor's counter-surveillance tactics; they'd had no other option than to abort. By now though, the exchange would be over. He looked at his watch. Razor would now have possession of the heroin and Jasper Nash would be history.

The wall mounted plasma screen came alive. It was Edward Levenson-Jones.

"Sharp! I'd like a word with you."

Vince looked up, surprised. "Sir!" he said, rising to his feet. LJ's expression was grave.

"Where's Dillon?"

"I don't know, sir."

"What's your opinion regarding this charge of bribery against detective constable Harvey?"

"Can I speak candidly?"

"Yes."

"Jake doesn't have a leg to stand on. He has no evidence that Harvey was accepting bribes. And a wad of cash doesn't constitute proof."

"Dillon told me that he was tipped off by Jasper Nash."

Vince felt his heart jump a beat for a moment. His stomach fluttered. "He's in touch with Nash?" He asked, unable to keep the surprise from his voice.

"Yes."

Vince grappled for some adequate response. "So that's why he hasn't had Nash arrested."

"Of course, he's been playing along with Nash because he knows that without his cooperation he wouldn't get the information he needs to complete his assignment. However, I've got MI5 crawling all over me for Dillon's whereabouts. They want a little chat with him."

"I'm not surprised, sir." Vince's mind was elsewhere. He wondered if Jake was with Nash now. No, he couldn't be. He'd just called. Perhaps they were setting up Razor. "There's something I don't understand. Why didn't Jake tell Inger or me? We've been floundering on the rocks for the last couple of weeks."

"Nash told him that Kane had a source inside Ferran & Cardini…"

Vince's mouth went dry. "That's ridiculous."

"Yes. That's one way of looking at it, but I'm not so sure now."

"You know what I think, sir? I think that Nash and Kane are very smart. I think they've invented the story-line to create smoke and mirrors. They're probably laughing their heads off."

LJ nodded, slowly. "This assignment has got out of hand. Dillon has taken his personal prejudice too far this time. I warned him at the outset that this would happen."

Vince nodded. He should have kept a much closer eye on Jake. He was clever; but because of his disrespect for protocol and rules, he could be easily discredited. "Apparently Max Kane was thought by Jake to be the sole cause of his then girlfriend's death. Something that was never proven, but Jake still believes it to be true, to this day."

LJ looked up, and blinked in surprise. He looked away from the camera lens, staring at a point in his office off to the right, deep in thought. He stood up and started to pace to and forth behind his desk. Finally he came to a decision. "Locate Dillon and tell him I want to speak to him - urgently. It's time to close this assignment down. It's been a charade from the start."

"I'll run a GPS search programme, I should be able to locate Jake's phone, even if it's switched off."

Vince watched his boss sit down at his desk and then the screen went blank. He heaved a sigh of relief, and sat down on one of the sofas.

Damage limitation - that was the first priority, and then he would find out exactly what Dillon knew, and then discredit him. That was all very well, so long as Dillon wasn't witnessing the meeting between Nash and Razor. He had to find Dillon; once LJ had spoken to him, they were all home and dry. And he'd have the second instalment paid into his Belize account.

Vince stood up and went up to the crow's-nest where Dillon preferred to work. He looked through the files on the desk searching for some unfamiliar lead. He shuffled through the bank statements.

He reacted automatically as the phone on the desk started to ring and immediately answered it.

"Dillon?" asked the voice.

"No. He's not here."

"Where can I reach him?"

"Nash is that you?" Vince asked.

"Yes. I need to speak to him urgently."

"Can I pass a message on? I'll make sure he gets it." Vince stopped leafing through the files. This is interesting.

"No. I need to speak to Dillon personally?" Jasper said.

"Well if he's not answering his phone, he obviously doesn't want to be contacted - does he?"

"Tell him I want to make a deal. Tell him I've located Martha..."

Vince listened, numbed. Perhaps it was time to step back and become a loyal Ferran & Cardini technical support officer again. He'd been careful. But not, he felt, careful enough - not if Kane was caught. There were too many questions and only Nash could answer them. Nash had found out about the derelict hotel. If Dillon spoke to Harvey he'd know that Vince had been told about that. A mistake like that was an embarrassment.

"What about Ryan Edwards?" Vince asked.

"Edwards?" Nash asked.

"Razor Edwards - how is he?"

"I'll let you know," answered Nash, enigmatically, before hanging up.

Vince replaced the receiver. It was always a question of being in the right place at the right time. He had intercepted a call which might have brought the whole deck of cards tumbling down.

Instead, Nash was about to enter a dead-end road.

* * *

The pain had become excruciating. Razor turned his head from side to side. He couldn't see. Every time he moved it felt as if his skin was being ripped from his face. He began to distinguish shades of light and dark. He could not work out whether they were shapes, but a panic welled up inside him. The flare that Nash had shot him with had ignited only after it had hit him in the stomach. Then there was the intense light and heat. He knew that he was blind. If he could reach a hospital maybe the doctors could do something. He didn't believe that bastard Nash was coming back. Cracker would sort out Nash when he got his hands on him; he was never coming back. He'd sort the woman too. Cracker would already be edgy; he was waiting for his call. Trouble was that Cracker didn't know that he was stuck on this boat. He had to get out.

He began crawling. He kept bumping into objects. The cockpit cabin was cramped. Every time his hands touched a surface the pain in his hands seared through his raw nerve endings. He sat down leaning against a stowage locker and rested. The effort required to move was immense and it took an eternity. But he hadn't come this far for it to end on some crappy old boat.

His blood pounded in his ears. He nearly fainted and his head lolled sideways, catching on something. The pain jolted him back to consciousness. At last he managed to get to his feet. He felt the rim of the helm against his back. Each movement made him wince, and with each wince he gasped with the pain. He took each step slowly until he came up against the glass of the cabin door. He'd be out soon. He'd call Cracker and warn him that Nash was on his way. He'd have Cracker deal with the bastard slowly. The thought made the pain bearable.

He leaned against the sliding door. It wasn't locked; he pulled it to one side and tumbled through, over balancing backwards, and landed on his head in the cockpit. The numbness evaporated in a blinding flash of agony as his head grazed the edge of the door frame. The pain stretched towards an ever increasing crescendo. He didn't know if he was screaming. It seemed an eternity before silence fell again.

"Help," he croaked.

There was no answer.

At least he was outside. He could feel the cool breeze, and he could just discern the diffused light. He leaned against a guard rail for a while trying to gain the confidence to move. At last he continued the slow journey towards the shore. He tentatively put one foot in front of the other to feel his way. He negotiated the ropes and other hazards on the deck. He found the lifelines along the side of the aging power cruiser. He'd soon be ashore. Progress would be quicker then. He would get onto the tow-path. Someone would help him to get to a telephone and then a hospital.

He eased himself on to the gangplank. Each step was gingerly taken. He shuffled along, pushing himself forward an inch at a time.

As he was falling he remembered why he had been so nervous when he first stepped on to the boat. The plank had only been resting on the edge of the deck. As he hit the freezing cold water he involuntarily breathed in with the shock, and the first mouthful entered his lungs.

* * *

Martha lay on the bed. She'd spent the past three days huddled in the foul smelling blankets, dozing in and out of consciousness. She tried not to think about her present predicament. It was so ludicrous it was unbelievable. She tried to ignore the cold and dampness of the decaying building. She closed her eyes tightly and thought of being at home. She wove daydreams in which she walked along the golden white sand of Sandbanks. Where the sun shimmered on the water and small waves lapped gently at the shore. She realised, without guilt, that Jasper made no appearance in these dreams. He was now a part of her past...

She lay focusing her hearing for any noises. Every time she heard a telephone ring in the distance it raised her hopes. It held the possibility of contact with the outside world. It broke her equanimity. This time she began crying. She couldn't help it. Her situation was hopeless. "Please help me," she repeated weakly between her sobs, as if it were a prayer. She heard the door open. Cracker was holding the mobile phone. He pushed it roughly towards her mouth and she gripped it with one hand. "Please help me," she muttered in to the handset. Then she heard Jasper's voice. He sounded normal. It sounded as if he were in control of the situation. She started to speak. He seemed to have no idea of what she was going through. Before she could speak again the connection was terminated. "Jasper," she repeated twice into the dead handset, before dropping it on the bed. He had rung off. "Bastard," she couldn't even count on him.

Cracker picked up the mobile phone. "Leave me alone," said Martha.

Cracker didn't leave. He sat on the edge of the bed. His presence jolted Martha into awareness. She tensed. She had made this room into her world, and now her privacy was being invaded.

"My sister looked a bit like you," said Cracker, winking at her. "They took her away from us."

"Why?" asked Martha.

"They said she was a danger. It was our dad, you see."

Martha didn't comment and didn't want to know any more details either. She wasn't going to waste her sympathy on this young thug.

"I bet you're wondering what the danger was. Well he used to get drunk every night. Then he would start using his fists on both of us. That is until he hit her once too often." He smiled at the memory. "You see she stabbed him with the biggest knife she could find. Plunged it right into him all the way up to the hilt, all the way into his fat gut, and then twisted it before drawing it upwards to his chest. Almost cut the bastard in two, blood everywhere there was."

"And that's why they took her away?"

"What do you think?" The riposte came sneeringly. "I shouldn't be talking to you like this. He told me not to talk to you."

"Who did?" Martha asked. She realised that Cracker had issues and a short fuse, and she had to humour him. The clock inside his head was ticking away.

"If they catch me talking to you they'll beat me."

"Who will beat you?"

"It's none of your business." Cracker said, and then fell silent. He looked at her. He wasn't seeing her. He didn't recognise her. She had become a figment of his warped imagination. For the first time she acknowledged that anything could happen to her in that dismal room, and no one would know - no one would come to help her.

Cracker's eyes flickered in the half light of the boarded up room. Then he seemed to re-focus, and looked her up and down for a long, long time. Slowly he picked up the hem of her dress and pulled it up to her thighs. Martha was too shocked to react immediately. She couldn't look at him. She pushed his hands away abruptly. He made her sick. She stared at the wall.

* * *

Dillon sat on the bright lime green coloured sofa in the small reception room, and impatiently flipped through a local glossy property magazine. Finally the door opened. The girl was young, no more than twenty years old, and pretty too. Dillon wondered why she was working as a call girl. Maybe she was supporting a drug habit or it was a way of paying her way through university; but he wouldn't make that any of his business unless it became absolutely necessary.

She wore a tight fitting black cocktail dress, black stockings and knee length black boots. She obviously knew what her punters liked. Her titian red hair was tied back in a pony-tail that gave her a look of innocence and vulnerability. She gave Dillon a friendly smile as she walked through the Orchid International Escort Agency's reception area into Carmen's office. She guessed that Dillon was the client, although she rarely met them at the office.

"Hello Lucy," said Carmen. "The gentleman in reception wants a word with you."

Dillon stood and approached the office as Lucy turned in the entrance. The friendly smile had gone, replaced with a wary look of concern. Men who wanted a word were definitely bad news.

"Thanks, Carmen," she said sarcastically. "You could have warned me. I wouldn't have bothered to put all my working gear on."

Carmen simply shrugged her shoulders.

Dillon was surprised by Lucy's voice. It was well bred and cultured, a little plummy but not offensive or stuck-up in a false way. "I want to ask you a few questions," he said affably.

"What about?" asked Lucy curtly.

"He's a spy," interjected Carmen.

"Oh yeah - well let's see some ID then." Lucy stared at Dillon. He reached inside his jacket and produced his fake MI5 identification card.

"Is there another office where we could talk in private?" asked Dillon, turning to Carmen.

Carmen couldn't conceal her disappointment. Her curiosity had got the better of her. "There's a small office next door to this one."

"That'll be fine," said Lucy. She leaned forward and picked up the remote control unit for the television mounted on the wall opposite Carmen's desk, and switched it on. She smiled impishly knowing that she had prevented Carmen from eavesdropping. She tossed the remote in to her handbag and closed Carmen in the office.

"So then, what do you want?" she asked sullenly, sitting on the edge of the desk. Dillon stood with his back to a wall, facing the doorway.

He stepped forward and showed her an image on the screen of his smart phone.

"I want to know about one of your clients." Dillon showed her a recent picture of Kane. "His name is Max Kane."

"I'm not big on remembering names of punters," Lucy said automatically. "Why should I?"

Dillon searched through the images and opened the picture of Kane in the company of Razor and Cracker. It had been taken three weeks previously. "What about the man in the middle?" He asked.

Lucy gave it a cursory glance. "I've never seen him before."

Dillon stared at her. "You're quite sure about that?"

She looked at the image again, and then handed Dillon his phone. "Of course I am."

Dillon felt taken aback. He couldn't have made a mistake. Was this another play of deception by Kane to misdirect him? Kane was definitely the punter she saw that night.

Dillon realised she wouldn't be readily forthcoming about anything until she was sure she couldn't be incriminated or arrested. He wondered whether she was one of Kane's regulars. She might tip him off. Perhaps Kane supplied her habit in return for personal services. Dillon had to take the risk.

"I could make life virtually impossible for you." He slipped off his jacket and placed it over the back of a chair.

"I could notify customs and revenue about your cash only income. I could have the police place you on a watch list," he adjusted the shoulder holster he was wearing, making sure the young prostitute spotted the Glock.

"Right now I could take you in for formal questioning and hold you for up to seventy-two hours. I could make your life absolutely intolerable." He paused to let his words sink in. Lucy stared at him and the gun with hard cold eyes. He had a hunch. "I could also drop in on your family and over a nice cup of tea, tell them exactly and vividly what you get up to every weekday afternoon from four o'clock until the small hours of the following day." Lucy's eyes flickered with doubt for the briefest moment. "They might not like to know what their lovely innocent looking daughter does for a living."

Dillon waited patiently for a reply. She remained silent. "But of course I don't have the time or the inclination to carry out all of that. However, if you don't help me now I'll do all of those things I mentioned. But I won't stop there. I'll keep the pressure on you because I will have no other option than to believe that you are guilty of aiding and abetting this man. Just when you thought everything was quietening down, someone will turn up, because I'm a vindictive bastard. You will have to look over your shoulder for ever more."

Lucy pursed her lips. "I can't help you, because I don't know him."

"Don't insult my intelligence. That's all bullshit." Dillon snapped. "I know you saw him last night."

Lucy didn't flinch. She took Dillon's phone from him, and frowned, giving the perfect imitation of someone in deep thought. Her movements were contrived and calculated. Most toms were liars, but this one was smooth with it. "Yes," she said at last. "It could be him. Most of the time he was wearing this black leather gimp hood. He was a right pervert this one."

"Can you recall where you met him?"

"One of those posh apartment blocks in Canford Cliffs."

"Can you remember which one?" Dillon asked eagerly.

"Sorry. It was dark."

"Would you remember which block if you were taken there?"

"What's in it for me?" asked Lucy.

"I'll owe you a favour if it's something in my power."

Lucy looked at him. She was surprised by the sudden sincerity in his voice. "Just pay the expenses I incurred coming here and getting back home later, and then forget you ever spoke to me," Lucy answered. She seemed to have come to a sensible decision. "This Kane is a nasty piece of work anyway."

Dillon picked up his mobile phone. The image was still on the screen, he realised that he didn't know where the shot had been taken. The police photographer had obviously been positioned at a location they all frequented. He looked at the picture carefully. The building in the background looked familiar. He shouldn't have overlooked something as obvious as that.

He slipped the phone back in to his jacket pocket. "Let's go." He said.

Outside Dillon led Lucy to where he'd parked the Panamera. "Fucking hell, what type of spy are you to drive a car like this?"

Dillon didn't answer. They drove off towards Sandbanks and Canford Cliffs. He sat tapping the steering wheel impatiently as they encountered heavy traffic on Penn Hill Avenue.

"You said that Kane was sick. What did you mean?"

"He's a pervert. Really weird, I hate people like that. Usually I try not to make value judgements. I mean it is only a job. After all, if it weren't for people being different I'd be out of pocket money. This one wanted to do all of the really strange stuff. Not just bondage. Usually they want to be tied up and dominated. Sometimes they want to wear my undies and for me to talk dirty to them. Sometimes they want nothing more than to be subjected to a little mild pain, nipple clamps and stuff like that. This one, he had a thing about doing it in a bath full of water. He tried to hold my head under water as he popped his nuts. I thought he was bloody well trying to drown me, I can tell you."

"I don't understand," said Dillon. Alarm bells rang in his head. All he could think of was Anna Westcott. She had drowned. Death by misadventure, they had said. "Can you run that by me one more time?"

"First of all we went into the bedroom. He had Champagne on ice and we started drinking. He insisted on taking my clothes off. I told him the price was for straightforward protected sex. He said not to worry about that. He'd pay for any extras." Dillon didn't want to hear this, but he couldn't help himself. He imagined the events of over twenty years ago. He imagined it was Anna talking to him as Lucy described in some detail the various violations which Maximilian Kane performed on her body.

"You didn't complain?" Dillon asked at one point.

"Everything has a price," said Lucy. "That's what he kept saying. But I stopped in the end. There's some stuff I won't do."

"Why do you do any of that stuff?" Dillon asked.

"I'm paying my way through university," said Lucy bluntly.

"What about the bath?"

"Some people get a kick being asphyxiated when they come. It's not unusual. Some men, and there are some women, who use amyl nitrates, it's a real heart stopper. Well, initially he wasn't interested in doing this to me. Oh no, he wanted me to hold his head under water while I spanked him with the flat of my hand. This was after the other stuff. I thought he was going to drown. He must have been under for a good three minutes. Then he said it was my turn. Thank God it wasn't a swimming pool." She paused. "Otherwise I would definitely have drowned." She looked at Dillon. He was staring straight ahead. He felt his face harden and the anger rising inside him.

"Why do you want to know? What's it all about then?"

He didn't answer at first. After a moment or two his face relaxed.

"Something from a long way back," said Dillon absently.

"What are you going to do?" Lucy asked.

"I'm going to stop him hurting people. Then I'm going to make sure he's locked up forever."

"Good luck," said Lucy. "That's nothing less than he deserves."

He looked at her and suddenly felt paternalistic. "Are you really doing this to pay your way through college?"

"Yes."

"What about your parents? Aren't they able to support you?"

"They think that I'm wasting my time."

"What are you studying?"

"I'm enrolled on a Psychology degree."

"Would you give this work up if you had a monthly allowance to support you?"

"Who wouldn't, but there's more chance of pigs flying." She scoffed at her own joke.

"Please don't take this the wrong way, Lucy. But I can arrange that monthly allowance for you. And ensure that it remains in place until you've graduated. The only undertaking that you would have to give is that you never do this work again and you get your degree." Dillon paused to allow the enormity of his offer to sink in.

"Where would the money come from? And how would I repay it?" She said sceptically.

"Suffice to say the money would come - each and every month. There will be no requirement to repay a single penny of it."

"But I don't understand - there must be a bloody big catch or you're a pervert too."

"You don't have to. I'm not a pervert and there's no catch - say yes and you will never have to place your life in danger ever again."

* * *

Vince drove past the rundown hotel just outside of Dorchester, and sized it up. There was no sign of activity. He might need a few tools to break inside. He had a set of lock picks and tensioners as well as one or two other tools of the burgling trade in the boot of his car. A sledgehammer, jemmy and screwdriver; was all that was needed to break into a property. There were few feelings to equal that of putting a sledgehammer through a locked door and hearing the splintering of wood and the crash of breaking glass. He parked the car in a layby about a hundred metres from the old hotel. He needed to be wary. It would be disastrous if he were seen in the vicinity. He wished he could speak to Nash, but couldn't risk calling him from his mobile as it would show his location on the grid at Ferran & Cardini and he would then have to explain the reason why he was there. It was better to leave Nash out of it. He wouldn't contact Nash as he had been indiscreet by mentioning to Dillon that there was an inside leak at Ferran & Cardini, and now Dillon was on high-alert. There was no knowing what Nash would do and say if he was caught, after all, there were the North Koreans to consider. Even Kane was turning into a high risk; but then, Kane had only been a stepping stone to Don Rafael, who held the key to the future.

For a moment Vince considered turning his back on the whole conspiracy. He was already ahead. He had his retirement fund in a Swiss bank. He wondered what had happened to Razor. Perhaps he had double crossed them. Perhaps Cracker had double crossed them and scarpered too, and the woman was waiting for Nash to be her knight in shining armour and save her; but then Nash wouldn't have called Dillon. No, it was wrong to back out. He was in too deep and had come too far. Now, he only needed to tell Razor that Nash was arriving and then they would have the heroin. If he could pull this off there would be more - much more.

Vince walked to the rear of the building. This was going to be a tricky operation. He knew Cracker, but Cracker wouldn't recognise him and wasn't likely to open the door to a stranger. If he persisted, Cracker would most likely let loose with a sawn-off shotgun. It was ironic that Cracker owed him a favour; if his picture had been forwarded to Interpol then he would have been identified as the mysterious Mr Kipper, who was wanted for questioning in connection with the murder of the Russian drug baron, Aleksey, in Paris. They would have soon realised that the description given by witnesses, all of whom noticed the prominent bags under the eyes of Mr Kipper, were nothing more than stick on latex and some very clever theatrical makeup. That Mr Kipper was really Conner 'Cracker' Hawkins. He wondered how Nash's girlfriend was coping; if the report into the death of Aleksey's girlfriend Natalya was characteristic, Razor and Cracker were both very nasty pieces of work.

He stood outside the door and listened. He looked around. A few grimy panes of glass still remained in their frames overlooking the cobbled courtyard, but there were no signs of life behind them. He noticed that the heavy duty padlock was unlocked. He turned the door handle carefully. It was locked from the inside. He checked the top and bottom of the door. There were no bolts. He decided to slip inside and make sure Nash wasn't already there. He would play it official, if he found Nash inside; then dispose of him one way or another later. If Cracker was alone he would terminate his contract with life immediately and save the British tax payer millions of pounds in the process.

He pulled out a small leather wallet from inside his jacket and slipped one of the picks into the lock, followed by the tensioner bar. After a few seconds, all of the internal locking pins aligned and the tensioner bar rotated under light pressure. The door swung open. He stood for a moment, peering into the filthy gloom of the interior. He entered, making sure there was no debris on the floor that could give his presence away. He closed the door quietly behind him and moved from room to room. The ground floor was completely deserted. As he climbed the stairs, he heard a muffled voice.

* * *

This was why Inger liked the job. Things changed so fast. For two days she had been cooped up in the rented house waiting for Jasper Nash to make contact; and her patience was exhausted. She was sick of waiting. She was sick of watching television, and she had become bored with staring out the windows at so much water. She had been on the verge of doubting Dillon.

One phone call changed everything. Dillon thought he had discovered where Max Kane was hiding, and she was on her way to meet Jasper Nash. Her instructions were to keep him in sight at all cost, and on no account tell anyone about what she was doing.

She wondered if Jasper had reached Martha before her. He must already have been on his way when he called. Suddenly it occurred to her that Jasper's phone call had not been as straightforward as she thought. Jasper was not telling Dillon he wanted a meeting, or that Martha had been freed. He was calling for help.

Inger pulled the hire car over to the grass verge. The road outside of the boarded up derelict hotel was deserted, devoid of life and light. She wondered if she had the right address. The car had to be parked somewhere where it couldn't be spotted from the road, she reversed up the road about twenty metres and backed the hire car up an unmade lane.

It occurred to her as she stepped out of the car that she had no authority or jurisdiction in the UK, and that what she was doing was stupid. She should never have been placed in this situation. If anything went wrong it would be her responsibility. She took out the phone and called Dillon's mobile number, only to find the call directed to voicemail. She tried Vince's number only to find that also went to voicemail. Now where had he disappeared to? She decided to find Jasper, stall him, and persuade him to wait for Dillon.

Chapter 18

Dillon had done it. He'd finally got the breakthrough he'd been waiting for. He had found out where Kane lived. In half an hour the apartment would be under twenty-four hour surveillance. The next time Nash called they'd work out a deal; if he called again. He might have done the exchange with Razor, and if he was lucky then Martha was now free.

Even if Nash never surfaced again there was a fighting chance of getting Kane now they knew where he lived. The moment he slipped up, they'd be on to him.

Dillon barely made it into the rented house before he was receiving a text message from Edward Levenson-Jones to standby for a secure video conference. He went through the luxury property, up the many stairs to the crow's-nest. He wanted to call Inger and find out what was happening with Nash. He needed to arrange the surveillance on Kane.

Priorities! LJ was the most important; he had to be kept in the loop. He must also tell him that he was now carrying a firearm - his old friend the Glock 20. He opened up the secure video link, and waited for LJ to accept the comm.

"So, Mr Dillon - what progress have you made down there in Dorset?"

"I've found out where Kane is living."

LJ was sitting behind his desk, nodded and said, "We need to have a talk Jake." He looked directly at Dillon through the camera lens.

"A talk - that sounds ominous."

"I've had a call from the Home Secretary himself. He has made it very clear that the PM wants closure on this affair, old son. He does not want a national security risk running around the Dorset countryside with a car boot full of heroin. If the tabloids got hold of this there would be hell to pay. There is also the allegation you made against detective constable Harvey.

The Deputy Assistant Commissioner of the Metropolitan Police insists that you substantiate this."

"That's not possible until this assignment has reached its natural conclusion."

"Your inability to offer me any concrete evidence is worrying. I have an unpleasant suspicion that your obsession with Max Kane is clouding your judgement, old son."

"We are in the throes of investigating a colossal conspiracy that reaches all the way up to the highest echelons of power. I'd hate to have to tell Dunstan Havelock that I'd been pulled off the assignment because you felt it was going nowhere - fast." Levenson-Jones went to speak but Dillon continued talking, "This investigation has two divergent elements to it. The first involves both Max Kane and Jasper Nash. They are involved in a sophisticated drug smuggling operation that has been operating for many years and which the conventional law enforcement agencies, have so far been ineffectual in busting open the chain of command. The second, we are rightly or wrongly assuming, involves Nash only. Who we suspect is passing on British military nuclear secrets to a Communist state. But, somewhere along the way, Nash has recruited another source. And as I've since discovered, he is now also able to sell highly sensitive United Nation strategic deployment blueprints to the highest bidder."

"Well. Admittedly, this does put a different slant on things, old son. Is there anything else?"

"Only that I resent having my integrity and ability questioned," snapped Dillon sharply.

"No one is questioning your integrity, Jake. As for your ability, I think you've proven that many times over, old son. Now if that's all, I think this video conference is over..." Dillon jumped in with both boots on.

"I'm pretty sure that Kane has someone inside Ferran & Cardini who is passing on information about this assignment to him."

It took a moment for the accusation to sink in. "Any ideas about who this person is?" LJ's voice was grave.

"I'm keeping that information to myself for the time

being. But, I'll get to the bottom of it by the time this assignment is over." Dillon knew he couldn't accuse Vince yet. LJ would sneer at such an unlikely suspect.

"You have until the end of the week to wrap this thing up."

The link was terminated and the screen turned blue.

* * *

"Cracker" The voice resonated down the corridor. It registered in Cracker's eardrums. He didn't know if the voice was even real. His head snapped round. He peered down through the gloom and picked out a shadowy figure at the far end of the corridor.

"I want a little chat with you."

The woman had been right after all. Someone had been watching. He took his hand from around her neck and stood up. He walked towards the voice.

"We don't have much time," said the accented voice. "You don't know me, but I know you. I've got a message from Max Kane."

Cracker could feel cold beads of sweat rolling down over his brow. He was struggling to keep his focus as he approached the figure. From six feet away he could see the face of Vince Sharp. He pulled out a Smith & Wesson snub-nose revolver from his jacket pocket and aimed at the obese figure in front of him. Each round left the barrel in quick succession as Cracker emptied the entire chamber into the figure's head.

* * *

From the front, the building looked impregnable. The windows were boarded up and the door had been obstructed with a large concrete block. Advertising posters were billed over the shuttering. Jasper looked suspiciously at the surrounding landscape, woods to the west and outbuildings to the east of the main building. He thought for one awful moment that Razor had given him the wrong address, but this thought was allayed quickly when he spotted a dim light coming from between the roughly fitted shutters of one of the first floor rooms. He stood still for a moment, listening intently for any signs of life. He walked round to the back. The carcass of an old 1980's Vauxhall Cavalier stood on construction blocks at the far end of a courtyard. Its wheels had long gone, the bodywork eaten away by the ravages of time and the rust that had ensued. He had expected Dillon and Inger to be there before him. He was surprised by the absence of activity. The back door of the old former hotel was ajar. He crouched low and moved quickly across the courtyard to the decaying car which offered a small degree of cover. He felt he was being watched from behind the dark windows of the outbuildings located around the far end of the courtyard.

He crouched down behind the old car and took Razor's Smith & Wesson revolver from his jacket pocket. It looked straightforward enough. There was a safety catch and a trigger. You just point and fire, what could be simpler. It had been a long time since he'd handled a firearm, and even then he had disliked the noisy things.

He looked at the door. There was still no sign of life. He held the gun beneath his jacket and ran quietly across the courtyard to the door. He looked behind him and saw someone watching him. It was Inger. He felt relief that he wasn't alone. He stood to one side of the door and beckoned her to join him. A moment later she was beside him.

"Where's Dillon?" He whispered.

She shook her head. "I don't know."

"Damn it!" hissed Jasper.

"I think he has found Max Kane," she offered by way of explanation.

Jasper smiled. "At last!" he hesitated for a moment. He took a deep breath. "Let's go in," he said.

"No," she said. "We wait for Dillon."

Jasper shook his head. He pushed open the door slowly, bringing up the handgun from under his jacket. Inger stared at it. Nash ignored her.

Ahead of him there was a short corridor. To the left was a door. He peered inside, into the gloom. Originally this area had been the below stairs staff toilets and washroom, he thought. He reached a swing door at the other end, and peered over the top into what had once been a large hectic kitchen. He pushed open the door. The spring on the hinge screeched in protest. Echoing around the darkened room, breaking the silence, and then for the briefest moment it was quiet. Then he heard the running footsteps. He looked, and saw Martha descending the stairs in the corner. She saw him, and hesitated for a moment, before she recognised him. Her dress had been ripped to the waist, and hung in tatters. Her attention was caught by something at the bottom of the stair well. Jasper couldn't see. She retreated up the stairs; horror on her face. She looked back at Jasper, as if begging him to do something.

Martha turned to run back, and her foot caught in the torn hem of her dress, tripping her. She fell awkwardly on the stairs. She rolled down, glancing off the walls, arms flailing in an attempt to break her fall.

"Martha!" shouted Jasper, starting forward to pick her up. He sensed movement to his right, swung round and saw Cracker standing there.

Jasper pulled the trigger of the gun, before he had fully raised his arm. He heard the shot, and instinctively knew it had missed. He pulled the trigger again. Cracker was almost on top of him. He caught sight of the knife blade. He saw the blood on Crackers sleeve. Whose blood? He took a wild shot, ducking away, and stumbling backwards. He kicked out at Cracker who was hurling himself at him, and rolled away.

Jasper brought up the gun, elbows on the floor, held it with both hands and pointed it at Cracker's chest, five feet away.

"No" He heard Inger's scream.

He pulled the trigger.

The gun kicked as the last round left the chamber.

Then there was silence. He stared at Cracker's body twitching involuntarily, and then nothing. He kept his aim steady at the head, at the bright crimson coloured hole. The smell of cordite and smoke filled the room.

Finally Jasper rolled away and stood up. He looked over at Martha, but Inger was quicker than him, and had an arm around her. Martha was gasping for breath, her mouth open in a soundless scream. She was swaying, her legs curled beneath her, and her hands clasping Inger's arm for security.

"Call the paramedics." He shouted at Inger. "Call nine, nine, nine now!"

"There's a phone in my handbag," said Inger calmly.

Jasper scrabbled in the bag, found the mobile phone and punched in the three nines. The call was answered almost immediately, the operator asking questions automatically.

"Name and address caller?"

He paced the floor, following the trail of blood around the corner and saw the bloody corpse. He hesitated, peering closely at the face, scared that it might be Dillon. It was too bulky to be Dillon.

"Caller - are you still there, caller?" The operator caught his attention. "What is the nature of your emergency?" He tried to sound calm. How much more information did they want? It seemed like an eternity before all of the details were recorded.

He pushed the end call button, and knelt beside Martha. He looked at Inger. "There's a dead body over there."

"Who is it?" Inger asked.

Jasper shrugged. "I don't know. He's definitely dead."

Inger didn't go to look. She felt Martha shivering and her skin felt clammy, and her eyes were lack lustre. "She's going into shock. Give me your jacket; it'll help keep her warm." She ordered, lowering Martha to the floor and raising her feet slightly to help circulation. Inger checked the other woman's pulse. It felt weak, but rapid.

Jasper took off his jacket and draped it over Martha. He took her hand. She pulled away.

"I'm sorry Martha. Truly sorry for the trouble I've caused."

It was a long time before Martha replied. She answered in a quiet voice. It was quite deliberate, quivering from the ordeal at the hands of Cracker. Her face was ashen, and beginning to glisten with perspiration.

"Leave me alone, Jasper. It's all over."

Jasper stared at her in bewilderment. He looked at Inger.

"Now you must call the police, Jasper," said Inger.

"No. I don't think so," said Jasper. He looked back at Martha, "I'm sorry, Martha. I hadn't foreseen this happening. I tried my best. But you're safe now."

"Leave me alone, Jasper. I never want to see you again," she said.

Inger shook her head at Jasper.

Then Martha screamed. A long loud, piercing scream which stopped him talking and startled Inger as well. The scream was born of frustration.

Jasper closed his eyes, and finally understood. When it ended, Martha buried her head in Inger's lap and cried; small gasps of despair.

Jasper stood up. He looked at Martha, her head buried, her hands grasping Inger's coat, her knuckles white.

Jasper looked at Inger. She stared back at him. Willing him to go - willing him to stay - praying for Dillon or the police to arrive. He saw nothing but his own selfish self-preservation. It was all over.

Jasper turned, looked with hate at Cracker. He picked up the Smith and Wesson, and put it in his pocket. He stood beside the corpse and prodded it with the toe of his shoe. It didn't move. And Razor could suffer on the boat for eternity; he dropped the mobile phone into Inger's bag.

He walked out of the door.

* * *

It was six-thirty the next morning. The Special Projects team at Ferran & Cardini International were still in shock by the news that one of their own had been killed whilst on an assignment. They waited for their instructions. They all felt that Vince's death could easily have been their own. They did not understand why it was taking so long for a directive to be issued. They wanted to be back on the case. They knew that the murder would fall under police jurisdiction; but the case itself was theirs.

In his office LJ prevaricated. He wanted to keep the

lid on the whole affair; but that was the only point on which he agreed with Dillon. The assignment should never have had doubt cast upon it; Dillon had fully vindicated himself, and now he refused to hand it over to the police.

Dillon was exasperated. "You can ignore the fact that Vince knew something about Nash's past that he had not imparted to anyone else. You can ignore Nash's tip off that Kane had someone placed in side of Ferran & Cardini. You can even ignore the fact that someone leaked the information of Aleksey's girlfriend's whereabouts. But what you can't ignore is that a man was seen talking to Cracker Conner fitting Vince Sharp's description by Nash's girlfriend, and she distinctly believed he was the enemy." The police could handle the murder. They could handle the abduction. They could even go looking for Max Kane. But Jasper Nash belonged to Ferran & Cardini, and to Dillon.

"Yes," said LJ, "but we don't know exactly what was said. Vince might have been negotiating the woman's release."

"We both know better than anyone else that is highly unlikely. Why didn't he call for back-up when he discovered where the woman was being held hostage?"

"Listen old son, it seems somewhat fortuitous that the very officer who cannot defend himself is being accused of corruption," said LJ.

"I'm willing to ignore that issue for the moment. There are more pressing things to concentrate on. We should make sure no mention of this is leaked to the press," said Dillon.

"If this gets into the news then Nash will be gone. At the moment he has no idea how badly things are going for him."

"I don't know if the police will accept that," cautioned LJ.

"I don't give a damn what the police like," warned Dillon.

LJ stared at him. He knew exactly what Dillon's warning meant; he was threatening to activate the biggest internal investigation into corruption the department had ever seen. It was best for morale if that didn't happen; and it never need happen, because Vince was dead and he had murdered

Cracker Conner. If Dillon was right about corruption, it was a convenient scenario. "What about Jasper Nash?" LJ asked.

"I don't know if he will contact us again. But I do know that the consignment of heroin changed hands, because Nash found out where Martha was being held hostage. That means that Villiers must contact Kane at some stage in order to pass over the drugs or the money."

"The police will want to put out an All-Ports-Warning in case Nash tries to skip the country."

"Fair enough, but if Nash is going to run he'll use his network of contacts to slip away quietly. Or, he might just run straight to the North Korean Embassy! Either way, we need to ensure that it doesn't get anywhere near the media. I'd much prefer a story was put out on Kane immediately, just in case he attempts to slip away while we're having this discussion."

LJ picked up the phone on his desk and dialled an internal number. "Have media affairs put together a piece on Maximilian Kane," he listened for a moment and then replied.

"Oh, something that will set the press packs after him with fervour," he hung up. "What's the news on Nash's girlfriend, Martha Hamilton?"

"Inger is still with her at the hospital in Dorset. She's suffering from shock. No interviews are being allowed until after midday tomorrow."

"So the police haven't been to interview her?"

"Not yet."

"They might well conclude that Cracker was working undercover, and that Vince found out."

"They might come to that conclusion," said Dillon, sceptically.

"And you're sure you can link this whole affair to Nash?" LJ asked.

"What, you mean the drugs or the espionage?" Dillon said bluntly.

"Both!"

"Yes."

"Then what are you waiting for, old son. Get on with it."

345

They looked at each other.

"Harvey?" LJ reminded Dillon.

"I think that's the least of our problems at the moment. I'm sure the Assistant Commissionaire will realise that our investigation is not complete."

LJ nodded. "Keep me posted of your progress, day and night."

"Of course I will," said Dillon. He didn't bother to tell his boss that he had already posted two field officers to watch Kane's apartment block before news of Vince's murder had broken.

* * *

Jasper knew he had lost everything. All he had left was his freedom, and he was not about to lose that. It was time to leave the UK. It was time to think about how he was going to do this. There was no way that Dillon or the police would allow him to simply walk away from a charge of selling top-secret information to a communist state like North Korea, and not forgetting a further charge of smuggling a 'class A' drug on a massive scale. He forced himself not to look back; it would only slow him down. He was surprised he was still at liberty, and if he could keep the momentum going he'd survive.

He had options. He still had the van safely hidden away in a back street lock-up, which had once been the start of a legitimate business. He tried not to think about those plans of a new life with Martha; they seemed so long ago. He would contact Jason, and beat Max to the money. He needed that money for the future. Max wasn't having it. He'd make sure Max knew who had taken it. He only wished he could be there when Max realised that it was his oldest friend that had ripped him off in the end.

Jasper had a friend who owned an airfreight operation flying out of Southampton, who would get him across the Channel. He'd make his way to Spain where he had contacts who could create a new identity for him. From there he would make his way across to the Caribbean, keep his head down for a year or two until the dust had settled and then return to the

UK. Perhaps he would see Martha again when the emotional scars might have healed, and maybe she would realise he was worth another chance.

For the briefest moment he was gripped by a terror that something bad was about to happen. He suppressed the fear. If he succumbed to the fears, then his freedom was meaningless.

He dumped Razor's BMW in the lock-up and picked up his van. It might be a mistake using it, but it wouldn't be for long. When he was out of the country he'd give Dillon a call, and tell him what he wanted to know, and who he should be looking for in the corridors of power. But first he had to make some phone calls.

* * *

Jasper met Jason in the underground car park of the supermarket at seven-thirty. They walked to Jason's car carrying bags of groceries. It was like old times; at the end of another job.

"You look awful mate," commented Jason.

"I've had a few problems," replied Jasper. "I've got to leave the UK."

"Have you been rumbled after all these years?" Jason asked, alarmed.

"No, it's nothing like that." Jasper lied. "But I've been seen in the wrong company."

"I was told that you'd already left the country," said Jason.

"Oh, I changed my plans," said Jasper. He decided it was better not to tell Jason the details after all. "How did things go with you?"

"Like a dream - no problems at all." Jason replied.

"I'm sorry that Max got in touch with you."

"To tell you the truth, I was really pissed off. I thought it was a bloody liberty all round."

"Did he give you a number to contact him on?" There was always the chance that Max had become careless.

"Yeah, he gave me a mobile number that I could call him on. Anyway, I'm glad you phoned. He had some really

347

complicated plan for handing over the money to some Swiss banker who was going to be in London next weekend."

"He never could keep things simple." They walked in silence for a moment or two. "Call him and tell him that I've already collected the money. You don't want any confusion."

"Don't worry, I will," said Jason.

"I won't be working with Max Kane again," said Jasper.

"He's become far too dangerous. Tell the good guys to keep well clear of him."

"Thanks," said Jason. The warning was unnecessary, and he knew better than to ask any questions.

They got into Jason's car and Jasper directed him to where he had parked. Jason opened the boot and took out four ordinary looking canvas holdalls with grip handles and loaded them into the van. He conspicuously handed the bag of groceries for the benefit of any onlookers. They were a couple of single blokes doing their weekend shopping after work.

"The money's all there. The final score was nine hundred and fifty kilos give or take a few grams. At today's rate, that makes four point eight million, less my commission of eight hundred thousand, leaves you with four million pounds sterling. Happy counting - it's always good doing business with you, Jasper."

They stood awkwardly for a moment or two. "Will you do something for me, Jason?"

"What is it?" Jason replied cautiously.

"Why don't you...?" he began, but Jasper interrupted him.

"We're not together anymore." Jasper said, and looked away. He felt a lump in his throat.

"I'm sorry, Jasper. Of course I'll do it."

Jasper pulled out one of the bags from the back of the van and passed it to Jason. "Give her that for me. Tell her it's my way of saying sorry and that I will always love her."

Jason nodded.

"Thanks Jason. I'll give you a call sometime. Maybe go for dinner."

Jason shook Jasper's hand. Jasper stepped into the van

and started the engine.

"Jasper!" said Jason. Jasper looked at him. "Good luck mate."

Jasper drove away. It was the first time he had left a meeting before Jason.

* * *

As he drove along the spur road towards the A31 at Ringwood, Jasper amused himself with the thought of how Max would react when he found out he had been ripped off. He liked the idea of Max catching up with him in the future. Max had always been paranoid about a rip-off. In all the years of running drugs he'd only experienced a fifty grand theft. New he was going to know how it felt to lose a couple of million. His worst nightmare was about to come true.

Jasper imagined a future meeting between them in some Cuban hotel or Spanish tapas bar. He looked forward to that encounter.

* * *

Jasper hunched over the steering wheel, driving carefully through a heavy thunderstorm, the raindrops killing themselves on the windscreen. It would only be an hour or so until he dumped the van and met up with Flynn in Eastleigh, and then he would be safe. He and Flynn had worked together on and off for over five years. He had helped Flynn with the finance to set up the airfreight operation. Now Flynn knew all the customs procedures, loopholes and scams at airports all over Europe. He was known by many of the officers because he did round trips to mainland Europe every week. He worked regular flights with his four turbo-prop aircraft. Most pilots who turned to smuggling were caught because they made stupid mistakes. They came into the country with unprofitable consignments or even empty cargo-holds. No company could afford to run an empty aircraft. The fly-by-nights set up an operation and bought older aircraft on the cheap for a few hundred grand. Flynn's fleet of four aircraft was worth a few million, and they paid for themselves legitimately. The others bought aircraft and created secret compartments throughout the fuselage, and then scratched their heads when Customs ripped open every panel and discovered the drugs. Flynn had purchased his first aircraft and ripped out the entire interior, replacing it with the exact same, but with the addition of new hollow panels, which became airtight once the dope was packed inside. This kept the sniffer dogs away and the panels were riveted back in securely after each trip.

They'd brought dope and cocaine into the country in this way hundreds of times, and taken the money out. Customs had even asked Flynn to report if he noticed anything suspicious about other airfreight operations. He had one of the best outfits because he'd set it up with Jasper. They'd had it made. They'd hit it off from the moment they'd met, and had never had a bad word between them, differences of opinion, but never bad words...

Max had blown it all. Max's greed had blown it all. Jasper wanted revenge. He suddenly realised he was doing this the wrong way. Max had to know who was responsible for his downfall. He wanted vengeance because Max had ruined his relationship with Martha. He wasn't going to let Max get away with ruining his life. Max Kane had to pay for all his wrong doings - ripping off a few million pounds wasn't enough. There were some things money could not buy.

When Martha heard about this, she might give him another chance.

Jasper pulled into the motorway service area. He phoned Flynn to change their arrangement. Afterwards, he felt better. He would enjoy dishing out his retribution on Max. When he'd done this, he wouldn't have to look over his shoulder in case Max tracked him down. Max would be otherwise occupied, locked away.

Chapter 19

It was late evening when Dillon arrived at Martha Hamilton's luxury apartment on the Sandbanks peninsula. He had parked the Porsche Panamera in a side road and walked the short distance back to Banks Road. Inger was just coming down the stairs into the main entrance hall on her way out of the building.

Inger had formed a bond with Martha, supporting her through her ordeal, and now that it was over, she felt empty. Dillon put his arms around her, and gave her a squeeze. She relaxed and folded into him for a moment, he responded by holding her a moment longer than he should have. They walked slowly back to the Porsche, the rain had stopped and the night sky was clear and they both savoured the sudden calm after the day's activity. He told her what had happened, and listened to the recount of her story.

"There's nothing more we can do tonight." He said.

"Except wait until the morning."

She slipped her arm through his as they walked. "Don't think about this assignment for now," she said.

"You're right," he agreed. "I'm tired of thinking. I've waited a long time for Kane. Nash also - anyway I've given it my best shot."

They walked in silence. "I think I'll go back to my house, have a drink and go to bed." Inger didn't comment, but he caught a look of confusion on her face. "I should have told you, I own one of the waterfront houses on the peninsula. LJ thought it safer if we rented a house, just in case things got rough."

"You don't owe me any explanations, Dillon. But I'm impressed all the same."

"Look, you don't have to come," he said. "You're probably sick of it all, and me, by now."

"If you want to be alone, maybe I should go back to the rented house," said Inger.

"That's not what I meant. I'd be happy if you'd come back."

"Do you have Champagne?" Inger asked.

Dillon raised one eyebrow, and said with a smile. "Is water wet?"

Inger smiled. She'd decided that she liked his sense of humour. She liked him after all, despite the bumpy start to their working relationship. He took out his cigarettes, and her hand slipped from his arm. She watched him, standing with his back to the breeze, face illuminated by the glow of the flickering flame. He was crying out to be loved, but he didn't know it. He kept himself so tightly closed; and she wondered who had hurt him in the past.

Dillon held the passenger door open for Inger to get into the Porsche. They sat in the luxurious interior and he was conscious of her warmth in the seat beside him. He looked across at her briefly, thinking what a gorgeous woman she was.

* * *

Dillon couldn't stop himself thinking about Nash. He wouldn't let Edward Levenson-Jones get away with simply sweeping the assignment under the carpet. He wasn't letting Vince Sharp, a man he had known for many years, and considered a close friend, be accused of being corrupt without carrying out a thorough investigation first. If the truth spoiled LJ's chance of being placed on the New Year's honours list, that was tough; and it would spoil his chances, because shit stuck. The whole Special Projects department would be smeared within the intelligence community.

He wouldn't pull any punches when he wrote up his report for Dunstan Havelock. He'd point out that there had been a lack of confidence in his handling of the assignment. That the reason for the lack of progress was largely due to his hands being tied by bureaucracy and over cautiousness on the part of his superiors. He knew that he would find proof of Vince's involvement with Kane, and he wouldn't have to dig too deep.

He would snout around the docks. Vince had been the one who had wanted that part of the assignment. Maybe something or someone would provide the key. Dillon would nail charges to Vince's coffin, and then see who turned up for the funeral. To hell with you, Cracker - you made a big mistake with your crooked smile and lips like a French Bulldog's arsehole.

* * *

"Relax Jake!" Inger said. She put her hand on his arm. "You are so tense. Your body is like a coiled spring. I think maybe you need a Swedish massage. What is wrong?"

"Nothing really, I was just thinking."

From what Inger knew of him, she knew that he would never open up. Old dogs didn't learn new tricks. He'd lived in that cage for too long. People like him were safe to have as friends. They made no demands on relationships, and never got too close unless invited. She liked it that way...

"Come over and sit next to me," she said patting her hand on the sofa cushion next to where she was sitting. She never could work out why she did some things. It seldom mattered. Life was a series of mysterious twists and turns and there was always some way of getting back home.

Dillon sat down next to her. For the first time in his life he wasn't sure about this situation or the stunning Scandinavian blonde sitting no more than twelve inches from him.

"Come," said Inger, and leaning towards him, gently removed the glass from his hand. She pulled him towards her and held him in her arms. He relaxed and almost as quickly resisted. She gripped his hair, pulled his face towards her, and kissed him. She parted her lips and slowly felt his tongue explore.

With urgency, Dillon's hands began work. His fingers slipped beneath her blouse and stroked her soft skin. He found her breasts, and caressed them for a moment, her breathing becoming laboured. For a moment they melted into one another.

"Are you sure this is a good idea?" he whispered in her ear.

"Can you think of a reason why not?" She answered,

quietly.

Dillon stood up and held out his hand and led her upstairs to the bedroom. They undressed each other slowly in the semi-darkness. She lay back on the bed, her naked body illuminated by a shaft of light shining through the half-closed door. He ran his hands from her thighs to her breasts, cherishing the firmness of her flesh. He pressed his lips lightly against hers, gently using his tongue to part hers, teasing her with things to come by moving it erratically inside her mouth.

His body was hardened and defined, unlike the soft untrained physique of her boyfriend in Holland. Dillon was gentle, he relocated his attentions away from her face, and she pulled him towards her - feeling him nuzzling provocatively against her inner thighs.

Back with a more urgent kiss her arms went around his torso, her legs around him - her hands over his battle-scarred flesh. He entered her with a loud sigh and moved in time with her writhing desperation. There were periods of love making interrupted by minutes of fucking until Dillon climaxed with a long satiated groan, he slowly withdrew and they both lay panting for a few moments, he twisted around and kissed her lips again, a long slow kiss, exclusive to new lovers. He wrapped his arms around her and holding her tight, and in the warmth of the bed, he could feel sleep overwhelming him. He moved his hand and stroked Inger's blonde hair before he drifted away.

Inger listened to Dillon's breathing. He was asleep. She could rarely let herself go the first time she made love to a new partner, male or female, but the novelty of the experience could never be repeated. She had no regrets. She ran her fingers over her breasts, slowly down her body; she closed her eyes and blissfully touched herself until the final moments when she stopped moving her fingers and let the rest of her body take over...

* * *

Dillon was still asleep when the doorbell rang. He struggled awake and gently disentangled his limbs from Inger's body. He looked at his watch, wondering who was calling at three in the morning. He got out of bed, slipped on a pair of jeans and went to the other side of the bedroom and pulled out his Glock 20 - ten millimetre automatic from where it was taped to the underside of a dressing table. He slipped it into the waistband of the jeans and padded barefoot along the landing and down the wide staircase to the main hall. He picked up his iPad and opened the app. that controlled the house security system, and recognised the voice on the line immediately. He tapped the icon to open the main entrance gates, and then tapped the one next to it to open the front door.

Dillon rushed back to the bedroom. He was wide awake and running on an adrenalin rush. "Inger!" he said, shaking her gently. "Wake up!" She moaned. "Wake up. It's Nash. He's back. Get dressed." He pulled on the rest of his clothes quickly. He was still buttoning his shirt when he heard the knock on the front door.

* * *

Jasper had left Eastleigh. He was committed to the plan now. He'd given the money to Flynn to keep for him. "I may be gone for some time. You'll hear from me every now and then. Spread this lot around. Maybe Belize or Lichtenstein, the banks there won't ask any questions about the size of the deposits you will be making. You can keep all of the interest for your trouble." He never questioned the faith he put in Flynn. If he started questioning the very few people he trusted, the whole deck of cards would tumble.

Flynn was big, solid and dependable. He smiled a big toothy smile in response to the instructions. His eyes twinkled as he peered into the bags. He stroked his cropped blonde hair with a large palm. He whistled when he saw the bundles of notes. "I thought you were too young to be allowed on the Brinks Mat heist."

"Cheeky sod," Jasper said jovially.

"It'll be here when you get back," said Flynn, gravely. And Jasper knew he meant it.

Flynn didn't ask any questions. He was used to Jasper's sudden appearances and disappearances. "Watch your back," he said, in farewell.

Then Jasper was driving west again, exhausted. He stopped at the motorway services for coffee, trying hard to stay awake.

* * *

Hello, Jasper," said Dillon. "I didn't expect to see you again so soon."

"Has Max Kane been arrested yet?" Jasper asked, dispensing with the niceties. If they'd picked up Max, then that was game over.

"I'm afraid not, Jasper."

"But you know where he is?"

"Yes we do," Dillon nodded.

"You've got him under twenty-four hour surveillance?"

"Naturally, I have three teams looking after Mr Kane." Dillon was already becoming bored with this cat and mouse question and answer game. Wondering from whom he had gotten his private address.

Jasper relaxed a little. That made things easier. "Good, because I've been doing a lot of thinking about Max, the police haven't got much on him, certainly not enough to bring a case against him. So they need to catch him red handed with the heroin - and I have the heroin."

"What happened to Razor?" Dillon asked.

"Max ordered him to kill me. He thought I'd be an easy target. Well he got that badly wrong - he came off worse!" Jasper shrugged.

"Did you kill him?" Inger asked.

"Not quite. He was alive when I left him. Not in great shape. But alive."

"Come on through to the living room," said Dillon. "You look exhausted. This is going to take a while, and I need to know everything you did after Razor gave our surveillance the slip."

Jasper told Dillon everything that happened on the boat, and its location.

"Any objections to me sending one of my field officers

to take a look there immediately?"

"No," Jasper shook his head. "By the way, if you don't find Razor. You might want to trawl the river bottom around the boat."

Dillon picked up the house phone and called the special op's coordinator at Ferran & Cardini International in Docklands, London. He instructed him to dispatch a field officer from one of the surveillance teams to Wareham

Inger emerged from the kitchen holding a tray with three mugs of freshly ground black coffee. Jasper started. He stood up defensively, before realising who it was. His nerves were shot.

"Coffee, Jasper?" Inger asked.

"Thank you. By the way - how is Martha since she returned home?"

"She's taking things a day at a time. That was a traumatic experience she had to endure and it'll take time for her to get back to normal - if she ever recovers at all from the ordeal."

Jasper was saddened by this news, and suddenly he only felt sorrow inside.

Dillon came off the phone to London. His expression was one of distrust, and suddenly he was looking directly at Jasper as if he were dangerous.

Jasper sank back into the luxurious soft hide of the sofa; he could tell that both Dillon and Inger were on high alert for any false moves he might be thinking of making. He began to doubt himself.

"So," said Dillon finally, "why have you come here?"

"I want to make a deal," said Jasper.

"You must be joking," Dillon said incredulously. He was authorised by the Home Secretary to deal with Nash if he had to. He might have to. "You killed someone, Jasper. That cannot be overlooked."

"You know as well as I do. A top-flight QC would get that reduced down to self-defence, and booted out of court as quick as you like. So why don't you get real and listen to my proposition. I will deliver the heroin to Max. In return you will ensure that no charges are brought against me for smuggling the drugs."

Dillon remained silent and kept his expression deliberately neutral.

"Look, I know you have the pull in the right corridors to make the drug thing go away…" Jasper said his voice was quivering a little.

"I do have the, pull, as you say, Jasper. To make your life very easy, but I can also make your life a living hell. However, I like your proposition so far - keep talking."

"OK then. We need to move on Max, before he makes a run for it."

"Why the change of heart now?" asked Dillon.

"Because of what he did to Martha - that's why. Max never liked the thought of me and Martha getting married, so he ruined the one thing he knew I cherished above everything else. All that the authorities have against Max Kane is circumstantial evidence. Even what I've told you about his financial affairs may not help, if he's already closed those accounts. There is the strong possibility that those accounts are not in his name. They'll lead investigators to other people, but not necessarily Max. This is the only way." He paused. "Anyway, I want revenge - just like you."

"You've thought about the consequences?" asked Dillon.

"Of course I have. Max Kane is not going to forget this betrayal in a hurry. He still has friends in far flung places. Even if this operation bankrupts him, they owe him favours, and I don't fancy my chances of survival after I've sold him down the road. Maybe you'll sort me out a new identity. Lock me up in a prison for traitors and spies. I've thought about it, and it's worth all that."

Dillon said nothing. He didn't know if Jasper would qualify for the Witness Protection Programme. He called the duty officer at Ferran & Cardini and told him to send three experienced field officers with firearms to join the two officers who were already watching Kane.

* * *

Dillon drove Inger and Jasper in the Porsche to the back street lock-up garage and retrieved the heroin for the BMW. Jasper sat in the back seat. "This is how I want to play it out," said Jasper. "I will deliver the heroin. I want a moment alone with Max. I want him to know what he has done. When I come out, then you can let the drug squad arrest him. After all, he will literally be holding the goods, and you'll have witnessed the transfer."

"He may refuse to accept the heroin. Especially if you tell him you're selling him out."

"I'm not that stupid. I won't be alluding to any sell out. I only want him to know his most recent antics and association with Razor and Cracker was ruined because of his greed. When he's arrested I want him to know I fingered him."

Dillon nodded, although he wasn't sure. There was still plenty which could go horribly wrong. It might be wise to simply let the drug squad boys arrest them both as they met, although Kane could deny he knew what was inside the bags.

"Can you open the bags inside his flat, so there's no doubt Kane knows what's in them?"

"Sure, I can do that," said Jasper. After a few moments he asked. "Tell me something. Why do you want Max so much?"

"About twenty years ago I was training to be an officer in the army at Sandhurst. I used to travel home most weekends to a small fishing village on the Cornish coast to visit my girlfriend Anna. Then a flash ocean going yacht came into port to shelter from a storm. Max Kane was aboard and he killed Anna."

There was stunned silence in the car. Inger looked at Dillon. Things were becoming clearer to her.

"I heard that it was an accident," said Jasper.

"That's what the coroner's court found. But it most certainly wasn't an accident." Dillon said. "But you'd know that wouldn't you Jasper?"

"I was there," said Jasper. "It was our first major smuggling operation. We were transporting cocaine for the Russian, Aleksey, in Paris. I can't remember how much now. I turned up pretending to be a sail maker and took the gear off the boat. I never went back again. It was some time later that I heard a girl had drowned there."

"That was Anna. Kane's first victim," said Dillon, heatedly.

"I'm sorry," said Jasper. "I'm very sorry to hear that." He paused, and then added. "So let's nail him good and proper. I'm counting on you to put him away for a long, long time."

Dillon surprised himself. He pulled over, turned in his seat and faced Jasper. He held out his hand, and the two of them shook hands. "You've got a deal. But this doesn't change anything. I've still got to bring you in for selling our national nuclear secrets to the North Koreans." Dillon said, and smiled grimly. He turned back, and drove on.

Dillon was such a complicated character, thought Inger. She wondered how he really felt, and whether he really believed that Kane's arrest would release him form this lifelong obsession. She hoped he didn't have too many expectations. Simply convicting Kane wouldn't change his life; it wasn't like that, not after twenty years. The habits and defences were too deeply etched into his character.

"We're approaching Kane's place," said Dillon. "It's a first floor flat of ten in the block. There's a…"

"I know which flat it is," interrupted Jasper. "He's a clever fucker, renting this place out all these years, so he could turn it back into a bolt hole when it suited him."

Dillon turned the next corner, and stopped. Across the road was a white Mercedes van; the driver raised his hand, to scratch his chin, as an acknowledgement of Dillon's arrival.

The drug squad were ready.

* * *

Jasper ascended the steps up to the main entrance of the block of flats. One thing was certain, if Max Kane was still in bed dreaming peacefully, he was about to wake up to his worst nightmare. A security light shone over the main entrance door. He placed the bags on the ground and pushed the intercom for Kane's flat. His heart began to race. It was curiously apposite that his partnership with Max should be ending where they had hatched the first operation all those years ago. He took out a cigarette and lit it. He inhaled deeply. He fingered Razor's gun in his pocket. For the first time he felt in control of a situation with Max.

He had a feeling that he might still be on the flight out of Southampton at dawn. The police wouldn't be expecting him to make a run for it. Their attention would be focused on Max. Hopefully, so would Dillon.

Jasper pushed the intercom again. He waited impatiently. There was no sign of life. Perhaps Max had already flown the country. No! Dillon was confident he was still in there. He rang the intercom a third and final time. He waited.

The intercom panel lit up as Kane answered. "Who is it?" His voice was angry at having been woken up.

"It's Jasper, Max."

"Jasper - what the fuck, are you doing here at this ungodly hour?"

"I'm delivering the drugs, Max." Jasper spoke in a quiet voice.

The door unlocked and Jasper picked up the bags and entered the building. He walked up the flight of stairs to the first floor. Kane's door was open and he was standing there in his dressing gown.

"Come in, Jasper, come in."

"I won't stay, Max. Just to let you know that I've got Martha, no thanks to you. But a deal is a deal."

Kane looked at the canvas holdalls suspiciously. "Bring them into the living room." Kane said, holding the door open. Jasper walked through and put the holdalls onto a low coffee table.

Kane closed the front door behind Jasper, and then switched on the light. He had obviously woken up from a heavy sleep and thrown on his dressing gown. He entered the living room, "Sit down," he said perching on the edge of the sofa.

Kane's brain was whirring into action. A knock on the door in the middle of the night was never good news, but he hadn't expected Jasper. How had he found out where he was hiding? Someone must have told him, but there was no one who knew. "So tell me, how long did it take you to find out where I was?" Kane asked, making sure his voice didn't betray his concerns.

"Someone told me," said Jasper.

"How intriguing, Jasper. And I wonder who that someone was?" Kane kept the anger out of his voice and his demeanour casual. That someone had to be Detective Constable Harvey or that spook Dillon. They must have found out somehow. It meant Jasper was attempting to broker a deal with the authorities. But Vince Sharp had reported that Jasper met Razor. Something had obviously gone horribly wrong.

"Who was that?"

"Your insider at Ferran & Cardini before Cracker decided to kill him."

Kane raised his eyebrows. "Why have you come here?"

"I came to fulfil my end of the agreement. To hand over the heroin," Jasper leaned forward and unzipped the bags. "It's all in there."

"Ah yes. The heroin," Kane mused. "You know, I thought you were going to rip me off, Jasper."

"Oh, I have ripped you off, Max," replied Jasper. "I've collected the money from Jason. I'm keeping it for all the trouble you've caused me."

There were more important things than money at stake now.

"I haven't heard from Razor or Cracker. Do you have any news of them?" asked Kane.

Jasper stared at Kane. He looked forward to seeing his reaction.

"Razor's dead. Would you believe it, that son-of-a-bitch tried to kill me. So did Cracker. I left him in a very poor state of health."

Kane raised his eyebrows. "Oh dear," he commented. Jasper was manifesting an uncharacteristic ruthlessness these days. "So you managed to resolve the thing with Martha?"

"This is bullshit, Max!" You put them up to all that. You were responsible for bringing Martha into this. And now you've fucked it all up - big time."

"It's a little disconcerting, Jasper." Kane shook his head. "You wouldn't be double-crossing me now, would you?"

Jasper looked at Kane. "I'm off now. I doubt if we will ever see each other again."

Kane nodded solicitously. He stood up and walked to the fireplace and picked up a packet of cigarettes, took one out and put it in his mouth. He looked around for a lighter. Walked across the room to where his jacket was hanging and reached into the pocket.

"You're playing a very dangerous game, Jasper. The way I see it, you're the only witness. Without you the authorities don't really have anything on me." Kane took the gun out of his jacket pocket.

He pointed the gun at Jasper's chest. "In case you're thinking that I wouldn't shoot you. Think again, because I will not hesitate to kill you. I am an extremely good shot."

Jasper wondered how long Dillon would wait before he came crashing through the door.

Kane smiled, and kicked the coffee table out of the way. Magazines and old newspapers slipped off onto the carpet. He yanked Jasper to his feet by grabbing his jacket and ripped it in the process.

"You can fuck off, Jasper. As usual you've got it all wrong. Your silence is my only insurance policy." He held the gun to Jasper's temple, pressing the muzzle into the flesh, turning it white with the excessive pressure that Kane was exerting. His face twisted with hate. "Fuck you now. You fucked up the biggest cocaine deal of all time." Kane pushed Jasper against the wall, kicking over a small occasional table and spilling coffee from a half full mug across the floor. The room was beginning to look like there had been a fight.

Jasper managed to grab hold of Kane's hand holding the gun as they struggled. He stared into Kane's eyes. "I have my own insurance policy, Max." He put his hand into his pocket and felt the gun.

"Really?" sneered Kane.

"Really, Max. I've done a deal," said Jasper. "This whole thing tonight is a set-up. There are at least four armed response officers and a team of drug squad officers outside. And they're waiting for you."

* * *

As Inger and Dillon watched Jasper walk up the steps to the main entrance of Kane's flat, Dillon said, "I think I'm going to get that bastard after all. But I need Nash as well, not only to be sure of getting Kane sent down for life, but I need Nash to give me the name of his source in the corridors of power."

"How do you think the court will find Jasper's position?" Inger asked.

"That depends on what he wants to tell us about the source of nuclear secrets that he's been selling to the North Koreans."

Dillon always felt a surge of energy flow through his body just before things kicked off. His alter ego came nearer to the surface when the shooting started and the world became a picture of black and white. No grey - just black and white. He wondered how long he should give Jasper. Five minutes, he decided.

Inger imagined the scene in the flat. She imagined Jasper opening the bags of heroin, and wondered how Kane would react. Suddenly she realised what it was which nagged at her. She could have kicked herself. When Jasper mentioned revenge, the word had made her uneasy. Now she knew why. Jasper still had the gun.

"Jake!" she said, "Jasper still has a gun."

Dillon looked at her puzzled, at first; then comprehension dawned.

"He said he wanted revenge, but I didn't think he meant to kill Kane," she said unnecessarily. Dillon was already talking to the officer in charge of the drug squad team, telling them to move in. They ran towards the block of flats.

They all heard the shot and then another.

They clattered up the steps and through the partially open main entrance door. Dillon banged on Kane's front door.

A police officer appeared with a door-breach ram, after three heavy swings of the twenty-three kilo ram the door's hinges gave way and the it burst open to the devastating sound of splintering wood.

* * *

Jasper struggled to stay awake, drifting into unconsciousness, struggling to remember where he was. It had been a long night. He jolted awake from time to time, drifting in and out of reality.

Flynn drove his truck through the torrential rain into the bright lights of Southampton airport and stopped at the security barrier. He had all his paperwork organised and ready for the border agency officials to inspect.

"I never thought I'd be taking you out of here. You all finished then?" Flynn asked. Jasper looked at the man with eyes that were heavily laden with burden. His exit from the UK was going according to plan. He was leaving the country. That was the only thing that mattered now.

"I really don't know," said Jasper. "I'm going away for a rest. Do you want to go on working?"

"The extra money is handy, for holidays and the like. And a bit extra always makes life a little easier."

Jasper's eyes darted around the immediate area outside the cab as Flynn moved forward towards the security checkpoint. Two security officers waved them down and gestured them to one side.

"What is it?" Jasper asked, anxiously.

"Nothing to worry about, Jasper," said Flynn. Jasper noticed that there were two more officers inside the office.

"Nothing to worry about, eh... I'll be the judge of that."

"It's been routine since they had a bomb scare in the main airport terminal. They tightened up on all security checks. Just relax, Jasper."

"I'll never get away from this bloody country at this rate." He shivered as the cold wind blasted through Flynn's open side window.

A moment later the truck moved forward again.

"You'd think that they'd know me and my truck after so many years. Shall I tell them, or do you want to?" Flynn stretched his arm out of the window to hand over the passports and his identification card. The young security officer scrutinised the documents to ensure they were in date and then handed them back, continuing his conversation with a colleague.

The barrier was opened and Flynn drove through and onto the airport. This was the point of no return. This was the turning point in his life - to become an exile from the UK, but Jasper Nash didn't plan to live in Paris or Geneva. He was going south to the sun, and a new life. Southampton airport didn't make him feel penitent about leaving this overcrowded island. There were too many cars and too many people and not enough land. He knew it all too well. He'd smuggled a few tons of cocaine into the country in his time. The biting wind whistled across the open tarmac, grasping at the baggage handlers high visibility jackets as they went about their duties. And as the truck parked alongside one of Flynn's private charter jets, Jasper relaxed and enjoyed the warmth of the cab for a moment longer.

He only felt a brief pang of remorse. He found himself standing on the tarmac apron, waiting to go aboard the aircraft. A young woman was standing next to him. It was Martha Hamilton. He watched outbound flights taking off, their navigation lights receding into the distance as they ascended. He wondered if he would ever see England again. He looked across at the private aircraft, its jet engines running, warming up. The rain was falling profusely now, obscuring visibility, and overwhelmed him. Moments later he came round, touched his forehead, and remembered what had happened only seconds before.

* * *

Jasper had watched Kane reel backwards. The side of his head obliterated, the wall spattered with blood and brain matter. Jasper went down with Kane as he crumpled on to the carpet. He knelt, quickly wiping his gun thoroughly with his handkerchief, and pressed his into Kane's left hand. He stood back and admired his handiwork. It looked like there had been a struggle. The blood was messing up Kane's cream coloured carpet. He smiled sardonically. A feeling of satisfaction, seeing Kane laid dead.

He stared at Kane's body with surprise. The devious bastard had actually planned to shoot him! He looked at the corpse with disdain. He disentangled Kane's fingers from the weapon he was holding in his right hand and carefully picked it up with his handkerchief. He dropped it into a clear plastic freezer bag with a sealable top.

Jasper heard heavy footsteps outside. He reached for the phone and dialled nine, nine, nine.

"Emergency Services," said the operator. "Which service do you require?"

"Police!" shouted Jasper.

He heard the men outside his front door shouting. As he walked to the rear of the flat with the wireless phone, he gave the address. He locked himself in the bathroom, and said. "My friend has just been shot in his living room during a struggle. I am barricaded in the bathroom. There are people breaking down the front door, and I think they are going to kill me."

"Please hold the line."

Jasper waited a moment while the police cars were deployed.

"Do you know if your assailants are likely to have firearms?"

"I'm confident that they are armed," said Jasper, and added. "They're inside the flat now." He could hear the bedroom doors being flung open. He didn't have long - just enough time for the theatricals and to add panic in to his voice.

"He's locked in the bathroom," shouted a male voice.

"Stand away from the door."

The bathroom door burst inwards and flew off its hinges. Jasper watched, from where he was sitting on the toilet, as Dillon came and stood in the middle of the open doorway.

"What the fuck, Nash." Dillon hissed. Jasper looked at the wireless phone in his hand. He guessed the police had heard and recorded everything. He terminated the connection.

"I don't think so, Dillon," said Jasper, insolently.

"By the way, there will be armed SO19 police officers here in a minute. They will want to know why you encouraged me to enter the home of a known criminal..."

* * *

Jasper Nash was taken from Max Kane's flat to the nearest police station and questioned by a senior investigating officer. Nash made the following statement.

I Jasper Nash, make this statement of my own free will. At four-thirty on the morning of 12th April, I went to the flat of Maximilian Kane, a man I had known for many years. I entered his flat, and was shown through to the living room. I had contacted Kane some weeks previously to ask him to repay a large sum of money that he owed me. He told me that he had insufficient funds available, and that he couldn't repay me right now. He then asked me for another loan for another new venture. The money he had borrowed previously had been for a new business that he had set up with two associates and had gone sour on him. He continued to beleaguer me with his requests, asking me to phone him at all hours. I took pity on him and tried to help him in practical ways.

On this visit Maximilian Kane appeared in a state of agitation. I asked him what was wrong and he proceeded to tell me about how his involvement in some nefarious activities had gone horribly wrong. He told me he had accidently killed one of his business associates during a struggle on his motor boat. I asked him if he had contacted the police. He told me he hadn't.

I tried to calm him down, but instead he blamed me for his current predicament and accused me of being deliberately disruptive. An accusation that I vehemently denied and told him not to be so paranoid.

I asked Maximilian Kane what was in the bags on the floor. He said they contained drugs, and proceeded to open one, from which he produced a gun and threatened to shoot me. At this point it was not obvious what he thought he was going to achieve. It appeared that he was attempting to frame me and had done a deal with the police to safeguard his own liberty. I was extremely anxious and when the opportunity presented itself I grappled with Kane for control of the gun. During this altercation the gun discharged itself and unfortunately shot Kane. I panicked when I heard what I assumed was Kane's associates at the front door. I locked myself in the bathroom and immediately called the police from a wireless phone.

At no time did any of the men identify themselves as law enforcement officers, and under the circumstances it is not surprising that I was petrified and in fear of my life.

When the bathroom door was smashed off of its hinges, I saw that there were at least six men in my hallway. The man I know as Jake Dillon appeared to be in charge. Shortly after this, the uniformed police officers arrived with an armed response unit and I was cautioned and arrested.

Signed

Jasper Nash

* * *

Dillon stood watching Jasper give his statement from behind the two-way mirror in the observation room next door. Inger was standing next to him with her arms crossed and a look of confusion.

"What's up?" Dillon asked.

"Jasper Nash is what's up!"

"What about him?"

"Why has he been brought to a police station when he should have been taken straight to a high security military unit for interview by someone skilled in counterintelligence?"

"I didn't have any choice other than to agree to him being brought here. The police know little if anything about the assignment that we have been running on Nash. Oh, and by the way, Inger. I've been de-briefing spies for over seventeen years."

"Oh, I didn't mean any…"

"I know you didn't mean anything by it." Dillon said amiably.

"So what happens now?" Inger said, turned and looked straight at Jasper Nash through the glass.

"Now we organise transportation to a Ferran & Cardini safe house, where I get to interview Mr Nash."

Chapter 20

Don Rafael believed in three things, his God, his right to extreme wealth and dire retribution for anyone who impugned the first two.

After hearing about the demise of Maximilian Kane, and the impounding of his heroin consignment by the UK police, he was certain he had been comprehensively cheated by Kane or one of his own principle associates there. The motive was simple - greed.

Don Rafael had become convinced that Kane had been playing the field with his heroin and cocaine, thus doubling the profits at his expense. His first reaction was to instruct his people to take revenge and to retrieve his narcotics from the police. This would be counterproductive, and only lead to the law enforcement agencies tightening up security at the ports in the UK.

The Colombian drug baron instead, decided to send two of his best assassins to tie up the loose ends left by Kane. Their instruction was to erase anyone associated with Kane; anyone who could potentially lead the authorities back to the Colombian cartel. The assassins arrived by way of different economy class flights departing from Bogotá El Dorado Airport: Colombia. One assassin used Lufthansa Airlines, via Frankfurt International Airport, arriving at London Heathrow. The other, flew United Airlines, stopping over at Newark International Airport, also arriving at London Heathrow.

For the next forty-eight hours the assassins left a trail of corpses from the container dock area in Poole, Dorset, up to London and, ending up in Manchester. They terminated everyone connected to Max Kane's drug distribution network. They had twelve residential addresses. Their orders were to destroy everything and leave nothing before the authorities could be mobilised. Only one person eluded them - Jasper Nash.

* * *

It took half an hour from the moment Major Kyung Sang Han of the Korean People's Army (KPA) terminated the call on his mobile phone. He felt a surge of power flow through his body as he stood inside the bunker about to witness the second test launch of his country's newest, and to date, most sophisticated long range nuclear missile. The order to carry out a test firing, without a warhead on-board, had come from the very top. The target on this occasion was a mock-up of a small town in the remotest regions of North Korea.

Han watched the engineers work; they had no intention of skimping their preparations just to appease their superiors. He had watched as the ground crew tanked the missile to its full 21,000lbs of fuel, giving it around 3,500 nautical miles airborne. A siren started to sound - it was time to clear the silo of all personnel and commence the countdown to launch.

Major Han was an officer in the KPA military intelligence department. For the last nine months he had been in charge of handling a British national turned traitor in England; who had been acquiring military nuclear secrets and passing them on to his embassy in London. This arrangement had been beneficial and extremely lucrative to both parties, until the traitor had become a liability to the cause and he had to authorise a wet squad to be sent to London to terminate him - that person was Jasper Nash.

* * *

They were on the lower fifth floor of the Ferran & Cardini International building in Docklands. Dillon looked across the glass topped conference table at Jasper Nash. They were done. After fourteen hours of questioning Dillon was satisfied that he had got as much information from Nash, as he was ever going to get out of him. Dillon called the Home Secretary's office to inform Dunstan Havelock that the assignment was over; that the name of the person instrumental in passing on military nuclear secrets to Jasper Nash would be sent to him by motorcycle courier once he had completed his report.

372

An hour later, Jasper Nash was transferred to a witness protection safe-house facility on the other side of London.

By eight-thirty that next morning - he was found dead. His throat had been cut, literally, from ear to ear. The blade had been skilfully applied with just enough pressure to severe the carotid artery but not to take off the head completely. The body lay crumpled in the corner, where the blood had flowed quickly onto the shower-room floor, to be washed away down the drain.

The witness protection officers, who had been minding Nash, reported that one of their colleagues had phoned in sick and another officer had been sent to cover for him.

This officer had been an imposter, an assassin sent to murder Nash.

Epilogue

The Porsche Panamera glided into the small Cornish coastal village, its driver stared around at the landmarks of his home, which he had not seen for many, many years.

North of the junction marking the centre of town he passed the war memorial, and at the junction of the high street and western approach, he toyed between stopping for a strong black coffee at Nell's Café, or something more at the pub. Then he noticed the new express supermarket and recalled that he would need provisions for the rented cottage he'd taken for the week on top of the cliff above the harbour. He parked the Porsche and entered the supermarket.

He filled a basket with essentials and ended up at the check-out. There was a young man, probably a student working his way through university as he had once done.

"Is there anything else, sir?"

"That reminds me," said Dillon. "I could do with a bottle of single malt whisky."

"Is it Scottish or Irish you're after? Asked the young man innocently, and then noticed that Dillon was looking strangely at him. "Right over there by the wine." He added quickly. Dillon thought it over. His doctor had told him to ease back on the whisky.

"Thanks, maybe some other time. And by the way, it would have been Scottish!"

* * *

It was the chauffeur of the brand new sleek silver Mercedes saloon picking up as usual from the fashionable mews house in London's Kensington, who raised the alarm. He was sure that his passenger was in residence. He had seen the man's housekeeper Mary coming out of a local supermarket with bags full of groceries on her way back to the house the previous day. Yet this morning he had not answered his door when he had pressed the door entry button, which he always did when he knew he was being collected. So on this morning he walked round the back of the property. To his surprise the gate to the walled garden, although seemingly closed as ever, opened to a light push. That was odd. Mr Levenson-Jones always locked this and answered by pressing a button inside to release the lock on the gate.

The chauffeur walked up the brick path to find one of the French doors partially open. He went pale and stepped back one pace when he saw Mary, who had looked like a harmless kindly woman, sprawled on the oak floor in the hallway, a neat bullet hole drilled through her forehead.

He was about to use his mobile phone to call nine, nine, nine for help when he saw the study door was also open. He approached in fear and trembling to peer around the jamb.

Edward Levenson-Jones sat at his desk, still in his leather wing chair, which supported his torso and head. The head was tilted slightly to the left, sightless blue eyes gazing contemptuously at the wall beyond. The pathologist would later establish he had taken just one shot through the centre of the forehead, the professional assassin's pattern.

No one in the British intelligence community or within the walls of Ferran & Cardini International, understood why.

When he watched the evening news, while eating his supper at the rented cottage in Cornwall, Jake Dillon understood why. It had had to be done and it was only right that he should have been the one to carry out the assignment issued to him by the Prime Minister. There was nothing personal about it. But you just cannot play both sides of the fence in matters of national security.

THE END

Until the next time...

Printed in Great Britain
by Amazon.co.uk, Ltd.,
Marston Gate.